PUBLIC SERVICE
LABOUR RELATIONS
IN A
DEMOCRATIC
SOUTH AFRICA

PUBLIC SERVICE LABOUR RELATIONS IN A DEMOCRATIC SOUTH AFRICA

Edited by
Glenn Adler

WITWATERSRAND UNIVERSITY PRESS

Witwatersrand University Press
1 Jan Smuts Avenue
2000 Johannesburg
South Africa

Published by Witwatersrand University Press in association with the National
Labour and Economic Development Institute (NALEDI)

NALEDI would like to acknowledge the funding of the Friedrich Ebert
Stiftung, which has made this publication possible.

FRIEDRICH
EBERT
STIFTUNG

© NALEDI 2000
First Published 2000

ISBN 1-86814-359-7

Cover photograph © William Matlala
Leadership of COSATU public service unions handing memorandum to
Minister of Finance Trevor Manuel at the conclusion of a protest march on
Pretoria during the 1999 wage dispute.

Cover design and typesetting by Sue Sandrock
Printed and bound by Creda Communications, Cape Town

'Democratising the public service: Co-determination, workplace
democratisation and transformation' by Imraan Patel was first published in
Engaging the State and Business (Witwatersrand University Press, Johannesburg:
2000)

CONTENTS

———— ✦ ————

ABBREVIATIONS/ACRONYMS

———————— ✦ ————————

ANC	African National Congress
ARD	Acquired Rights Directive
CCMA	Commission for Conciliation, Mediation and Arbitration
CCT	Compulsory competitive tendering
CFA	Commission for Administration (currently the Public Service Commission)
CLGF	Commonwealth Local Government Forum
COSATU	Congress of South African Trade Unions
CSS	Central Statistical Services
DENOSA	Democratic Nursing Organisation of South Africa
DET	Department of Education and Training
DPSA	Department of Public Service and Administration
ELRA	Education Labour Relations Act, 1994
ELRC	Education Labour Relations Council
EPSU	European Federation of Public Service Unions
EPU	Education Policy Unit
FEDSAL	Federation of South African Labour
FEDUSA	Federation of Unions of South Africa
FFC	Financial and Fiscal Commission
FORCE	Federation of Organisations Representing Civil Employees
GDP	Gross Domestic Product
GEAR	Growth, Employment and Redistribution strategy
GEPF	Government Empoyees' Pension Fund
GNU	Government of National Unity
HAD	House of Assembly Debates
HOSPERSA	Hospital Personnel Trade Union of South Africa
HWU	Health Workers' Union
ICFTU	International Confederation of Free Trade Unions
IFP	Inkatha Freedom Party
ILO	International Labour Organisation
IMF	International Monetary Fund
IPS	Institute of Public Servants

JAC	Public Service Joint Advisory Council
LRA	Labour Relations Act, 1995
MASA	Medical Association of South Africa
MEC	Member of the Executive Committee
MMF	Mandating Ministers Forum
MP	Member of Parliament
NACSO	National Civil Service Organisation
NALEDI	National Labour and Economic Development Institute
NAPCRU	National Public Civil Rights Union
NAPSA	National Public Servants' Association
NAPTOSA	National Professional Teachers Organisation of South Africa
NCHF	National Consultative Health Forum
NEC	National Executive Committee
NECC	National Education Crisis Committee
NEDLAC	National Economic Development and Labour Council
NEHAWU	National Education, Health, and Allied Workers' Union
NEUSA	National Education Union of South Africa
NETF	National Education and Training Forum
NGO	Non-governmental organisation
NNF	National Negotiating Forum
NP	National Party
NPSWU	National Public Service Workers' Union
NTUF	National Teachers Unity Forum
NUMSA	National Union of Metalworkers of South Africa
NUPSAW	National Union of Public Service and Allied Workers
NZPSA	New Zealand Public Service Association
OECD	Organisation for Economic Co-operation and Development
PADA	Pioneer Agency for Development in Africa
PAS	Personnel Administration Standard
PAWUSA	Public and Allied Workers' Union of South Africa
POPCRU	Police and Prisons Civil Rights Union
PRC	Presidential Review Commission
PRP	Performance related pay
PSA	Public Servants Association of South Africa
PSAAWU	Public Servants and Allied Workers Union

PSC	Public Service Commission (formerly the Commission for Administration)
PSBC	Public Service Bargaining Council
PSCBC	Public Service Co-ordinating Bargaining Council
PSF	Public Service Forum
PSI	Public Services International
PSPRU	Public Services International Research Unit
PSL	Public Service League
PSLRA	Public Service Labour Relations Act, 1994
PSTF	Public Service Transformation Forum
PSU	Public Service Union
PTA	Parent-Teacher Association
PTSA	Parent-Teacher-Student Association
PUSEMO	Public Servants Movement
RECES	Research Committee on Education Structures
RDP	Reconstruction and Development Programme
RSA	Republic of South Africa
SACE	South African Council of Educators
SACP	South African Communist Party
SADNU	South African Democratic Nurses Union
SADTU	South African Democratic Teachers Union
SAHPSWU	South African Health and Public Service Workers' Union
SAMA	South African Medical Association
SAMWU	South African Municipal Workers' Union
SANA	South African Nursing Association
SANDF	South African National Defence Force
SAOU	Suid Afrikaanse Onderwysunie
SAP	Structural Adjustment Programme
SAP	South African Police
SAPOS	South African Post Office Service
SAPRI	Structural Adjustment Programme Review Initiative
SAPS	South African Police Service
SAPSA	South African Public Servants' Association
SAPSAWU	South African Public Service and Allied Workers Union
SAPU	South African Police Union
SARS	South African Revenue Service
SASA	South African Schools Act
SGB	School governing body

SGT	Self-governing territories
SOE	State-owned enterprise
SPO	Special Programme Officer
SSSBC	Safety and Security Sectoral Bargaining Council
TBVC	Transkei, Bophuthatswana, Venda, Ciskei
TFC	Teachers' Federal Council
TNC	Transnational company
TPA	Transvaal Provincial Administration
TU	Transformation Unit
TUAC	Trade Union Advisory Committee
TUPE	Transfer of Undertakings Protection of Employment
UDF	United Democratic Front
UNIPSA	United National Public Servants' Association of South Africa
UP	United Party
VSP	Voluntary severance package
ZCTU	Zimbabwe Congress of Trade Unions
ZLADDFWU	Zimbabwe Local Authority and DDF Workers' Union
ZUCWU	Zimbabwe Urban Councils Workers' Union

PREFACE

◆

The chapters in this book were commissioned by the National Labour and Economic Development Institute (NALEDI) as part of its long term research project on Public Service Labour Relations in South Africa. NALEDI is a not-for-profit research non-governmental organisation, established in 1993 by the Congress of South African Trade Unions (COSATU) to conduct research and policy analysis on issues of relevance to the labour movement.

In late 1996 NALEDI embarked on this project to investigate the dramatic changes occurring in the public service. During the transition to democracy, the public service was one of the most conflictual labour relations arenas as workers launched campaigns for union recognition and organisational rights and for improvements in wages and conditions of service. Labour's campaigns prioritised the broader aim of democratisation as well as the transformation of the state itself.

With the advent of democracy public service workers have for the first time in South African history been included under the ambit of the Labour Relations Act. The new law – and democratisation more generally – thus set the stage for public service workers to improve their conditions of service. In the few years since public service workers were granted bargaining rights, they have made considerable progress. Union membership has increased rapidly. Black workers have gained job security. Minimum wage levels have risen dramatically and above the rate of inflation. Most impressively, the wage gap has narrowed from 64:1 in 1989 to 15:1 today.

However the public service remains untransformed. Work organisation is archaic and overly bound by convoluted rules. Decision-making remains overly centralised. Productivity is low and quality of services poor. Staffing is marked by gross racial and gender distortions. The public service is not yet a 'model employer,' nor has it been restructured to contribute to transformation.

Indeed, these two goals may be contradictory. First, improving conditions for black workers will come at the expense of the previously privileged, who have considerable power to block change. Such groupings are highly organised and are now able to pursue their interests through the same labour law that empowers and protects black workers.

Nor can the state buy its way out of this problem by being all things to all employees. Not only does government policy seek to reduce the proportion of the wage bill as a proportion of overall public expenditure, but the demands of increasing spending on infrastructural development and services means that difficult choices must be made. These will inevitably generate labour relations conflicts, not only between the state and workers, but between different groups of workers. Moreover these conflicts will not always be confined to old cleavages defined on the basis of race or political outlook.

Second, those who are comfortable in the present order will be threatened by efforts at restructuring aimed at making them work both smarter and harder. It is difficult to achieve these goals while extending job protection to workers that makes retrenchment, discipline and dismissal more difficult.

In both of these ways public service transformation is fundamentally a problem of labour relations. But while these problems are in many respects similar to those in the private sector, the public service is different. It is the largest employer in the country, and its decisions about wages and employment levels therefore have a dramatic effect on other sectors as well as on the overall level of effective demand in the economy. Furthermore, despite efforts at revitalising the private sector, the public service remains the single most important agent of development in the country. For many citizens it is the provider of last resort, and its services – or the lack of them – often mean the difference between life or death. Its ability to perform this role is to a large extent bound up with the quality of its labour relations.

In all these respects, the public service is currently – and for the foreseeable future – perhaps the single most important labour relations arena. For this reason NALEDI launched its long-term research project, with the aim of building a more systematic understanding of the development of labour relations in this crucial sector.

To this end NALEDI commissioned eleven original research papers from labour-based researchers and academics for whom this is a specialised field of study. Nine of these reports appear in this collection.

The results were first made available to COSATU's central executive committee in 1997 and to the full range of public service unions in a one-day conference in late January 1998. A selection of revised papers appeared in a special focus issue of the *South African Labour Bulletin* v. 22, no. 3 (1998).

We are grateful to the Witwatersrand University Press for agreeing to publish the revised contributions in this collection so that the work may be communicated to a broader audience in South Africa and abroad.

If the research began soon after the formal development of labour relations in the public service, it is being published at a time when these processes are more clouded by controversy than at any time since 1994. The acrimony between unions and management generated in the 1999 wage negotiations continues. It is difficult to see how the two sides can be reconciled to deal with the many issues confronting the sector. Yet much progress has been made in the PSCBC, and in principle the government's and labour's positions overlap. Whether they have the skill, political will, and luck to find common ground remains to be seen. Whatever the outcome the public service will be an important area for investigation and investigation for many years to come.

Policy-oriented research always runs the risk of becoming dated before it finds its way into print, not only because the research addresses ephemeral questions, but because the object of the research itself is rapidly changing. However for the reasons mentioned above we believe that the research presented here will remain of value well beyond the period in which it was conducted and the moment in which it is published.

The researchers whose work is reproduced in this book are keenly interested in the fate of public service labour relations. However they represent a spectrum of views on the matter, and there are some disagreements in position. Though we held three researchers' workshops to develop common questions and methodological approaches, no attempt was made to present a common set of conclusions, which remain the responsibility of the authors alone. Moreover, while NALEDI is closely linked to COSATU – many current and former trade unionists and allied scholars sit on its board – the organisation is independent of the federation and its research findings do not reflect nor are they bound by COSATU's policies.

If the research reflected in the contributions to this collection is a first assessment of public service labour relations, it is also by definition incomplete and tentative. We attempted here to investigate a number of key issues: bargaining, union structure, the character of management and worker participation (co-determination). We also commissioned a contribution on global trends within the public service. Finally we examined the dynamics of these key issues in the context of two critical case studies where labour relations has been a central issue: education and the police. There are a number of areas we did not investigate, including affirmative action, dispute procedures, and the dynamics of labour relations in the civil service itself. Furthermore, we did not assess labour relations in the public sector more broadly: state-owned enterprises and local government are not included.

Nonetheless, the present volume marks a beginning. In 1999 NALEDI launched further long-term research projects on the public service, and we hope that this book, combined with subsequent work, will begin to fill in the story of public sector labour relations.

We wish to thank the Friedrich Ebert Stiftung, especially Ulrich Golaszinski, Bethuell Maserumule and Sven Schwersensky, for valuable support at all stages of the project, including financial assistance with publication. We wish to thank the NALEDI staff – Edson Phiri, Emily Radebe, and Dolly Vundla – for their administrative support. The shop stewards, organisers and office bearers from the public service affiliates who participated in our 1998 conference in Johannesburg gave the authors valuable inputs which were of enormous help in their efforts to clarify their work. Finally we wish to thank the editors at Witwatersrand University Press, for bringing this collection to readers.

Ravi Naidoo
NALEDI Director
Johannesburg, June 2000

ACKNOWLEDGEMENTS

———— ♦ ————

In 1996 NALEDI's board endorsed a new thrust for the institute: the creation of a number of 'long-term' multi-author research projects on complex problems facing the labour movement. First among these projects was the investigation of labour relations in South Africa's public service, a topic that has never before been investigated in a systematic fashion. These efforts allowed NALEDI to draw on the talents of an array of experts to generate new insights based on substantial and original investigation. The board's commitment to research has been impressive as it runs against the grain in a policy milieu increasingly driven by rapid-fire responses based on limited investigation.

I'm sure, however, that the board had little idea how long 'long-term' would be! We compensated by presenting the research-in-progress to the labour movement in a variety of formats, including a major workshop and publication of selected reports in the *South African Labour Bulletin.* I am deeply grateful that NALEDI saw merit in publishing this book so that our work could reach a wider audience. In particular I would like to thank the board and its chair, Vusi Nhlapo; NALEDI's director, Ravi Naidoo; and the Friedrich Ebert Stiftung. I also wish to thank the Witwatersrand University Press and its commissioning editor, Hyreath Anderson, for their sterling efforts to produce this volume.

The project would never have succeeded without the intellectual and administrative support given by Jeremy Baskin – who initiated the long-term research efforts in 1996 – and Imraan Patel: past NALEDI directors whose innovative research is represented in three chapters in the book. It is important to mention my predecessors at NALEDI, Neva Seidman-Makgetla and Julia de Bruyn, whose work on the public service provided a foundation for this project, as revealed by the numerous citations of their publications in the notes.

Three general secretaries – Fikile Majola of NEHAWU, Thulas Nxesi of SADTU and Jacob Tsumane of POPCRU – helped shape the project's presentation to labour while their ideas contributed to the development of an on-going NALEDI research programme on the public service, now ably managed by Ebrahim Khalil Hassen.

I am grateful to the Sociology of Work Unit at the University of the Witwatersrand for seconding me to NALEDI, and to the Staff Development Committee of the Sociology Department and the Dean of the Arts Faculty, Gerrit Olivier, for approving the arrangement.

Finally, I wish to thank the ten contributors to this book, which would never have been possible without their insights, hard work, and persistence.

Glenn Adler
Johannesburg, June 2000

1

THE NEGLECTED ROLE OF LABOUR RELATIONS IN THE SOUTH AFRICAN PUBLIC SERVICE

————— ✦ —————

Glenn Adler

INTRODUCTION

As a consequence of South Africa's transition to democracy, public service workers now enjoy trade union and collective bargaining rights for the first time in the country's history. These changes provide public servants with opportunities to bring their conditions of service into line with industrial relations 'best practice' in the private sector, and for black workers in particular, to redress decades of racism, employment insecurity, and low pay.

Yet these reforms occur at a moment of straightened economic circumstances, which constrain possibilities for wage gains and employment growth. Moreover, the public service is undergoing massive restructuring, not only to overcome legacies of racial inequality and authoritarianism, but to transform the state into a more effective agent of development. The problems – under conditions of austerity – of addressing workers' wage demands and concerns for job security while redressing the legacies of apartheid will likely generate considerable conflict between workers and managers as well as between different groups of workers.

These difficulties exist in many areas of the South African economy. But labour-management conflict in the public service is not a narrow industrial relations issue of interest to the parties alone. The public service is, with more than 1,1 million employees, the largest single employer in the country. Through its procurement policies it is the largest single consumer of goods and services. The wages and benefits it provides have a massive impact on effective demand, particularly in provinces where public servants make up a large proportion of total employment. Through its direct expenditure on social services and development, and indirectly through the economic effects described above it is the most important single agent of reconstruction. Finally, for vast numbers of citizens the public service is the provider of last resort: its actions literally determine whether people live or die.

Thus labour relations conflicts in the public service will have crucial and long-lasting consequences for restructuring the state as an institution, and therefore for the government's ability to promote fiscal integrity, economic development, and service delivery. Such conflicts will thus inevitably spill beyond the boundaries of the public service to have an important impact on all citizens. But labour relations are not simply a 'problem' to be avoided at all costs, for example by limiting public servants' right to organise or strike, or by exempting the service from labour relations legislation. If labour-management conflicts point to the existence of a problem, they also hold out the promise of a solution. Negotiated agreements between government and organised labour may provide means for finding constructive solutions to the tangle of difficulties currently confronting the public service.

Public service labour relations are thus an important factor shaping the prospects for development in South Africa, and with it the fate of democratisation itself. But the possibility of developing modern labour relations practices in the public service, given its legacies of racially based paternalism and authoritarianism, and given fiscal constraints is a tall order. These practices do not emerge automatically as a consequence of the legislative inclusion of the public service in the Labour Relations Act and the extension of substantive and procedural rights to the sector. In the private sector these rights evolved over decades of intense conflict, and remain imperfect, unevenly applied, and subject to reversals. It is difficult to imagine that the growth of labour relations in the public service will be any less fraught. However, if public service labour relations go wrong, the consequences will be profound for all South Africans. Thus the public service will be perhaps the single most important labour relations arena in the future.

Yet the subject is almost entirely unresearched in this country. Much of the existing published material is descriptive and technical, oriented towards training officials in the rules and procedures of the public service itself. While such texts have their role, they are not sufficient for preparing unionists, public servants, students and academics to understand and confront the key issues in a public service undergoing transformation. The chapters in this collection are a first attempt to come to grips with this difficult but fascinating area of investigation.

WHAT IS THE PUBLIC SERVICE?

The public service is part of the broader *public sector*, and though the terms are often used interchangeably, they may refer to very different things. As this book focuses on the *public service*, it is important at the outset to define the term.

The public sector refers to all institutions under public control where direct or indirect political control is exercised through appropriate legislation. In this light, the public sector includes a wide range of components: national and provincial departments, state-owned enterprises, and local authorities. These differ in terms of the form of political control, relationship to the national budget, the method of wage determination, employment numbers and conditions, and the form of regulation and ownership (see Figure 1.1).

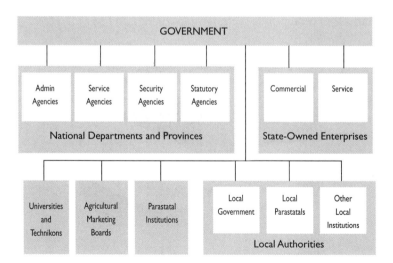

Figure 1.1: The South African public sector
Source: NALEDI

Public sectors vary greatly in scope and organisation between countries, depending on their own historical experience, politics, and needs. Moreover, in the last two decades the very nature of the public sector has undergone change under the influence of new market-based ideologies of governance and in the face of political shifts that have favoured right-of-centre political coalitions. As Waghorne points out in his chapter in this collection, there are no fixed definitions of either the public sector or, more narrowly, the public service that apply everywhere and for all time.

In South Africa the public sector as a whole employed nearly 2 million workers in 1996 (CSS, 1997). It included:

- the public service, defined as national and provincial departments, which was the single largest component of the public sector, accounting for more than two-thirds of all employment
- state-owned enterprises, such as Transnet and Telkom, which accounted for another 15% of employment
- local authorities, including city councils, municipalities, town councils, and the former regional services councils, which together employed approximately 13% of all public sector workers
- and other components, including universities and technikons, marketing boards, and associated insitutions which accounted for less than 5% of total public sector employment (see Figure 1.2).

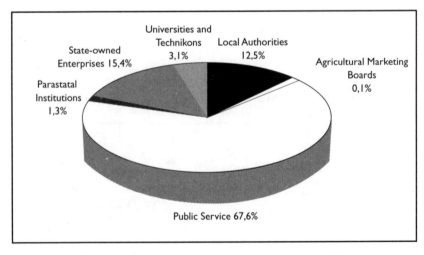

Figure 1.2: Public sector employment, December 1996
Source: NALEDI

This book examines only the first of these four components: national and provincial state departments. The emphasis means that some important dynamics in other areas of the public sector are ignored, such as privatisation of state-owned enterprises, local government restructuring, or the transformation of tertiary education. On the other hand, the narrower definition brings a number of advantages. By treating the public service as a single 'industry' (albeit one divided into different sub-sectors) covered by common legislation, the discussion is focused on relations between a single 'employer' and a limited range of unions. Both the employer and the unions bargain in the same institution: the Public Service Bargaining Council (PSBC) was established in 1993 and reorganised in 1997 as the Public Service Co-ordinating Bargaining Council (PSCBC). The approach not only simplifies discussion of a complex subject, but allows for clear comparisons and for somewhat stronger generalisations to be drawn.[1]

Prior to 1994 the South African public service was complicated by the division of the country into 15 distinct administrations serving 11 different 'governments' which included the 10 apartheid-era 'independent states' and 'self-governing territories'.[2] The 1993 Interim Constitution of the Republic of South Africa, which came into effect following the first democratic elections in April 1994, eliminated these apartheid-era creations by establishing a single public service for the country as a whole composed of a central administration and the administrations of the nine newly created provincial governments.

As can be seen from Figure 1.2, the public service is the single largest component of the public sector. It includes national departments, provinces, and statutory agencies. It also covers educators employed in terms of the National Policy for General Education Affairs Act, 1984; personnel employed under the Correctional Services Act, 1959; and police personnel employed under the South African Police Service Act, 1995. The public service also includes the South African National Defence Force (SANDF), the National Intelligence Agency, and the South African Secret Service.

It is useful to sub-divide further the public service into a number of different types of agencies:

- *service delivery agencies*, such as health and education
- *security agencies*, such as the South African Police Service (SAPS) and the South African National Defence Force

- *administrative agencies,* normally referred to as the 'civil service', specifically established to ensure the effective administration of governmental functions
- *statutory agencies,* which include the Public Service Commission (PSC), the Financial and Fiscal Commission (FFC), the Gender Commission, and the Auditor-General, agencies established by the constitution or by subsidiary legislation. These agencies do not fall under the PSCBC: they determine their own terms and conditions of employment, though in practice they tend to use the agreements, grades and salary structure determined in the PSCBC.

In 1996 total employment in the public service was nearly 1,3 million, though this had fallen to slightly more than 1,1 million by the end of 1998. (For a detailed breakdown of public service employment see Baskin, Chapter 7.) The vast majority of these workers were employed in the service delivery and security agencies.

Since April 1994, greater clarity has emerged on the division of powers and functions between national government and provincial government and this has affected the location of public service workers. As both the interim and final constitutions defined many service delivery functions – such as education and health – as provincial competencies, the majority of public service workers are in fact employed in the nine provinces.

LABOUR RELATIONS IN THE SOUTH AFRICAN PUBLIC SERVICE

In focusing on labour relations the contributions to this collection examine the range of interactions between the employer (the state) and organised workers in the public service. In the main these interactions focus on remuneration (wage and non-wage) and conditions of service (including job grading and training, discipline, dispute resolution and affirmative action). However in both practice and law this relationship extends to a number of issues well beyond the employment relationship, including involvement in policy making in areas such as public service transformation.

For most of the twentieth century the public service was one of the most inhospitable sectors for worker organisation in South Africa. The public service as a whole was excluded from the ambit of the Labour

Relations Act (LRA), a condition that undermined collective action by all public servants, white or black. The very notion of 'labour relations' scarcely applied: no public servants, white or black, enjoyed the right to join a registered trade union and bargain collectively with the employer. They did not enjoy the right to strike, nor were they covered by mutually accepted procedures for discipline, retrenchment or grievances. Instead white public servants benefited from the range of discriminatory practices that served all white workers: citizenship rights, job-reservation and social welfare. Moreover they were enmeshed in a deeply paternalistic system founded on patronage within Afrikaner nationalism. By contrast, black public servants faced the barrage of restrictions imposed on all black workers: the denial of basic citizenship rights, exclusion from the industrial relations legislation, repression by the security forces and employer hostility. In addition through the 1970s they were largely excluded from the racialised patronage networks within the state, except in the black homelands. While the wave of unionisation that washed over South Africa in the 1970s and 1980s swept away much of the employer unilateralism that characterised the workplace in the private sector, the public service remained an island where the employer's power reigned supreme.

Since 1912 the Public Service Commission (PSC) administered all aspects of the employer-employee relationship, including the determination of wages and conditions of service, discipline, and grievance handling (see Macun and Psoulis, Chapter 4, in this collection). It unilaterally determined the nature of work through the determination of a Public Administration Standard (PAS) for each occupation, and developed a welter of regulations and legislation governing employment. No issue was too large or too small to be determined by the centralised PSC.

White permanent civil servants (almost exclusively male) gained a measure of collective representation with the establishment of the Public Servants Association (PSA). But in line with the apolitical and professional public service ethos instilled by the British colonial model of administration, this was a restrained body that played a limited consultative role in the Public Service Joint Advisory Council. On the rare occasions when the PSA pursued an issue of importance to its members it could be ignored by the PSC.

Yet the PSA's constituents did not lack reasons for complaint. As Posel argues in her chapter in this collection, white public servants were continually frustrated by the PSC's below-inflation rate wage increases, sanctioning of unfair dismissals, and deaf ear to employee grievances. Curiously the PSC's arrogance never provoked the PSA to take collective action, and for Posel, the explanation is bound up with the system of patronage created by the National Party (NP).

Labour relations under apartheid

The NP politicised the PSC in efforts to remake the public service into an instrument for realising its apartheid policy, neatly reversing the long-standing demands for public service neutrality it expressed while in opposition before 1948. Instead the NP treated the public service as a vast pool of patronage for party loyalists, even if this meant appointing incompetent whites unable to find employment elsewhere in the expanding post-war economy.

In restructuring the state to pursue apartheid policies the public service was itself remade in apartheid's image. Not only did this entail the notorious creation of separate administrations for the TBVC states and self-governing territories, but it also led to a flurry of regulations to entrench the position of whites within the public service. These provisions contributed to duplication of work, the proliferation of occupational classes, a bewildering array of bonuses and allowances, and a massive wage gap marked by high levels of inequality on the basis of race and gender.

The legacies of this political approach continue to structure employment relations in the public service as these very regulations were preserved during the transition. The legislative drafters of the LRA (1995) – largely ignorant of conditions in the public service – relied on the advice of senior bureaucrats who secured the conversion of all existing public service regulations into collective agreements. As a result, the same officials who had written these regulations to promote their own interests – such as favourable voluntary severance packages, extensive non-wage benefits, and generous leave provisions – ensured that these would be virtually enshrined in the new democratic order.

If NP hegemony created infinite ways to deliver benefits to Afrikaners, it also bound public servants in a subordinate position to the party and state elite. Most civil servants could not easily find work in the private sector, and were equally vulnerable should the impediments to recruitment of black public servants posed by job reservation be relaxed. As Posel argues, they knew 'that they depended on the party for their jobs, which could be revoked just as easily as they were supplied. The pressure for conformism and compliance were thus enormous'. These tendencies are clearly revealed in the chapters by Garson and Marks in this collection, which describe the authoritarian staff culture common in schools and the police. In both cases promotion – if not survival – depended on fulfilling the commands of one's superiors.

Public service labour relations, according to Posel, were characterised by an increasing gap between the formal rationality of the bureaucratic PSC and the NP's party political project. Nor was the NP keen to resolve this tension. As PW Botha's 'total strategy' gathered momentum from the late 1970s the NP could use patronage to maintain loyalty while simultaneously deploying a public service discourse to discipline avowedly right-wing civil servants bent on undermining reforms.

In this context the NP had little interest in pursuing the Wiehahn Commission's recommendation to extend labour rights to public servants. In the face of the historic upsurge in union organisation in the private sector during the 1980s the PSC ignored the Commission's advice and chose instead to extend the PSA's 'diffident and polite', 'non-adversarial' (in Posel's words) model to other public servants on a racial basis. Thus the 1980s witnessed the launch of a number of relatively toothless staff associations defined by race, occupation and geographic location.

The apartheid public service under pressure

The decline of paternalistic unitarism in the public service occurred in tandem with the transition to democracy. In the second half of the 1980s the new union movement began at last to make inroads into the public service. Union advances led by affiliates of the Congress of South African Trade Unions (COSATU) came first in those state departments most implicated in the state-society conflicts beginning in 1984. As state institutions became targets of township protest, increasing popular pressure came to bear on the black public servants responsible for services in black areas: teachers, police and soldiers, health workers. These workers had accumulated their own complaints as a consequence of years of discriminatory policies produced by the PSC. Now many were being asked by mass movement organisations to take sides in the growing civil conflict, by observing stay-away calls or embarking directly on industrial action, as in the 'chalk down' protests by teachers or the rolling mutinies by soldiers in 1989 (see Garson, Chapter 9 and Marks, Chapter 10).

In these actions, black public servants' material grievances – apartheid on the job – merged with their own and their communities' wider discontent with NP rule. As elsewhere in the economy this yielded an explosive combination that produced militant social movement unionism. The budding unions in the public service were from the outset highly politicised, in the first instance because they were the only formations in the labour movement that faced the apartheid state both as oppressor and as employer. Where in the past this combination put black public servants in a highly vulnerable position and retarded union development, under conditions of mass mobilisation and widespread conflict with the state it transformed the public service into perhaps the most volatile labour sector in the country. With the growth of the mass democratic movement during the state of emergency and in the renewed defiance campaign of 1988 and 1989 it became difficult for the state to pursue any strategy of unilateral reform from above: labour protest had helped transform the state itself into an unreliable instrument of NP rule.

Such volatility was heightened – not diminished – by the unbanning of political organisations in 1990 and the onset of negotiations over South Africa's constitutional future. Ordinary labour repression was made virtually impossible once the NP had committed itself to a negotiated transition and free political activity was restored. Moreover the signing of the Laboria Minute in 1990 between the government, COSATU, the National Council of Trade Unions and the South African Consultative Committee on Labour Affairs (a representative business body on labour relations issues) committed all parties to fundamental revision of labour law which included the long-delayed recognition of public servants' labour rights within a single Labour Relations Act.

COSATU's efforts to establish a union beachhead in the public service date from 1987, with the founding of the National Education Health and Allied Workers' Union (NEHAWU). However these organising efforts bore little fruit until 1990. In education the federation played a central role in drawing together the disparate staff associations and more radical teachers' organisations that formed in opposition to the official bodies. The South African Democratic Teachers' Union (SADTU) was launched in 1990, uniting teachers across the disparate provincial and racial education authorities. In 1989 and 1990 police and correctional services officers staged a number of dramatic strikes, workplace occupations, and protest marches, and launched the Police and Prisons Civil Rights Union (POPCRU), which began as an independent union, joined COSATU in 1994 (see Garson, Chapter 9 and Marks, Chapter 10).

Between 1989 and 1993, these three unions were largely responsible for the biggest strike wave in the history of the public service. As Macun and Psoulis write in their chapter in this collection, many of those who participated were not union members at the time, but joined after taking part in the strikes. The issues motivating the strikers were in nearly all cases the same: wages, union recognition, solidarity with dismissed or harassed workers, and discriminatory treatment. There were few strikes in the civil service, still the preserve of the PSA and the other old-guard staff associations, and weakly organised by the COSATU affiliates. But civil servants did take action in the homelands, whose own repressive labour laws became a major target.

These strikes finally yielded a new labour relations dispensation, which saw core labour rights extended for the first time to public servants as a whole, with separate dispensations for educators and police personnel.[3] The legislation allowed for recognition of public service unions and collective bargaining, created dispute resolution procedures and established a bargaining council for the public service with separate councils for teachers and police (see Patel, Chapter 6 and the chapters by Garson and Marks).

The new public service unions demonstrated considerable militance stemming from their double protest against apartheid and against the apartheid state as employer. During the transition this led to a dual role: using industrial muscle to block unilateral state restructuring (which would harm their members and hamstring a future African National Congress (ANC) government) and to push for transformation of the public service. In the context of the transition these interlinked imperatives made the new public service unions the COSATU affiliates closest to the ANC.

Under these circumstances the new public service unions grew extremely rapidly after 1990. However after 1994 these conditions produced a strange inversion. Under successive ANC-led governments the politicised unions would find themselves under pressure to conform to the policy orientations of their political ally. At the same time, the old staff associations would transform themselves from the 'diffident and polite' organisations of the apartheid era into more effective representatives of their members' interests.

LABOUR RELATIONS IN A NEW DEMOCRACY

Power changed hands in April 1994 to the ANC-dominated Government of National Unity. However, daunting obstacles stood in the way of developing a public service, in the words of the Reconstruction and Development Programme (RDP), 'capable of and committed to the implementation of the policies of the government and the delivery of basic goods and services to the people of the country' (ANC, 1994: 126).[4]

These obstacles posed problems for the government and the unions alike, notwithstanding that in the few years since public service workers won labour rights they registered their greatest gains ever. However these advances occurred in an increasingly contradictory context, in which the fruits of democratisation for workers (improvements in wages and conditions of service, job security, bargaining power, involvement in decision-making) would increasingly run up against competing imperatives of boosting expenditure on services (delivery), transforming the state itself (reconstruction), and maintaining fiscal discipline. These tensions were temporarily contained with the adoption of a landmark three-year collective agreement in early 1996, but intensified with government's adoption of the Growth, Employment and Redistribution program (GEAR) in 1996. With the expiry of the agreement in 1999 the contradictions erupted into the first major conflict in the public service since the early 1990s.

Transformation

Given that its reason for existence was the promotion of apartheid, in both its culture and in its very institutions the public service was ill-suited to serving the development needs of the majority of the population. The NP's political projects shaped who was hired and promoted, where they were deployed and the character of their jobs. Most notably, the public service inherited by the ANC was strongly structured by a racial and gender division of labour resulting from decades of preferential hiring of white male Afrikaners. The priority given to party-political appointments meant that many public servants at all levels were hired for their loyalty rather than their ability to perform their jobs.

Moreover, the apartheid project shaped the very institutional integument of the public service. It was characterised by an uneven racial/geographic distribution of its services, the racial duplication of entire – incompatible and financially wasteful – administrative systems, and the preponderant power of the coercive institutions of the national security state.

Finally, the PSC's centralised rule-making power not only meant that modern labour relations practices were non-existent, but also made the public service highly inflexible. Ordinary workers were of course subject to its authority in the determination of wages and conditions of employment, but so, too, were senior public servants. Under PSC-rule senior officials were not managers in the conventional sense of the term: decision-makers with responsibility for the outcomes of their choices. Instead they were reduced to the status of administrators carrying out functions defined by the PSC within fixed regulations over which they had little influence. At both the top and the bottom of the public service hierarchy initiative, innovation, responsibility (and, therefore, accountability) were largely absent.

Given these legacies, transformation was as much about destruction as creation: not simply grafting new institutions and practices onto the old, but an ambitious program to change the public service's purpose, structure, and personnel composition. As a result, it was quintessentially a labour relations matter as the remaking of the public service simultaneously meant the reconstruction of workers' jobs, their relations with other employees, with their superiors and with the public they were expected to serve. From this point of view transformation entailed overcoming racial and gender imbalances, a commitment to education and training to develop public servants' skills, eliminating discrimination in salaries and benefits, and changing the public service's authoritarian culture and outmoded work practices.

Under the terms of the new LRA and in the common understanding of both government and labour, these changes were to be brought about through new *processes* of labour relations. On the one side these involved allowing workers to organise and bargain freely with managers; on the other it required a change in the nature of authority, breaking the centralised power of the PSC and transforming administrators into managers endowed with decision-making power and responsibility. In short it entailed replacing the paternalistic model that had grown under apartheid with the system of labour-management bargaining that had developed in the private sector since the 1970s.

Given the enormity of transformation it is remarkable, looking back on the mid-1990s, that little explicit attention has been paid to its deeply contradictory character.[5] It was occurring in a politically sensitive milieu defined by 'sunset clauses' negotiated in the transition talks which made it difficult to replace the senior old-regime personnel who were transformation's very targets.[6] It was expensive: redirecting public services to those who were once systematically denied such benefits entailed infrastructural and personnel expenditure of monumental proportions. Even assuming the goodwill of all parties and sufficient finances, these were – and remain – enormously complicated technical tasks: misguided policy and outright mistakes would be expected, and would inevitably cause delays. Transformation was rendered all the more difficult as service provision was to be maintained even as the instrument of delivery was undergoing change.

Finally, transformation generates its own conflicts, not only between employer and employees, or between old and new or white and black public servants, but within and between these categories as well. Transformation creates new winners and losers, and spawns new collectivities and alliances as well as new adversarial relations. These will not always coincide with the cleavages inherited from the apartheid public service, and will likely cut across established patron-client relationships. Indeed, in some cases they may create new ones. Given these difficulties associated with transformation, it is remarkable that it has not provoked either widespread breakdown or all-out civil war within the public service.

A strong case could be made that peace was maintained as a result of labour relations, which yielded improvements in wages and conditions of service, job security, and a relatively strike-free environment for most of the life of the Government of National Unity. However the means used to avoid war will not be readily available to the parties in the future.

Democratisation: Worker rights and collective bargaining

The Public Service Labour Relations Act (PSLRA) came into operation in August 1993 followed by enabling legislation in the education and police services sectors. These separate pieces of legislation were promulgated despite the agreement in the Laboria Minute to include the public service within the general labour relations dispensation.The separate Acts aimed to solve an immediate crisis in the public service, which could not be systematically addressed outside of a legislative framework. Yet the LRA itself was scheduled for fundamental renegotiation immediately following the installation of a new government. The PSLRA was thus an interim measure to create, virtually from scratch, appropriate bargaining structures and powers, as well as agreements about appropriate representation from the employer and workers, and about which issues would be bargained.

The Public Service Bargaining Council (PSBC) was established under the PSLRA and covered workers employed under the Public Service Act, excluding educators. According to Patel, both employer and employee representatives were weak and divided. The PSC – which had previously administered the public service unilaterally – was unable to adjust to the exigencies of bargaining, while its negotiators lacked basic labour relations skills. Employee representatives were similarly inexperienced and divided into two blocs, one composed of old-guard staff associations, the other of progressive unions led by NEHAWU. These problems entrenched adversarialism in the PSBC. Nonetheless, a number of agreements were struck, including a wage settlement for 1994/1995. But agreement on a settlement for 1993/1994 was interrupted by the F.W. de Klerk government's unilateral implementation of an across-the-board (and below inflation) 5% increase.

Union, membership increased rapidly, and in June 1999 stood at 981 816 out of 1, 016 440 employees, giving an extraordinary union density figure of more than 96% (PSCBC, 1999).[7] SADTU provides a good example of the rapid growth: its membership increased from 40 000 in 1993 to more than 210 000 in 1999, an increase of better than 420% (see Figure 1.3 below; for complete union membership figures see Macun and Psoulis, Chapter 4).

Though union density and growth rates are impressive, these do not provide an accurate index of union strength. Given the much more permissive labour law environment after 1994 and the relatively union-friendly orientation of government it would have been surprising if unions *did not* grow rapidly. Their achievement is not, in this respect, exactly comparable to the organising gains registered by certain private sector unions in the labour-repressive context of the 1980s.

Nor does density indicate the unions' degree of organisation. By contrast, in the 1970s and 1980s many private sector unions grew comparatively slowly, but on a factory-by-factory basis where they laid down strong shop-floor organisation. Their emphasis on democratically elected shop-steward structures not only gave these unions a deep pool of leadership, but provided them with the capacity to respond to members' needs and the ability to embark on disciplined action in pursuit of their interests (Friedman, 1987; Adler and Webster, 1995). For the most part unions in the public service have not grown in this fashion, and workplace and intermediate-level organisation has lagged behind. This is certainly the case among the old staff associations, which never professed to operate as representative trade unions, but also remains true of COSATU affiliates, despite their federation's long-standing commitment to shop-steward organisation and leadership.

As Marks reveals in Chapter 10 on labour relations in the police service, neither the South African Police Union (SAPU) nor POPCRU have effectively translated into practice their in-principle commitment to developing shop-steward structures. Effective organisation at shop-floor and intermediate levels remains elusive and is not encouraged by the still highly centralised character of both public service bargaining and administration. The unions' capacity problems at these levels may compromise their ability to bargain in newly created provincial bargaining councils, and their ability to interact with management at all levels.

Finally, membership does not imply organisational loyalty. There is a marked tendency towards multiple union membership – where workers

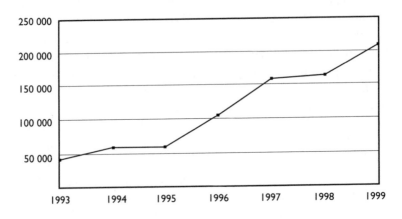

Figure 1.3: SADTU membership growth, 1993-1999
Source: NALEDI (1999: 9)

join one union to obtain benefits and another for political reasons – informally estimated at 80 000 or close to 10% of the total membership in the public service. This phenomenon has been relatively unknown in the private sector, where for black workers in particular union membership historically entailed a risky act of identifying with a union's goals. Moreover 'agency shop' provisions further dilute the meaning of union membership. Unions may now receive 'agency' fees from public servants who are not members, but who nonetheless benefit from many of the collective agreements negotiated in the PSCBC. High agency shop fees serve as an inducement for workers to join a trade union, whether or not they believe in its goals.

Taken together, these factors suggest that high union density in the public service does not mean that the organisations are strong enough as a whole to convert these numbers into effective power in their interactions with the employer. Their priority will need to shift to converting their massive numbers into organisational strength, especially as there is no room for further growth except through mergers or by poaching from other organisations. Those who fail to convert quantity of membership into quality of organisation may well find themselves victims of their more successful rivals' poaching efforts.

The three-year agreement

In the 1994 bargaining round in the PSBC unions collectively put forward a set of demands that combined the old-guard staff associations' interest in a high overall increase and the progressive unions' interest for uplifting those at the bottom. The position called for a R1500 minimum monthly salary and an across-the-board 15% increase. The unions expected that these demands would be met, given their membership growth, a new labour relations dispensation and the perception that the new government would be amenable to improving public servants' conditions of service.

However the proposal was rejected by government, which offered slightly more than a R1 000 per month minimum wage and a freeze on salaries at the high end. The offer was rejected by all the unions, many of whom threatened to walk out of the talks. Government then offered a variable increase, starting at 20% for employees in the lowest grade, falling to 5% at the top, but the PSBC nonetheless deadlocked. The impasse was broken through high-level political intervention by then-deputy presidents

Thabo Mbeki and F.W. de Klerk, and a wage agreement was reached only after commitments were made to create task teams to conduct a comprehensive investigation of the public service salary structure. The investigation was not completed in time for the 1995 round of negotiations, but the process was accelerated by a wave of wage strikes in the private sector and a particularly fierce wildcat strike among unorganised public service nurses.

The disparate positions of unions and government were eventually consolidated in a three-year agreement which not only went beyond the unions' original 1994 demand, but awarded the largest wage increase in the history of the public service, if not of the country as a whole. According to Baskin (Chapter 7), the three-year agreement made a significant improvement in the minimum wage rate, which increased from R13 200 to R17 100 per year. The largest increase went to the lowest paid: grade 1 workers received a healthy 29,5% increase, grades 2-6 all obtained increases higher than 35% (Jacklin and Machin, 1998: 14). No employee received an increase of less than 7,5%.

These increases – as large as they appeared – were made even more substantial by changes to the 'rank and leg' system of promotion. Where these promotions normally occur on an individual basis every two or three years, in 1996 all employees on grade 1 were automatically advanced to grade 2, whether or not they qualified on the basis of a performance review.

Plans for further increases in 1997 and 1998 were not realised, given problems in financing the agreement (see below). Still, in both of those years public servants received average increases at or above the rate of inflation, though improvements for those in the bottom grades were considerably higher, while senior managers' salaries were frozen.

As a consequence the agreement made major inroads into the public service wage gap. This legacy of the apartheid public service was reduced from 64:1 in 1989 to 25:1 in 1995 (after the first negotiations between the unions and the new government), then to 17:1 after the first year of the three-year agreement, and finally to 15:1 in 1998. (See Bhorat, 1997 and Patel's chapter on collective bargaining in this collection.) Closing the wage gap through an improvement in conditions of the lowest-paid was one of the COSATU unions' core demands, and reversed the long-standing emphasis in the PSC to reward those at the top at the expense of the mass of black unskilled workers.[8] The three-year agreement also sought to simplify and extend the range of non-wage benefits available to public service workers. For example, women were ineligible for the public service housing subsidy, while many General Assistants (and other categories, including some teachers) did not receive pensions and 13th cheques as they were considered to be casual workers (see Baskin, Chapter 7).

The hallmark of the three-year agreement was the link between wage improvements and broader restructuring and transformation of the public service (see Patel, Chapter 6 and Baskin, Chapter 7). Improved conditions for those at the bottom were a key element of this vision, as were a reduction in the unwieldy occupational structure to 16 grades, reducing wage differences between grades, introduction of a new skills-based grading system, and a measure of job security through a moratorium on employer-initiated retrenchments. The new grading system aimed at overcoming the existing complex and arbitrary occupational hierarchy, which had been shaped by imperatives of maintaining the racial and gender hierarchy of the public service, rather than by an objective evaluation of job content or workers' skills. It was meant not only to break the apartheid division of labour, but to provide workers with career paths that could deliver advancement and further real improvements while developing the skills base of the public service.

Under the agreement wage increases were to be financed through 'right-sizing' the public service. According to Baskin, the parties agreed in principle to 'right-sizing': that 'the size of the public service be related to "available financial resources"', though the meaning of right-sizing remains contested. For government this meant reducing the public service wage bill as a proportion of public consumption expenditure, while the unions stressed that employment levels must be determined by service delivery requirements. In the context of a moratorium on retrenchments 'right-sizing' was to be achieved through a management plan and a skills audit to provide an accurate account of existing employment and skills levels and a link between these and service requirements. In addition, the agreement emphasised freezing or abolishing vacancies, a program of voluntary severance packages (VSPs), attrition, and in the last instance, retrenchment of 'supernumerary' officials, though only after all possibilities for 'redeployment' had been exhausted. Finally, the parties agreed to restructure pension benefits, both to make early retirement more attractive to long-serving public employees, and to achieve savings through a reduction in the state's contribution from 18% to 15%.

The high-water mark of worker participation

Not only did the post-1994 public service rapidly develop the familiar institutions of pluralist bargaining, but both unions and government alike shared a commitment to developing deeper forms of worker involvement in decision-making (see Patel, Chapter 8). The workplace forum provisions in Chapter 5 of the new LRA stimulated important debates in South Africa on the merits of co-determination: the development of forms of consultation and joint decision-making between management and employees. However, Chapter 5 was not the stimulus for the extension of worker participation in decision-making; indeed, the public service was in fact exempted from the relevant sections of the new Act.

To a significant degree the interest in public service co-determination was impelled by temporary institutions and practices developed during the transition. Progressive unions made a concerted effort to check the unilateral prerogatives of the apartheid state by promoting the creation of broad transformation forums in public institutions in which a measure of power would be shared out among stakeholders. Many of these innovations survived the transition and provided models for new forms of public governance which were prominently featured in the White Paper on the Transformation of the Public Service (DPSA, 1995). The White Paper envisioned worker representatives becoming directly involved in fundamental policy formulation as well as in implementation and monitoring at the enterprise level.

At many levels prospects for worker involvement in decision-making are far greater in the public service than elsewhere. Central bargaining in the PSCBC not only gives unions a powerful platform, but the scope of issues bargained extends beyond conventional distributive issues. According to Patel (Chapter 8) many unionists believe they have the ability to raise a wide range of issues in central bargaining and through transformation structures at the institutional level, and hence have little need for the comparatively modest powers available in Chapter 5 of the LRA. Moreover sectoral bargaining councils in education and the police allow for consideration of broader policy questions in those areas.

Given the improvements in wages and conditions of service, involvement in policy-making and implementation, and the moratorium on retrenchments, it is not surprising that the public service was one of the least conflictual sectors in the country from 1994 to mid-1999 (Andrew Levy and Associates, various). Where the public service had been perhaps the most strike-prone sector in the years 1989-1993, with health workers, police and teachers embarking on lengthy strikes, from 1994 this changed dramatically. Except for a prominent wildcat strike by nurses, largely in Gauteng and the Eastern Cape, there were no major strikes in the public service during this period, and comparatively few person-days were lost due to strikes.[9]

The nurses' strike ironically demonstrated the efficacy of public service labour relations. Their actions were prompted by pent-up frustrations over wages and working conditions, especially the increased workload caused by the extension of free health services in 1994. Moreover, public service nurses were unable to express these demands due to the absence of an effective nurses' union.[10] Far from a repudiation of the emerging labour relations dispensation in the public service, the strikes were an unfortunately clumsy effort by one occupational group to find a way of processing their demands *through* the system. In the aftermath of the strike most nurses did join unions, and participated in subsequent bargaining rounds in the PSCBC. Moreover, there has been no repeat of the 1995 wildcat strike.[11]

Failings of the three-year agreement: Quick fixes, deferred problems

If the three-year agreement contributed to labour peace, it was unable to produce the conditions for sustainable transformation. Each of its key elements would in time come undone.

Voluntary Severance Packages

VSPs were the most glaring failure. They were meant to cut public service employment levels while freeing up funds to pay for the wage and non-wage increases. They did nothing of the kind. According to the Presidential Review Commission, very few posts vacated by VSPs were in fact abolished; most were filled by new appointees. In some cases the very same public servant who received the VSP returned through the 'back door' as a consultant, though this practice violated the severance terms. As a result, 'although the long-term savings … are … likely to be much smaller than predicted, the short-term costs have been much higher' (PRC,

1998, 3.2.4.2). The VSPs did not succeed in shedding 'dead wood' or undesirable 'old guard' employees, but rather provided a lucrative escape for public servants with marketable skills. These departures were felt particularly sharply in health and education. Crucially, the VSPs did not yield anywhere close to the kinds of savings that were expected. As such savings were to be a source for funding the general wage increases granted in 1996 and projected for 1997 and 1998, the failure of VSPs put intense pressure on the fiscal sustainability of the wage settlement.

The retrenchment moratorium

The VSPs are not the only examples of unintended consequences issuing from the three-year agreement. A similar fate befell the moratorium on retrenchments, seemingly a major union victory. According to Baskin (Chapter 7), the moratorium did not prevent the loss of nearly 170 000 jobs or more than 13% of the workforce as public service employment fell from 1,25 million in 1996 to less than 1,1 million at the end of 1998. Ironically the cuts fell most heavily on the constituencies organised by the COSATU unions that fought most vigorously for the moratorium. The cuts were heaviest at the bottom grades, affecting NEHAWU's membership most severely, and causing an 8,5% decline in the police workforce. These changes had a dramatic effect on the skills profile of the public service, as the total number of jobs in the lowest grades (1 to 5) declined by over 19% while those in the middle category (6 to 9) increased by over 7%.

However, as the decline in police numbers attests, these cuts were not made according to delivery or development priorities. Instead they appear to have been motivated by managers' desires to defend their budgets by cutting back on the unskilled beneficiaries of the wage increases and extension and equalisation of benefits. However, employment growth in the relatively expensive middle-range categories put upward pressure on the wage bill and offset any savings from the job losses at the bottom. In this manner the decline in employment delivered neither cost savings nor a closer fit between policy priorities and personnel. It was in some ways the worst of both worlds for unions and government: neither cost-saving 'downsizing' nor good 'right-sizing'.

Financing the agreement

Given these developments, it is not surprising that the fiscal basis for the 1996 increases quickly eroded. Total personnel costs as a percentage of the budget (excluding interest expenditure) increased from 46,6% in fiscal year 1995/1996 to an estimated 50,6% in fiscal year 1999/2000. The situation was worse in the provinces, where personnel spending rose from 53% of provincial budgets in fiscal year 1995/1996 to more than 59% in fiscal year 1998/1999. It is this rapid increase in recurrent expenditure that provoked government demands for a review of pay policy and for ending the retrenchment moratorium, proposals that would guide their position in the 1999 wage dipute. Increasing personnel costs were said to be 'crowding out' other spending. COSATU argued that personnel costs actually fell in real terms since 1996 while non-wage expenditure fell even faster, due to government's aggressive deficit reduction efforts. Instead of cutting the wage bill COSATU has called for a review of deficit targets and the expansion of non-wage spending.

This problem highlighted a larger issue: the lack of alignment between government's budget process and annual wage negotiations in the PSCBC. This problem would intensify with the adoption of the Medium Term Expenditure Framework (MTEF) from 1997. Under the MTEF budget planning would be projected in three-year cycles, largely fixing expenditure on the wage bill well in advance of PSCBC negotiations. Collective bargaining would become less about the size of the wage bill and more about its division. From the unions' perspective this fundamentally undermined collective bargaining.

A skills-based grading system?

If the sustainability of the wage increases came under scrutiny, so too did the basis for determining remuneration. The three-year agreement announced a shift towards a skills-based grading system, borrowed directly from private sector developments. Other union-initiated remuneration reforms were based on this foundation: reducing the number of job grades, narrowing differentials within and between grades, closing the overall wage gap. The new system promised opportunities for training and career advancement.

In practice the agreement ushered in no such thing. In a detailed study of public service wages and grading, Jacklin and Machin (1998) argue that the three-year agreement failed to include other initiatives on which a skills-based grading system depends: the delivery of training, changes to work organisation arrangements and a reformed performance appraisal system. The inadequate opportunities for training meant that workers – especially those at the bottom – would have limited opportunities for advancing within the system, and would likely be consigned indefinitely to their existing broad band.

The consequences of failing to move to a real skills-based grading system were made worse by changes to the 'rank and leg' promotion system. Public servants are normally eligible for promotion every three years, or every two years if they are deemed 'preferentially promotable'. The benefits of promotion are substantial: rank promotions can result in as much as a 20% improvement in income. In the main, advancement within a broad occupational band (composed of a number of ranks) does not depend on either a vacancy or on funding for the post, nor in practice does it require meaningful assessment. Though in principle workers must be deemed 'promotable', in practice almost no one is held back. The 'rank and leg' system amounts to a regular bonus for employees unrelated to either individual performance or a rational assessment of the public service's skills requirements. Indeed, if a higher grade position is unavailable, workers will be paid at the higher rate even while continuing in their old job. The 1996 agreement did not change this, and in one respect made the problems worse through the mass promotion of grade 1 workers.

Recent figures from the South African Police Service illustrate the perverse effects generated by the promotion system (see Table 1.1). The fact that there are nearly five times as many sergeants and twice as many inspectors as constables is a reflection more of police officers' desire for and success in achieving promotion to senior positions than of the country's policing objectives and of the labour requirements necessary for achieving these. Nor do the figures reflect the police officers' skills nor the real content of their jobs. In cases where officers have been promoted to the rank of sergeant they may in fact be working as constables, though with the more senior title and its commensurate higher salary.

In addition to rank and leg promotions, workers may also apply for promotion between the broad occupational bands – a 'post' promotion – but success depends on the availability of a vacant funded post and workers must possess appropriate qualifications. Grade 1 workers – including general labourers – may have been promoted en masse to grade 2, but in the absence of proper training programs, they have few opportunities to gain the qualifications necessary for a post promotion into grade 3 jobs, such as clerical positions. In general, the same applies to more skilled workers applying for promotion from grades 7 to 8 – from

Table 1.1:   SELECTED RANKS AND SALARIES IN THE SAPS AS AT
                JANUARY 2000

Rank	Number of employees	Salary (in Rands)
Constable	11 217	34 557
Sergeant	55 312	40 881
Inspector	25 620	63 042

(Source: DPSA)

clerical to administrative officer positions – though such advances are relatively easier than for labourers attempting to move up.

In short the changes to the grading system, in the context of 'rank and leg' promotions, produced destructive results. Not only is promotion expensive, but it remains unrelated to either worker performance or the public service's employment needs while – in the absence of proper training programs – workers are effectively consigned to a life within their broad occupational bands. As Table 1.1 indicates, changes to the promotion system would not only allow a better fit between employment, remuneration and needs, but could in fact finance an expansion in employment at lower levels.

The three-year agreement was signed two months before the launch of the government's new Growth, Employment and Redistribution (GEAR) macroeconomic strategy. And while it is probably true that the deal could never have been struck after GEAR, the strategy itself was not responsible for the three-year agreement's contradictions. Even before GEAR the government had been committed to a reduction in government expenditure as a proportion of GDP, and to a reduction in the public service wage bill as a proportion of total government spending to make resources available for infrastructure development and other services. This put government in a very tight box. The equalisation of conditions of service could come about either through maintaining employment levels while reducing wages and benefits or improving remuneration while cutting numbers. Both parties accepted the latter formulation, though with a priority on attrition, freezing posts, and eliminating ghost workers. Expansion of the wage bill would put pressure on other forms of government expenditure, in the absence of increased borrowing or increases in revenue through higher taxation or privatisation. But such steps are politically difficult and fiscally problematic in the context of an untransformed state unable to spend effectively those resources it already commands.

Given this context the three-year agreement was inadequately costed while additional elements crucial to its success (like adequate training programs or a means to effect real personnel reductions) did not materialise. Many of its possible consequences – such as the likely effect of VSPs – were obvious to observers at the time, but were not addressed. Moreover its authors were generally unaware of the complexity of public service systems, and entered agreements with little understanding of their likely effects. ANC officials depended on advice from 'old guard' senior civil servants, who often ended up drafting new regulations with more concern for protecting their own prerogatives than for promoting transformation.

Viewed as a way of transforming government under tight constraints, the three-year agreement must be seen as a failure. If viewed as a crisis management exercise adopted with imperfect information, it was a qualified success. It certainly helped ensure labour peace, though at the cost of deferring core problems.

From agreement to conflict: 1999 and beyond

If the PSBC was able to defer long-term problems, its successor body, the PSCBC, had no such luxury. Not only were the defects of the 1996 bargain well known, but negotiations for a new agreement began in late 1998 in the midst of South Africa's worst economic crisis of the decade.

The unions' initial common position was for a 15% across-the-board increase, while government responded with an offer of an average 5,7% increase. This massive gap remained through the announcement of the budget in March. At a PSCBC meeting at the end of April the government proposed a task team to review salary progressions, but would determine for itself whether to increase its offer based on the task team's recommendations. At this point all the unions in the PSCBC declared deadlock.

In July the dispute was referred to arbitration, but within days the government improved its average offer from 5,7% to 6%, with employees in the lowest grades receiving 6,2%, and those at the top 3,5%. At the end of July, following a one-day strike led primarily by the COSATU unions, government's offer was improved to an average of 6,3%, with a 6,8% increase for teachers. By this time the unions had reduced their demand to an average of 7,5%, with a somewhat higher increase for teachers (PSA, 1999; Fraser-Moleketi, 1999).

In early August a number of unions again embarked on a legal strike – supplemented by public demonstrations organised by unions that had stayed out of the earlier protest. This was an unprecedented development in public service labour relations: the first time that progressive and old-guard worker organisations pursued a common program of industrial action. In fact, the strike marked the shift by many of the old-guard unions to a more robust form of unionism. To an extent they have begun to shed their diffidence and politeness, and have made use of the new possibilities in labour law for exercising power.

At the same time, the unions linked to COSATU were caught between their commitments to their base and their participation in the alliance with the ANC. In the past the tripartite alliance had yielded many benefits when the COSATU unions had been able to break deadlocks through appeals to the party, and especially to President Mandela. In the run-up to the 1999 elections alliance discipline effectively diverted COSATU unions from pressing their case in the PSCBC or in the streets. And after the elections, the alliance route was effectively closed.

Indeed, leading ANC figures attacked public servants' profligacy, labelling the unions as having selfish special interests. Informal efforts to broker a compromise failed, and on 7 September government unilaterally implemented its final offer – a step taken previously in the short history of public service labour relations only by F.W. de Klerk in 1993 (Fraser-Moleketi, 1999a).

In issuing its unilateral increase government offered to 'work' with the unions on the 2000/2001 round of salary negotiations, and to develop a comprehensive remuneration policy. However, the invitation to return to a forum in which the unions had expended considerable energy in return for a mere 0,5% improvement on the employer's offer – which was then unilaterally imposed – must have seemed eminently resistable. Indeed, at the time of writing the unions continue to boycott the PSCBC, on the grounds that the wage deadlock continues – and some of the unions have pursued the matter through arbitration.

A 'score card' approach to assessing industrial conflict is seldom useful, but is even less appropriate here. Notwithstanding that the employer imposed its solution on labour, in fact neither party addressed the fundamental questions facing the public service: effectively linking budget, staffing levels, remuneration, and delivery priorities. This failure will have important consequences in the future.

Given the enormity and difficulty of these questions it is unfortunate, but not surprising that the bargaining turned on the issue of wages rather than the unresolved transformation matters. Informants close to the PSCBC negotiations indicate that an agreement was in fact forthcoming on a new remuneration policy, including fundamental changes to the rank and leg system. However, given the obvious attractions the old policies hold for public servants, unions rightly calculated that they could not sell the agreement in the absence of a real wage increase.

Explaining government's refusal to compromise is more difficult. In part its position was informed by the dynamics of the June 1999 elections. It effectively delayed proceedings in the PSCBC until after the poll. Then, as a result of the ANC's overwhelming mandate for a further five year term – with a near two-thirds parliamentary majority – government was in a politically unassailable position from which it could substantially increase its autonomy from its alliance partners and respond to other interests in the party bent on curtailing the unions' influence. The ANC likely concluded that the public service unions would be unable to mount a strike that could impose sufficient costs to force government to reconsider its position. Given the coordination between new and old guard unions COSATU's strategic and tactical choices were limited by the need to maintain a common front with partners untested in mass action. In addition, its choices were restricted by the exigencies of maintaining public support, which would not be easily forthcoming if the unions were seen to be disrupting 'delivery' in their fight against a popular government. Both of these conditions – government's unprecedented freedom of manoeuver and COSATU's equally unprecedented constraints – no doubt reinforced the position of those in and outside government committed to a strict interpretation of GEAR and the maintainence of fiscal discipline. The PSCBC negotiations enabled these interests to steal the line of march on the trade unions.

However, government's resolute stance holding the line at 6,3% creates a number of problems on its side. First, its stand defers consideration of restructuring for yet another year. Meanwhile, the animosity generated by the dispute creates its own dynamics that make it more difficult to come to terms with these issues, when in the future – as is virtually inevitable – the parties must seek each other out to implement meaningful transformation of public service labour relations. The problems are qualitative, not merely quantitative, and depend on agreement between the parties; they cannot be resolved through victory in a labour relations 'war'.

KEY ISSUES IN PUBLIC SERVICE LABOUR RELATIONS

It is difficult, in the current climate of mutual recrimination, to discern a means that would bring the parties back to good faith bargaining in the PSCBC. Yet it is equally difficult to perceive a route for restructuring the public service that does not pass through the PSCBC. On every dimension of transformation the parties are faced with balancing competing imperatives that have been mutually acknowledged. There are few easy solutions. What are the key issues?

The budget

Since the beginning of formal labour relations in the public service a fundamental – and still unresolved issue – has been aligning negotiations over wages and non-wage benefits with the budget. Government draws up the budget beginning in the year prior to presenting it in parliament, in consulations between the Department of Finance, national departments, and provincial governments. Now that the Medium Term Expenditure Framework is in place, these discussions occur within three-year rolling budgets that to a major extent fix allocations. The budget is then presented to parliament where its allocations may be interrogated.

At its heart the issue concerns two competing and difficult-to-reconcile principles. Government draws up budgets, and parliament is supreme: it alone has constitutional power to approve money bills. On the other hand wage agreements in the public service depend upon good-faith bargaining between parties in the PSCBC not only over the allocation of funds available for salaries and benefits, but over their total amount. As personnel expenditure is by far the largest single item in the budget, even small changes can have a massive effect on government's ability to meet its other obligations.

A bargaining process that generates agreements with little regard to these wider obligations would either upset other public priorities or would effectively render the agreement a dead letter. But the reverse is equally problematic, where the integrity of the budget trumps public servants' right to engage in collective bargaining, not only about the allocation of expenditure, but about its overall size. At present this is the case. In 1999 the budget effectively capped the amount available on personnel expenditure; the unions were unable to persuade government to change the allocation significantly nor could they marshal effective power to force it to do so. This is a common problem in public services in every democratic society. However, particular circumstances in South Africa add to the difficulty. GEAR targets limit room for manoeuver, but these are not the origin of the difficulty. The overwhelming imperatives of service delivery and infrastructure development place burdens on government that for the foreseeable future will put pressure on the size of the public service wage bill. Attempting to overcome the legacies of the apartheid division of labour while at the same time retaining skilled public servants makes it difficult to trade off the needs of one employee constituency against another. Moreover, given the single-party dominant political system and the leadership's tight discipline over the parliamentary caucus, public service unions can exert little pressure on government to change the budget, either through lobbying or through the electoral process.

There is no easy or logical answer, but the present arrangement is unsatisfactory: it has produced repeated conflicts since 1994 that are wasteful of time and resources and generate considerable ill-will. Furthermore it generates perverse consequences for government's own plans for public service restructuring. As Baskin notes in Chapter 7, limiting bargaining to dividing up a pre-set amount will tend towards majority rule at the PSCBC:

> and this is likely to take the form of 'across-the-board' increases, or larger increases at the lower end of the salary scale. In the medium-term this will lead to erosion of the bargaining unit as lower-end employees are replaced by contracting out arrangements, and as higher-end ... employees attempt to leave the bargaining unit ...

A way forward is offered by the Medium Term Expenditure Framework (MTEF), though this will severely test both parties. The MTEF enables all citizens to learn government's long-term budget priorities. Such transparency for the first time allows for government to be held accountable for its performance. A major problem arises, however, if the MTEF's three-year commitments are perceived to be imposed from above or are unresponsive to needs.

The MTEF includes – at least in rhetoric – mechanisms for popular participation in its formulation. But in practice such participation is de-emphasised by Government, whose priority has been to establish executive authority over the budget process and to insulate it from external participation (Gelb and Bethlehem, 1998). Such insulation effectively extends to Parliament, notwithstanding the invocation of the 'supremacy of Parliament'. Arguments that prioritise Parliament's supremacy as against public service unions' involvement in the budget obscure the fact that Parliament's budget-making powers are severely limited. Though the constitution gives Parliament the power to amend money bills, such powers must be activated by a separate Act – which has not been passed. This state of affairs 'renders the [parliamentary] budget process largely symbolic as the budget is determined wholly by the executive with Parliament having little or no say in its contents' (Adair and Albertyn, 1999).

The test for government will be whether it will tolerate even minimal forms of involvement in developing MTEF priorities – including the allocation for personnel expenditure – from civil society groups, including the public service unions. This would be in line with the values expressed in the White Paper on the Transformation of the Public Service and the Presidential Review Commission report, both of which stress partnerships with civil society and empowering citizens to share the responsibilities of governance (PRC, 1998: 3.1.2, 3.2.3).

At the same time such participation would present a major challenge for the public service unions. It would require formulation of initial negotiating positions a year in advance, development of sufficient economic research capacity, and the development of capacity to engage with the MTEF process at the many provincial and departmental sites where and when it occurs. It also requires sufficient sophistication to engage with state technocrats and other stakeholders and the will to press the matter if their approaches are rebuffed, through public campaigns if necessary. Short of such an effort, their wage claims will carry little sympathy if presented as a fait accompli after the budget has been tabled in Parliament.

Bargaining structures

Public service collective bargaining structures grew in equal parts from improvisation and imitation. Educators and police were able to gain a measure of recognition as a result of the crisis precipitated in these sectors by the struggle against apartheid. Whether or not there was a legal basis to do so the authorities in these sectors were forced to address workers' collective demands simply to ensure the continuation of state services (see Garson, Chapter 9 and Marks, Chapter 10). The existence of separate bargaining councils is thus a by-product of the conflict that attended democratisation, reinforced by the fact that historically ministers in these areas have legal authority to set wages and conditions of service.

But the structures also evolved in imitation of the private sector and the development of centralised bargaining elsewhere in the economy. The PSBC was created as a vehicle for bargaining at the highest level of the public service as a whole. Its creation was facilitated by the existence of the PSC; unlike other sectors of the South African economy the determination of labour issues in the public service was already very highly centralised. In an odd way the establishment of centralised bargaining could occur much faster in the public service than elsewhere, as it meant transforming the existing PSC into a truly bipartite structure.

However, unlike almost any other sector, the public service was composed of but one employer and a multitude of distinctly different 'industries' that were further divided into nine different provinces and more than 30 national departments. The federalism implicit in the Constitution further complicates matters: some departments of state – education, welfare, health – are joint competencies of the national and provincial governments. Most of the managers and workers in these areas are in fact employed by the provinces. To further complicate things, different provinces organise their affairs in different ways, combining in one department functions that are housed in separate national departments. It has been a daunting task developing bargaining structures that suit the contours of the public service, without compromising the coherence of the sector as a whole and centralised bargaining. The same can be said about the kinds of issues bargained and the levels at which they are determined.

The model of industry-wide bargaining councils provided under the new LRA was crudely extended to the public service, creating an unwieldly mix of more than 40 provincial and departmental bargaining institutions, alongside the PSBC, the Education Labour Relations Council (ELRC), and the National Negotiating Forum (NNF) (Adair and Albertyn, 1999). The framework was not wanted by anyone, however a replacement was not immediately perceived.

Notwithstanding the conflict in the PSCBC over wages, considerable convergence occurred over the shape of bargaining (see Baskin, 1999). Unfortunately not all the issues were resolved, nor formalised in agreements, and progress was thwarted by the dispute. In 1999 the NNF was replaced by a new Safety and Security Sectoral Bargaining Council (SSSBC), and its membership was extended from police to all employees of the SAPS, including civil servants. In 1999 two other structures were established, the Health Sector Bargaining Council (HSBC) and the General Administrative Bargaining Council (GABC). The former includes all employees of the Departments of Health and Welfare (national and provincial) as well as public health and health and welfare professionals in other departments. Given that health is a provincial competence, the HSBC intends to establish provincial chambers for negotiating more detailed agreements. The GABC includes all employees not covered by the other bargaining structures. The ELRC continues to exist, and has developed provincial chambers in each province. While considerable progress has been made on the structures of bargaining there is less agreement about where issues are to be bargained. The underlying issue is finding a balance between common standards across the public service and accommodating the specific needs of the different provinces and departments. If wages and conditions of service are negotiated solely at the PSCBC, the sectoral and provincial institutions will be largely irrelevant. On the other hand the complete devolution of bargaining to the sectors and/or provinces could lead to intolerable conditions: either growing inequality between provinces or competition in which sectors attempt to outbid each other in pursuit of skilled staff. Solutions include converting bargaining in the PSCBC into agreements over minimum and maximum wages and progression ranges, rather than actual wages, or allowing it to ratify agreements made in other bargaining councils.

Restructuring management

A strong system of labour relations in the public service depends not only on strong unions, but also on capable management. However public service management – in the true sense of the word – is a post-1994 phenomenon and remains more rhetorical than real. One of the main aspects of transformation has been overcoming the centralised structure of administration symbolised by the old PSC. As Adair and Albertyn write in Chapter 5, this logically entailed the devolution of authority to lower levels of the public service and converting adminstrators into managers endowed with both power and responsibility.

As mentioned in the previous section, the Ministers of Education and Safety and Security already possessed powers to determine terms and conditions of employment for educators and police. Amendments to the Public Service Act in 1996 extended these powers to national ministers and, at the provincial level, to Members of the Executive Committees (MECs), who were given original powers to organise their departments, including the hiring and dismissal of employees. This parallels other legislation and regulations that make 'executing authorities' responsible for financial matters in their departments. The PSC's rigid provisions for disciplining employees were replaced by a collective agreement reached in the PSCBC in January 1999, which now allows for discipline to be managed according to standard labour-management procedures in a flexible manner and at the appropriate level.

However managers have not yet been given power to determine pay and conditions of service for their employees. These powers are still vested in the Ministers of Education and Safety and Security for educators and police and the Minister for Public Service and Administration for all other public servants. In practice these are determined through bargaining in the PSCBC. Even the new powers granted under the 1996 amendments to the Public Service Act are limited. According to Adair and Albertyn 'executing authorities' may determine the organisational structure of their departments:

> however they may not retrench surplus employees and they must organise their department within the prescribed nationally determined grading system, which is inflexible and does not take account of sectoral needs and differences.

Though extending responsibility with one hand, the amendments take power away with the other, as executing authorities' scope for autonomous action is highly constrained by decisions at the highest level. Moreover, 'even within the departments and institutions, all decisions, no matter what they are, have to be made by the highest authority' as executing authorities who do not readily delegate powers to lower levels of management in their departments.

According to Adair and Albertyn, 'decision-making thus remains highly hierarchical with senior and middle management having very little decision-making power'. The state of affairs fosters neither accountabilty nor responsibility, nor does it allow for meaningful interventions by workers or their trade union representatives, except at the very highest levels. Notwithstanding massive efforts to transform the old public service, and the increasing importance of collective bargaining in place of the unilateral determinations by the old PSC, 'managers still do not "manage". They are responsible for ensuring that employees abide by a complex set of rules and regulations, rather than concentrating on output and service delivery'.

The extension of financial responsibility to senior managers under these constraints produces perverse effects. Managers must fit their decisions about personnel deployment into calculations for meeting their financial obligations within fixed standards on wages and conditions of service. Personnel decisions are thus oriented towards budget concerns instead of being rationally linked to service delivery needs. Management tasks are made even more untenable as retrenchment has been blocked by the three-year agreement's moratorium, while redeployment is difficult, and dismissal – even for cause – is so time consuming as to be virtually impossible. The present conditions discourage creativity and initiative, and break the link between spending, development priorities, and the deployment of personnel.

But even if one could find an appropriate balance between national norms and standards and decentralised decision-making, this is not the most profound management problem. Far more difficult is overcoming the legacy of apartheid-era hiring practices that allowed vast numbers of unqualified people to become managers. A system that is able to develop centrally-determined norms and standards while encouraging managerial flexibility depends ultimately upon skilled managers. Indeed it demands highly sophisticated men and women who can understand and effectively maintain this delicate balance. These are not – in the main – the kinds of managers that the apartheid public service bequeathed to the new order. Their lack of proper managerial training is most glaring in the areas of financial management and labour relations, which seriously weaken their effectiveness in linking budgets and personnel with policy objectives (DPSA, 1997).

These problems are of course uneven: some provinces are worse than others (especially those that absorbed former TBVC and SGT administrations), and the same is true of national departments. But a number of high-profile public scandals have brought the problem of public service management into sharp focus. Recent reports from the Auditor General have shown that many departments are forced to roll-over their allocated budgets because they cannot disburse money. The Departments of Welfare and Health, for example, were unable to spend substantial portions of their national funds for poverty relief and AIDS prevention. Allegations of wide-spread corruption in the Department of Correctional Services have revealed that practices of patronage common in the old regime persist into the new, albeit deployed along ethnic – rather than merely racial – lines. These three cases are extremely worrying as they occurred at the national level of these departments, where it is assumed managerial competence is greatest.

Adair and Albertyn argue that new legislation will need to be passed that completes the transformation of management in the public service. Nonetheless the task of developing and training management to perform the responsibilities thrust upon it remains an overwhelming – and exceedingly long-term – priority of transformation. Good management is a necessary condition for good labour relations in the public service.

Right-sizing

As mentioned above, one unfortunate consequence of the 1999 wage dispute was to defer yet again progress on 'right-sizing' the public service. The unintended consequences of the three-year agreement's retrenchment moratorium and VSPs have still not been addressed, thereby stymying efforts to align the size and deployment of staff with development priorities and the budget. Right-sizing still means different things to management and labour. For the former the priority has been reducing the public service wage bill as a proportion of public consumption expenditure, while for the unions employment levels are to be determined by service delivery requirements.

However both parties – at least in principle – recognise the other's priorities. Cutting the wage bill to reduce public expenditure without regard to the government's development goals makes a mockery of the budget, transforming it into an end in itself rather than a means to achieve political goals. In principle this position is rejected by government in all its policy documents, not only those on the transformation of the public service. The Presidential Review Commission observed that right-sizing:

> should be located within the macro-economic constraints established by GEAR, but should nevertheless be driven primarily by the need to improve the efficiency and effectiveness of service delivery rather than by narrow budget considerations. (PRC, 1998: 3.2.7)

The DPSA's recent report on its skills and service audit suggests that restructuring is a qualitative matter that does not easily produce savings, and that savings may come at the cost of affecting basic service delivery (DPSA, 1999). The audit revealed that the public service as a whole is not overstaffed; rather many departments are seriously understaffed, or have inappropriate staff complements for their needs. For example provinces that incorporated old homeland bureaucracies have an oversupply of unskilled labourers, but a serious undersupply of higher-level managers, professionals, and support personnel.

In another example, the audit showed that many township and ex-homeland schools suffer from a severe undersupply of support staff, essential to effective education. The report advocated an active redeployment strategy, rather than simple retrenchment (itself an expensive step).

On the other hand, determining staffing by reference to service delivery alone – without reference to budget constraints – is even more problematic. Yet this position is rejected, at least implicitly, in a number of union policy documents. For example, the report of COSATU's September Commission on the Future of the Unions advocates an ambitious program for 'building a public sector that can deliver efficiently and effectively, and improve the working life of the members of the public sector unions' (COSATU, 1997: 3.2).

For COSATU this entails 'taking some responsibility for co-managing transformation', by exposing corruption and ghost workers. At the same time, the approach acknowledges:

> there are limits on government resources, and unlimited needs. COSATU should reject the limits defined by GEAR, and continue to contest them. But even without GEAR, there would be limits. This implies trade-offs between different priorities. (Ibid.)

COSATU still believes that a 'bigger, more labour-intensive' public service is necessary, but accepts that 'Participation with government ... would mean that whatever choices are made, even hard ones, the unions would be willing to take joint responsibility for their implementation' (Ibid.).

A similar position is at least implicit in a recent assessment of the public service strike written by two leading NEHAWU unionists. Though they disparage the notion of 'crowding out', they do not reject the idea of trade-offs between components of the budget (Makhura and Phadu, 1999).

There is thus, in principle, considerable overlap between positions. It remains to be seen whether the parties are able to reach agreements that resolve this key problem of transformation. And, even if agreements are reached at the PSCBC, it is questionable whether either management or labour have the capacity to implement and monitor these at sectoral, provincial and institutional levels. Even if both sides find an accommodation that enables them to escape from the current impasse, neither has the capacity as yet to ensure compliance from their constituencies at the sectoral, provincial, and enterprise levels. Faced with an unreliable management echelon itself in need of change, management's victory in the 1999 bargaining round may prove short-lived: it will find it difficult to fight a two-front war with both labour and its own managers.

This state of affairs does not augur well for public service transformation. It also suggests a third possibility: that many managers and workers will find common cause in defending their inherited privileges against the restructuring agendas advanced by both government and organised labour. In this scenario, poor management structures may permit both old- and new-guard civil servants to direct public resources towards maintaining their own positions. There are many disturbing signs – as in the Department of Correctional Services – that apartheid-era patronage not only persists, but has opportunities to flourish in a situation precariously poised between the paternalism of the old order and the rational labour relations of the new. There is considerable danger that the contemporary public service will recapitulate the situation under apartheid where the formal rationality of bureaucratic rules became increasingly distant from the real paternalistic relationships between management and labour. The public service may have been brought under the LRA, but it has not yet been remade in its image.

Faced with these possibilities, recent suggestions by ministers and senior officials that the public service be exempted from many provisions of the LRA and the Basic Conditions of Employment Act may in fact backfire. Rather than promoting management hegemony or even fiscal discipline, such steps might in fact encourage practices of patronage quite at odds with formal models of managerial control. Though many may reject the notion, an employer truly interested in transformation of the public service and service delivery may have much to gain from bolstering effective unions and developing sound labour relations practices.

CONCLUSION

In the few years since South Africa's first democratic elections, incredible progress has been made in the development of a modern system of labour relations in the public service. Not only have unions and bargaining structures been established, but these have reached successful agreements on a range of distributive and non-distributive matters. The system has, for the most part, produced labour peace in what was until recently a storm-centre of industrial protest. These are remarkable achievements, not only considering the distance the parties have had to travel from the racist and authoritarian past, but also considering the fiscal and skills constraints facing the public service.

At the same time, the labour relations system has been more adept at deferring major problems than resolving them. In part this stems from the inherent difficulties of the issues. In part it is a result of mistakes, and the unintended consequences of agreements reached in haste and under political pressure. In 1999 the system broke down in a dramatic wage dispute, which saw government acting in a unilateral manner not seen since F.W. de Klerk's presidency. Yet the attention given to the dispute obscured the agreements made over the same period on the structure of bargaining, management, and other issues. It also masked the fact that the parties' principled positions are not significantly different and that they have a mutual interest in reaching an accommodation.

Whether the new labour relations system can deliver agreements on the outstanding issues remains to be seen. The private sector has had nearly three decades in which to develop labour relations institutions, and effective managers and trade unionists to make them work. The public service has to catch up in less time, while facing more daunting issues, higher expectations from its intended beneficiaries, and the full glare of publicity when things go wrong. The stakes are high: labour relations will either unlock or slam shut the door to public service transformation, and will help determine whether the state can fulfil its obligations for development. To a great extent the fate of democratisation in South Africa rides on the outcome.

2

LABOUR RELATIONS AND THE POLITICS OF PATRONAGE

A case study of the apartheid civil service[1]

———— ✦ ————

Deborah Posel

Posel's chapter is the first assessment of the historical relationships between the apartheid state and white civil servants in the old public service. Her analysis is crucial for our consideration of labour relations in the contemporary public service as it not only identifies important legacies, but examines some of the lessons that this history may hold today. The National Party used the Afrikanerisation of the civil service as a strategy of industrial discipline in the public service. White civil servants came to depend on the party for jobs, and patronage functioned as a highly authoritatian instrument of control. If white servants ever had any doubt about this relationship, the Broederbond possessed mechanisms of surveillance to remind would-be obstreperous civil servants exactly where control really lay. The Public Servants Association (PSA) was often powerless to neutralise this kind of patronage, partly because of the state's power but also because the PSA played by the rules, which were crafted by the state to circumscribe the organisation's effectiveness. White civil servants were privileged, but they wore their privilege like a golden handcuff: they were relatively powerless in their relationship with their employer because, not in spite of, the dynamics of white racial privilege. This history is relevant today. Trade unions need to play a crucial role in protecting labour relations as a system above political loyalties. In this respect all trade unions, irrespective of their different histories and traditions, have a common interest as trade unions in their relations with their employer.

INTRODUCTION

This book looks at the public service in South Africa since 1994. Why, then, is it necessary to dwell on the old public service? This chapter is written in the conviction that the character of the apartheid public service provides lessons and legacies for current efforts to refashion the public service and its relationship to the state as employer. Relying heavily on techniques of political patronage, the apartheid state turned the public service into an agent of a party political project. A political culture was created which was authoritarian and secretive. This thwarted the possibility of open industrial relations. The prospect of successful collective bargaining within the new public service depends on eradicating this political culture. This, in turn, presupposes an understanding of what needs changing.

Many studies of worker organisation begin with a dramatic story of an important strike or some other flashpoint in the conflict between workers and employers. In the case of the South African civil service during the apartheid years, the story seems much duller. It is the story of the recurring absence of strikes and other visible struggles – despite a string of grievances and high levels of frustration among civil servants – reaching a 'state of rebellion' at times (*Sunday Express*, 14/10/1973). A huge, disaffected workforce, with the potential to bring the advance of apartheid to a complete standstill, chose not to use its powers to mobilise against its employers, the apartheid state.

Why was South Africa's civil service in the pre-1994 period so passive and compliant? This is as much a question about the character of the apartheid state as it is a question in labour history. Indeed, an answer depends on understanding the interconnections between these two sets of processes, as they unfolded from 1948.

The chapter is divided into two parts:

- the first charts the changing character of the apartheid state (from 1948 until the 1980s)[2]
- the second considers how the nature of the state impacted on the prospects for worker organisation.

THE APARTHEID STATE: BALLOONING BUREAUCRACIES

The most obvious feature of the state's development during the apartheid era was its unremitting expansion, or what the National Party (NP) proudly referred to as 'an abnormal growth under this government in every sphere'. The number of state departments increased, as did staff complements (House of Assembly Debates, 1964: 11-5944).[3]

This process began as soon as the NP was installed in power, and went hand in hand with the making of apartheid. One of the striking features of apartheid doctrine was an enormous confidence in a big, strong state as the solution to all manner of social problems. As far as the ideologues of apartheid were concerned, the key to their success lay in creating a state which was sufficiently large, powerful and centrally co-ordinated to keep each race in its 'proper' place (Posel, 1999).

The Department of Native Affairs took the lead in this process, rapidly transforming itself from a minor, under-resourced department into the vanguard of apartheid policy-making. By the mid-1950s, the growth and number of state bureaucracies was evident across the board.[4] In 1939, state departments employed a total of 57 000 people of all races in permanent positions. By 1950, the number had risen to 110 000 and to 139 000 by the end of 1958 – an increase of 144% in twenty years (RSA, 1962: Annexure A). This process of expansion surged ahead throughout the 1960s and 1970s. By 1967, the number of permanent appointees in the public service had grown to 212 788, a substantial increase of 53% over the 1958 figure.[5]

These figures do not include the many thousands of civil servants who were temporary appointees. Taking these employees into account provides an even more dramatic picture of expansion. Statistics for the civil service alone are not available, but figures for the public service as a whole give a good indication of trends that were mirrored in the civil service. A total staff establishment of 140 042 in 1930 had doubled by 1950, shooting up to 454 692 by 1960 and rising by a further 21% to 549 865 in 1970 (Seegers, 1994: 42).

At the same time, the number of government departments steadily increased. On the eve of the NP takeover, there were 26 departments; by 1970 there were 41 (Roux, 1971: 82).

Afrikanerisation

The expansion of the civil service was closely associated with efforts to change its ethnic composition and political leanings. With the energetic help of the Afrikaner Broederbond, the NP introduced what amounted to a tacit policy of affirmative action for white Afrikaners. Afrikaans-speakers were actively recruited for positions of influence in as many social, political and economic organisations as possible, including the state. English-speakers, particularly those in powerful or prominent positions, were discouraged, or forcibly prevented, from holding office, while Afrikaans-speakers formed a growing proportion of new appointees (O'Meara, 1996: 61).

The Department of Native Affairs once again led the way, with its policy of replacing officials considered 'liberal' with more pliable, loyal Afrikaner nationalists (Posel, 1991: 70). This trend soon became a conspicuous and controversial feature of the state as a whole. By 1959, Afrikanerisation had advanced to such an extent that, of more than 40 departments and sub-departments, only six had English-speaking heads. The 'financial specialist departments' – the Treasury, Inland Revenue, and Customs and Excise – remained the 'last bastion' of English civil servants (*The Star*, 14/7/1959). Even here, there were moves to evict them. The experience of a Mr Paige, Collector of Customs and Excise in Durban, who was forced to take early retirement at the age of 55, was not uncommon. No official reasons were given to him, other than that his retirement was in the interests of 'organisational reforms', commonly understood as a euphemism for the Afrikanerisation programme (*The Star*, 1/8/1959).

By 1974, English-speakers accounted for only 20% of senior staff in government departments (*Rapport*, 26/5/1974), and even less in 1976, when only 7 out of 146 senior posts were held by people with English surnames (*The Star*, 12/12/1976).

Staff shortages

One of the more bizarre features of the apartheid state was that it continued to expand in the midst of crippling personnel shortages. The problem of staff shortages was inherited from the previous regime. In 1944, the president of the Public Servants' Association (PSA), the principal organisation representing white public servants, 'issued a serious warning that things are going from bad to worse in the public service and the number of resignations is increasing' (*The Public Servant*, 4/1944). As a result, 'the supply of labour for other than purely routine work is not equal to the demand' (Ibid., 7/1943). It seems that the NP's ambitious plans for expanding the size and scope of the state had been launched without devoting any thought to this problem. The strategy of Afrikanerisation then made the problem worse, with the available labour supply falling seriously short of escalating demand.

In 1959, government departments reported around 5 000 vacancies, a figure which grew in subsequent years (*Rand Daily Mail*, 7/9/1959). By 1961, staff shortages in the Department of Inland Revenue and the Auditor General's Office were already considered 'critical' (*The Star*, 19/4/1961). In 1962 the annual Conference of (governmental) Department Heads devoted itself entirely to discussing this problem.[6] By 1965, staff shortages were reported as 'crippling' across the board (*Sunday Express*, 14/1/1965). Many departments complained of further deterioration since 1963, when one out of every five permanent state posts had been unfilled (*Rand Daily Mail*, 2/4/1965).

Still the state continued to swell. By 1966, 11 000 new posts had been added – despite the fact that only 6 305 people joined the service that year and 5 557 resigned (*Rand Daily Mail*, 22/2/1968a). By 1968, the situation was so bad that the PSA issued one of many public warnings of 'total dislocation and disintegration of the service'. Some departments were now up to 60% understaffed (Ibid., 24/10/1968). And attempts to investigate the full extent of the problem were themselves 'held up by staff shortages' (HAD, 1969: 26-4454)!

The PSA drew particular attention to the widening gap between upper and lower personnel strata, which made filling senior positions increasingly unlikely. As an editorial in the association's journal, *The Public Servant*, put it: 'we cannot be accused of being alarmist if we say that with the present trickle of matric recruits, let alone graduates, the gap will sooner or later become unbridgeable' (quoted in *Rand Daily Mail*, 19/3/1969).

In bureaucratic circles this was, to some extent, old news. But, with the Public Service Commission (PSC), the body responsible for staff recruitment, defensively inclined to underplay the seriousness of the problem, it was only in the late 1960s that Parliament suddenly woke up to the staffing crisis. In 1968, the United Party (UP), noting the serious staff shortages and a 'virtual collapse of administration in many spheres,' (Ibid., 22/2/1968a) called for an immediate probe into conditions in the civil service. The following year, a parliamentary Select Committee produced 'shattering revelations of staff shortages' in many important branches of the civil service. The Financial Institutional Division of the

Treasury (which controlled all financial institutions, such as banks, building societies and insurance companies) was reported to be on the verge of collapse because of staff shortages. A similar situation existed in the Department of Inland Revenue which consisted of 501 posts. Of these, 90 were unfilled and 104 were filled by temporary appointees who lacked appropriate qualifications (HAD, 1969: 26-4457). In the Department of Agriculture, only 20 out of 31 posts in the personnel division were filled. Of these, only four incumbents had more than six years' service in the job. In this department's accounts office, the 57 established posts had experienced 248 staff changes over the previous ten years. Only 59% of the 1 853 posts in the Department of Labour were properly filled (Ibid.). There were several reasons for this staffing crisis.

Firstly, the labour supply for the civil service was seriously limited. A matric was the minimum requirement for permanent, graded posts in the service. The matriculation rate amongst Afrikaners was, however, still relatively low. English-speakers on the other hand, were increasingly unlikely to consider a career in the civil service, having been alienated by the NP's affirmative action programme. Indeed, many left to join the Rhodesian civil service.

Secondly, the 1960s was a period of economic boom. With job reservation policies still largely in place, white people with any hint of talent or experience were bound to find more lucrative jobs in the private sector. As one personnel manager in the motor industry put it: '... any genuine white worker who presented himself at your gate and ... hadn't been to prison for six or seven months in the last two years, you said "Okay, give him a try. He's white." ... You didn't actively kick whites out' (Quoted in Adler, 1993: 51).

Thirdly, the 1960s saw alarming rates of resignations from the public service generally, and the civil service in particular. Poor salaries and working conditions were typically cited as reasons. In 1961, the PSA reported an attrition rate from the public service of between 200 to 250 per month (*Rand Daily Mail*, 21/6/1961). By 1964, this had increased to 3 158 for the year (*The Star*, 23/6/1965). Between 1956 and 1964, a total of 22 106 public servants resigned (HAD, 1964: 11-5932). In 1967 the overall resignation rate was 10,3% of the establishment. Almost as many people resigned as were hired (HAD, 1969: 27-7170 and *Rand Daily Mail*, 4/6/1968).

In 1968 the Prime Minister, BJ Vorster, attempted to deal with the situation by appointing a special committee of inquiry (*Rand Daily Mail*, 21/2/1968b and 22/5/1968), but this rather feeble effort had little effect. Resignations continued to accelerate, rising to 12,7% of the establishment by 1974 (*The Star*, 11/2/1975). In 1975, more people left the public service than joined, despite the fact that the establishment grew by up to 20% in some divisions (*Rand Daily Mail*, 7/1/1975).

Effects on the composition of the workforce

The combination of a bloated state increasingly ambitious in its social engineering efforts, and deteriorating staff shortages, had devastating effects on labour productivity and efficiency. Once again, this was a problem with a much longer history. The president of the PSA had pointed out in 1943 and 1944 that mediocrity was already a worrying tendency within the public service generally. At this stage, the problem seems to have been the result of the absence of any training whatsoever for new appointees, along with an inappropriate management culture:

> Public servants are recruited and, without being given any instruction in the various activities of the state service, they are left to pick up information in the best way they can ... by sheer accident, he lands in a department, the functions whereof he understands little and then proceeds with the assurance that he will regularly receive his salary and that one day when he becomes senior in the grade, he will receive promotion, often to another department where the work is entirely new. (*The Public Servant*, 4/1944)

In 1960, a short orientation course was introduced for new white junior recruits to the civil service, but by then the problems of poor service had taken on completely new dimensions. By the late 1960s, inefficiency and low productivity had plunged to spectacular new depths. An internal government investigation in 1969 found that about 50% of officials in the public service had held four or more jobs outside the service before entering it. As the author of the report put it:

> In view of the more advantageous working conditions that apply in the private sector, the question inevitably arises

whether many of these people, figuratively speaking, are not
'factory rejects' who were not competent to make a living in
the more competitive labour field outside the public service.
(*Rand Daily Mail*, 15/8/1968)

The Auditor-General made a similar point: 'In the past, the public service
only accepted the better matriculants, but now we grab anyone, no matter
what his attainments are' (*Sunday Express*, 20/12/1970). And the UP drew
Parliament's attention to the:

cases where people were transferred into highly technical
departments while they had no knowledge of the department
and yet within two or three years they become the secretary
without even knowing details of the technical functioning
of the department. (HAD, 1969: 27-7166)

The lack of adequate expertise and training reached farcical proportions
in civil service legal posts. Repeated complaints had surfaced during the
1960s about a dearth of suitably qualified legal staff. This led to the
appointment of people without the appropriate skills, on the understanding that they would register full-time for a B.Juris degree – drawing
full salaries while studying. Yet, by 1976, only 153 out of 653 posts for
legal assistants were filled by officials with anything resembling the
desired qualifications. In this year alone, 250 out of the 675 officials doing
the B.Juris degree were withdrawn from the degree because of
'unsatisfactory progress'. Yet they retained their jobs – as legal officials
(*The Star*, 26/2/1976).

The effects of job reservation on the staffing crisis were highly ironic.
Intent on protecting privileged spheres of employment for whites, the
apartheid state created its own labour shortages. Whites were streaming
into better paying jobs in the private sector with little competition from
blacks. Yet the very same job reservation policies prevented the state from
training black people in sufficiently large numbers for the civil service
positions which the available white labour supply was too small to fill.

The staff shortages were so severe that efforts to keep the civil service
white were bound to fail. Black people[7] made substantial inroads into the
civil service in the 1960s. When the UP pointed out the contradictions in
this situation, the Minister of the Interior insisted that black public servants

were 'chiefly messengers' (HAD, 1969: 11-5942). Had he been correct, this would have produced a veritable army of messengers. According to one set of figures the number of black people in the public service as a whole increased by more than 100% in 1963 alone (*Rand Daily Mail*, 8/8/1964). In government departments, the number of blacks employed had outstripped the number of whites by 1960, and the differential continued to grow.

The number of white women employed in the civil service also grew during the 1960s, a result once again of the staffing crisis. In 1965, the PSC formally decided to employ more white women, even in the higher posts from which they had previously been barred. For the first time, women with matric or a degree could be appointed to special grade and senior clerical posts without the departments first having to find out if men were available for the job (*Sunday Express*, 21/2/1965).

Still there were definite limits on the work prospects of both black people and white women in the civil service. When the Secretary for the Interior told a conference of departmental heads that the service was 'losing its backbone', what he had in mind was the mounting absence of 'promising, productive men in the middle grades' (HAD, 1969: 26-4454). Or, as a Mr Van der Merwe of the Transvaal Provincial Administration put it: 'Where are the people going to come from to fill the senior posts in future if the public service cannot appoint and keep young men?' (*Rand Daily Mail*, 21/5/1969) It goes without saying, of course, that such men would be white.

As the economic boom faded and the recession of the 1970s set in, the many problems facing the civil service did not ease. In fact, in many respects, they continued to worsen. As a senior official of the PSC put it in 1975: 'All the time the service is responsible for providing more and more services as the country expands, but the loss of staff is constantly getting worse' (*Sunday Express*, 21/2/1965). By 1976, the public service reported a turnover of more than 50% of its staff in only three years (*The Star*, 26/2/1976).

The government's homeland policy only made matters worse. As the number of homelands increased, so, too, did the number and size of their own bureaucracies. This meant more bureaucratic red tape, compounding inefficiency and incompetence problems. In 1969, an internal investigation found that the Department of Pensions was administering 41 different pension schemes (*Rand Daily Mail*, 29/8/1969).

By 1976, with seven self-governing homelands, the main government departments were replicated another seven times each.

Although a sense of crisis was expressed within bureaucratic circles as early as 1961, very little was done to address the problem before the late 1970s, when PW Botha took office as Prime Minister (the title was later changed to State President). In fact, during the 1960s, the reaction from the Cabinet to reports of an incompetent, inefficient or oversized public service was defensive and accusatory. Such talk, it was said, 'was peddling a crises-mindedness' *(Rand Daily Mail,* 17/6/1969). However, big business had begun wielding its political muscle by the mid-1970s. It posed embarrassingly public and probing questions about the ailing, bloated state bureaucracy. Botha tried, in some ways, to take the problem in hand. The PSC was roped in and a plan was produced for the rationalisation of the service. Schlebusch, the newly appointed Minister of the Interior, announced the need for a 'thorough-going reorganisation' of the civil service, in particular, which had proved itself 'incapable' of providing the necessary 'manpower requirements under present conditions' (*The Star,* 17/9/1979).

The number of government departments was progressively reduced from 39 to 22. Botha also initiated the creation of the rank of Director-General – a new 'super-managerial' position, with salary and perks designed to compete favourably with the private sector (although the salary scales and benefits were never made public). These posts were intended to woo new talent into the civil service from the private sector.

Botha's strategy was, however, less a thorough-going rationalisation programme than a political manoeuvre to marginalise right-wing opposition within the civil service, which had become one of the strongholds of Afrikaner reactionaries resistant to his reformist agenda.[8] The enormous apartheid bureaucracy gave senior officials potentially lethal powers to block reform. Botha's primary concern, therefore, was with reconfiguring power relations at the top levels of the service. Senior bureaucrats who were considered obstructionist found their authority superseded by the new director-generals drawn from outside the service. Compliant secretaries were rewarded with internal promotions to the same position. Furthermore, in the name of 'rationalisation', Botha greatly enhanced the scope of his own office: all planning functions were now reallocated there, giving him autocratic powers within both bureaucracies and the cabinet.

Apartheid's bureaucratic absurdities ensured that the civil service continued to expand – 'rationalisation' notwithstanding. Indeed, the PSC, in rather cryptic vein, assured civil servants that their numbers would continue to grow: 'This is inevitable in any increasingly industrialising country ... but the rationalisation process will definitely lead to a smaller increase in the long run' (*Rand Daily Mail*, 8/12/1979). With the 'long run' a long way off, the problem of staff shortages still loomed large. By 1981, public servants were speaking openly about the 'near collapse of the public service' (*The Star*, 25/2/1981). NP cabinet minister, Dr Piet Koornhof offended civil servants deeply when he compared the civil service to a tortoise: If you leave it alone, he said, it will proceed at its own pace, but if you push it, it will stop dead (*Rand Daily Mail*, 16/7/1980). But on the reptilian scheme of things, the more profound description came from UP Member of Parliament (MP), Marais Steyn, in 1968, who compared the civil service to 'a dinosaur with a massive body and a small brain' (Ibid., 3/8/1968).

IMPLICATIONS FOR WORKER ORGANISATION

In some respects, it is surprising that the apartheid years did not produce more concerted pressure and resistance from white civil servants.

The massive expansion of the state, the vast complexity of the apartheid system and the strongly administrative bias of much apartheid legislation all contributed to the enormous powers wielded by civil servants. Their support, co-operation and commitment were absolutely essential for apartheid to function. By 1976, 'observers of the workings of Pretoria, especially Nat [NP] businessmen' were reportedly highly anxious about this trend. There were now no less than 1 650 laws and 6 000 proclamations on the statute books. Apartheid legislation had become so prolific that 'not even a superhuman minister could hope to cope with all the decisions that theoretically are expected of him. He must simply delegate to the officials.' Bureaucrats, concluded *The Sunday Times*, 'do, in fact, "run" their ministers. So power is separated from accountability, much more than we admit' (*Sunday Times*, 3/10/1976). Civil servants also wielded power as a large bloc of Afrikaner voters – whose disaffection with the NP *en masse* could have been politically catastrophic.

While they formed the backbone of the apartheid state, civil servants were also generally a frustrated and often highly disaffected bunch. As early as 1962, the PSA noted that 'the word "frustration" (has) become a somewhat overworked word in the public service' (*The Public Servant*, 9/1962). The association complained regularly, if politely, of a range of grievances, of which salaries were the most frequent. Salary levels were set by the PSC, which was the 'central agency of the public service ... responsible for position classification, recruitment, selection, placement, training, remuneration, merit assessment and promotion, negotiations with employee associations and employee services.' With no system of collective bargaining, the PSC set wages through a process of 'joint consultation' in a 'public service joint advisory council,' consisting of ten members nominated by the recognised personnel associations and five by the PSC. (Salaries for black public servants were excluded from this process (Roux, 1971: 89-90).) Any recommendations made by the council required the approval of the Treasury. During the 1960s, the Treasury was intent on limiting inflation within the public service. When wage increases were awarded (and this did not occur every year), they fell far short of those common in the private sector, especially during the period of economic boom. This was all the more the case for the increasing proportion of women and black people in the service, who had even less prospect of influencing negotiations. Although the PSA did call for equal wages for equal work (for whites) as far back as the 1950s, the bulk of its membership was male, and its organisational priorities reflected this fact.

Dissatisfaction with the system of wage determination ran deep amongst civil servants. In 1958, the PSA lodged an appeal for a more structured, impersonal mechanism for wage negotiation and arbitration (*Rand Daily Mail*, 20/11/1958). But the PSC adamantly refused to consider any changes to the system. From its vantage point, setting wage levels through 'personal consultation' was the principal virtue of the existing system: 'We have this to thank for the remarkable peace and quiet which has marked our public service.'[9]

Working conditions also caused much resentment and stress. Staff shortages meant that many civil servants were poorly trained for the jobs they were doing. This created an enormous burden for those who were competent and experienced, as they found themselves totally overloaded.

By the 1970s, faced with what seemed insoluble staff shortages, particularly at senior levels, the PSC went along with cabinet pressure to recruit top appointees from outside the civil service. This practice –

increasingly common as the decade progressed – became a major grievance, particularly for senior civil servants.

During the 1950s and 1960s, in their quest to colonise the civil service for the *volk*, the Nationalists had placed more emphasis on quantity than quality in the recruitment of civil servants. By the 1970s, the legacy of this policy had become increasingly inconvenient. Not only were the reformists forced to entrust the administration of 'reform' to often incompetent and ill-trained bureaucrats, many of these people were also reactionaries intent on preserving the apartheid system of old. The Cabinet thus proceeded to pull the carpet from under the feet of the very people whose jobs and prospects it had sponsored just a decade previously. Whereas in the past, promotion was based on length of service and seniority achieved by rising steadily through the ranks, the PSC now regularly went over the heads of long-serving officials by appointing outsiders to top positions.

Civil servants also complained of inadequate grievance procedures. In terms of the 1957 Public Services Act, the PSC was responsible for civil service appointments within the central state authorities. On paper, the PSC was intended to function in much the same way as similar institutions elsewhere in the world:

> The original objective of the PSC … was to make the officials independent of the politicians, i.e. to prevent nepotism and/ or unfairness in appointments, salary adjustments, promotions and termination of service. (Cloete, 1992: 156)

In practice, however, impartiality and fairness did not rank amongst the PSC's strongest points. For example, in 1966 the PSA reported that:

> Widespread dissatisfaction exists among public servants, because, they claim, their complaints are not being taken seriously enough by departmental heads and the PSC … The fact that seniors often refuse to treat complaints seriously or victimise juniors for making them, is regarded as one of the most important resignation factors in the service.
>
> (*The Star*, 14/1/1966)

The problem was compounded by the regulations laid down by the 1957 Public Services Act. For example, if a complaint was laid against an official, that person was not guaranteed an opportunity to respond, nor was he or she necessarily informed about the substance of the complaint (Ibid., 23/ 2/1970). The PSA's journal often reported dismissals without any reasons being given. Lodging an appeal of any kind was cumbersome and unrewarding. The association complained of the 'inadequate and evasive' provisions of the Act under which an official could appeal a decision on his or her working conditions. 'To call the present provision an appeal procedure would be an overstatement,' said the editorial in *The Public Servant*:

> There is only one single public service regulation giving him a very limited right to appeal ... However, there is no obligation on a head of department to respond to these charges within any particular time period. As a result, the provision of this directive lost much of its value.
>
> (Quoted in *Rand Daily Mail*, 14/4/1964)

In 1971, the PSA called for an official inquiry into the public service, to cover a range of issues, including overlapping services, serious shortages of qualified staff, problems of retaining workers, defects in the merit system and negotiations machinery and delays in the handling of pensions. The call was flatly rejected by the PSC, and the PSA capitulated (*The Star*, 2/6/1971).

In 1973, feelings were running very high amongst civil servants. *Rapport* disclosed a 'state of rebellion' in the Department of Prisons and the Department of Tourism (*Sunday Express*, 14/10/1973) and further investigations revealed similar conditions in the departments of the Interior, Foreign Affairs, Labour, Transport, Posts and Telegraphs and Information. The *Sunday Express* reported 'discontent among public servants in almost every major state department ... over the Cabinet's administrative policy and other interference by the Cabinet in the running of internal public servants' affairs' (*Sunday Express*, 14/10/1973). Civil servants dismissed the PSC as 'useless' in addressing their grievances; nor was the PSA any more effective, having remained a rather toothless organisation.

Senior officials began taking their complaints directly to opposition MPs to expose them in parliament, rather than using established channels of communication within the state or the NP (Ibid.).

With the appointment of the Wiehahn Commission in 1977, the PSA saw a new opportunity for the overhaul of labour relations in the public service. Although the issue of public service labour relations was not included in the brief of the Commission, Wiehahn was prevailed upon by the PSA to consider it. The Commission recommended far-reaching changes:

> The Commission is of the opinion that many of the existing and future problems relating to industrial relations in the public sector could be solved by extending collective bargaining rights to public sector employees – either under the general or under specific legislation. Although not the prime reason for this view, such extension would also be in line with the general trend experienced elsewhere in the world. (RSA, 1980: para 4.65.20)

The Commission mentioned, as one of the potential advantages of such a system, that 'decisions taken by the state would be more readily accepted by public servants if they have some sense of participation, however limited, in such decisions' (Ibid.). But these recommendations were, however, still-born.

Whatever their powers and grievances, public servants were either unwilling or unable to mobilise and organise collectively to assert their interests more forcefully. Both the political culture of the time and the self-imposed limits of the PSA accounted for their apparent quiescence.

Political culture of Afrikaner nationalism

Afrikaner nationalists rejected the British notion of the state as properly the neutral arbiter of popular interests. Instead, they saw the state as the instrument of the *volk* (O'Meara, 1996: 62), in pursuit of the apartheid project

For much of the NP's rule, this view of the state was, in fact, at odds with the letter of the law. The Public Services Act of 1957 reproduced its British colonial heritage in barring public servants from playing any part in party politics. In practice, the law was completely ignored. Hundreds of thousands of Afrikaner civil servants remained loyal and active participants in the NP. The tacit affirmative action policy in the civil service was effectively a strategy of patronage on the part of the NP. Most civil servants knew that they depended on the party for their jobs, which could be revoked just as easily as they were supplied. The pressure for conformism and compliance was thus enormous.

The politics of job reservation heightened this dependency. Indeed, if it was a hindrance to the NP's ambitions for expanding the civil service, job reservation was also a powerful aid in disciplining this workforce. It was NP policy to keep the civil service white – or, under the circumstances, as white as possible. As the staffing crisis in the public service deepened, the UP became more and more vociferous in its calls for the civil service to be opened up more fully to black employees. The prospects of having to compete for their jobs against a huge black labour pool must have reminded white civil servants that their meal tickets remained with the NP, their grievances and complaints notwithstanding.

Afrikaner politicians tried hard to maintain the pretence that the civil service was neutral. Every now and then, however, the politics of patronage were exposed for all to see. In 1967, for example, the Secretary for Transport, Danie Joubert, admitted that there were many people occupying posts in the civil service, including his own department, for which they were wholly unqualified. Incompetence, he declared, was a small price to pay for political loyalty:

> What would happen if you gave them their walking tickets? They would be thrust out in a hard commercial world with which they would not be able to cope. These officials invariably have wives and children … at present they have their self-respect and the children can thrust back their shoulders at school because their father is employed. Maybe the salary paid to the father is higher than his service warrants, but at least it is helping to bring up children who may one day be good South Africans. (*Rand Daily Mail*, 20/10/1967)

The contradictions between the terms of the law and the NP's political practice produced many an outcry from opposition parties – for example, when a senior civil servant in the Department of Bantu Administration and Development became the NP's candidate for the Innesdal constituency, the same year that a UP candidate in another state department was expressly warned that participating in elections was grounds for dismissal (Ibid., 17/9/1969).

Partly in response to jibes from the opposition, Afrikaner civil servants lobbied the NP to change the Public Services Act in their favour. Their reasoning was unashamedly to the point: 'When we were in opposition, we did not want civil servants to take part in politics because they acted against us, but now that we are in power the position has changed' (*The Star*, 20/9/1967).

The cabinet, however, preferred to keep things the way they were – the law remained a useful device in undermining the emergence of political opposition within the service. In 1970, however, the law was finally amended, at which point the changes rapidly became self-defeating. An expression of the NP's confidence in its hold over the civil service, the new law threatened to create an unforeseen obstacle in the way of 'reform'. By permitting the open politicisation of the civil service, the new law gave openly reactionary civil servants powers to pursue their own political agendas in the course of their jobs. This only intensified the politics of patronage. Fearing disloyalty amongst their ranks, ministers were now even more likely to offer 'jobs for pals', bending the rules when necessary. As one academic commentator put it:

> The pattern is always the same. Direct ministerial or State President appointment to the positions that are not advertised. In this way there cannot be competition or merit appointments. The situation gives politicians a glorious opportunity to reward allies or party hacks at the taxpayers' expense. (*Sunday Times*, 30/2/1977)[10]

The growing schism between pro- and anti-'reform' factions in the apartheid state raises the question of why the disaffected reactionaries, betrayed by their political patrons, did not use their powers of opposition more effectively. This probably has a lot to do with the weaknesses of the PSA as a vehicle for organised resistance.

Organisational cultural and power of the PSA

With membership ranging from approximately 23 000 in 1953 to about 40 000 in 1981, the PSA was the single largest organisation representing the interests of white public servants (Louwrens, 1996: interview). Yet its powers were remarkably slight – the result of a combination of the state's intimidatory tactics and the culture of service deeply ingrained within the PSA from its inception in 1920. The PSA found its hands tied, bound by its own scrupulous adherence to the rules and norms which the state, as employer, openly flouted.

As an avowedly 'professional' staff association, the PSA was anxious to present itself as an apolitical organisation, which did not stoop to populist rabble rousing: 'The PSA steers clear of any issues which have a political flavour,' it insisted (*Rand Daily Mail*, 21/7/1959). Since the NP had succeeded in politicising virtually every appointment and dismissal in the public service, this seriously limited the PSA's sphere of operation.

The PSA's style of operation was diffident and polite. It prided itself on its non-adversarial relationship with government, and disdained any 'militant' tactics. 'Let it never be said that we, in our dealings with the authorities, deserved the ugly stamp of agitators' – such was the organisation's rallying cry (*The Public Servant*, 10/1962). So in 1964, for example, when 300 angry public servants attending a meeting of the PSA in the Orange Free State called for an independent commission of inquiry into the public service, the PSA stressed that 'there was no intention ... to wash dirty linen in public ... the meeting was urged to carry the motion so that matters could be rectified without embarrassment to the service' (HAD, 1964: 11-5931). Likewise, during 1965 (a time of economic growth and expansion of the private sector) the PSA called on its members to be patient in their demands for salary increases:

> Members should bear in mind that the respect in which the association is held in government circles was founded on a broader basis than the mere welfare of its members. Let us say unequivocally that the association will in no circumstances lend itself to any action which will carry the slightest taint of incitement of its members.
>
> (Quoted in *Rand Daily Mail*, 22/9/1965)

The same thing happened in 1968: while wage increases for whites in the private sector were well beyond inflation, the PSA agreed to accept government's decision to impose a public sector wage freeze and to ask only for increased fringe benefits (Ibid., 1/2/1968).

The PSA's own frustration levels clearly rose – ever so politely – as the decades wore on. Adhering scrupulously to the rules laid down by the PSC – that all consultations take place through the Public Service Joint Advisory Council, with final decisions made by the PSC – it nevertheless found itself regularly ignored and humiliated. Unanimous decisions taken by the PSA and endorsed by the Joint Advisory Council, were rejected by the PSC, with no reasons given (*The Public Servant*, 3/1961).

Still, the PSA stuck doggedly to the rules, even while being emasculated by them. It justified its practice in the name of the British colonial tradition, 'to serve the government of the day ... the real professional public servants try to serve with efficiency and dedication' (Louwrens, 1996: interview).

The association's room for manoeuvre was further constrained by the NP government's efforts directly to manipulate labour relations in the civil service. As Mr A Louwrens, long-serving office bearer of the PSA explained, if civil servants brought grievances to the PSA in the hope of a more muscular encounter with the employer, 'government got to know about our discussion ... that raised concern ... not direct threats, but veiled and indirect warnings that if we persisted with this type of action, things could become bad for us.' For example, the government would threaten to cut off the PSA's stop-order facilities (the basis of its funding). Threats against individual employees became an effective means of restraining the PSA itself. 'From the top down, the message could come, that if you are a member of the PSA, that could be used against you in promotion. Once this message spread, people got scared ... they didn't want to become seen to be active in the PSA' (Louwrens, 1996: interview).

The machinations of the *Broederbond* made these tactics even more effective. The Broederbond had set up a number of 'task forces' to monitor and police personnel and policy areas within state bureaucracies (Wilkins and Strydom, 1979: 397-405).

In short, the NP leadership was able to manipulate the white civil service in ways which promoted its quiescence: with the decisions of the PSC regarding individual reward and promotion closed to any outside scrutiny and based on 'personalised consultation', and the PSA largely a damp squib, the best chance that ill-trained, unproductive civil servants had of success was to work the system from within, currying favour with their superiors, rather than relying on a toothless staff association to take up their cause within the rules of an anachronistic system of consultation.

CONCLUSION

Literature on the apartheid state during the 1950s and 1960s tends to assume that the civil service was a contented, well-served beneficiary of the NP's affirmative action and job reservation policies. This chapter has shown that the picture was more complex. Afrikaner civil servants were certainly beneficiaries of NP patronage, but their indebtedness and dependency masked mounting dissatisfaction and disquiet within their ranks. The NP succeeded in politicising industrial relations in ways which disabled the prospect of organised resistance or pressure on the part of civil servants, whose conditions of service deteriorated as the apartheid project expanded.

Since 1994, South African civil servants, for the first time, face the prospect of organised collective bargaining, which promises the opportunity to transcend the traditions of bias, patronage and authoritarianism which characterised labour relations in the civil service in the past. However, the success of this shift will have much to do with the manner in which the state itself is restructured. The new system of collective bargaining is predicated on a particular model of political authority: it assumes a mutual acceptance on both sides of what Max Weber termed a 'legal-rational' notion of authority. In terms of this model, impartial and binding rules structure bargaining procedures that are pluralistic, open and bureaucratically uniform. This model of industrial relations rests, in turn, on similar assumptions about the character of the state: it, too, should operate according to the same mode of bureaucratic rationality, its procedures open to scrutiny according to widely publicised, uniform and accepted rules of procedure. This chapter has shown that the notion of bureaucratic rationality operative within the apartheid state was profoundly distorted by a lethal combination of inefficiency, incompetence and over-ambitious strategies of social engineering, compounded by the effects of a tacit affirmative action strategy tied to a party political project. The African National Congress (ANC) has inherited a state that still bears the imprint of this past. Rationalising industrial relations within the civil service will depend, in profound ways, on the ANC's capacity to resist the temptations to which the NP succumbed: allowing the state to grow independently of the numbers of appropriately qualified and experienced personnel to staff it, and then wielding political patronage as an instrument for industrial discipline.

If it does not succeed, one of the more ironic aspects of transformation of the civil service may be that long-serving, white civil servants, incapacitated by the previous regime of labour relations, use the new system of collective bargaining to rediscover their powers.

3

GLOBAL TRENDS WITHIN THE PUBLIC SERVICE

—————— ◆ ——————

Mike Waghorne

Waghorne's chapter provides an important dimension to the collection. He surveys issues confronting public service unions around the world and their implications for industrial relations procedures. He argues that trade unions need to look closely at the full range of structural adjustment, public sector reform, commercialisation and related policies to develop strategies for defending the public service and their members' jobs and working conditions.

This chapter, unlike the others, looks at the broad public sector, in part because the boundaries between it and the narrower 'public service' differ dramatically between countries. Moreover, the issues confronting public service unions traverse these borders as services are redefined and moved out of the public service, as narrowly defined. Unions elsewhere have not been defensively trapped in government's plans. They have developed their own vision of what they think the public sector should be and have developed tactics for achieving that end. In the process they have protected the rights, jobs and working conditions of their members. Unions should consider the concept 'offensive co-operation', an approach in which unions are prepared to co-operate with government, but on the basis that they be treated as genuine social partners. If government does not do so, then the co-operation ends and the 'gloves come off'.

The promotion of public sector reforms, industrial action and international public sector solidarity all have distinct risks. Members may accuse union leaders of 'class collaboration'. Some members will lose out in the changes and take independent or 'wildcat' action. There have been many (often temporary) splits in the public sector union movement. But public sector modernisation and commercialisation can have positive effects on workers and trade union rights. A case-by-case approach is often the only way that a public sector union can best serve its members' interests and be perceived to be acting in the community's interest by promoting flexible and accountable services to the people.

INTRODUCTION

We are all familiar with the story. The government decides to privatise a loss-making public utility. A 'socially responsible' transnational company (TNC) offers to take it off the government's hands for a good price, considering the risks involved. The World Bank finances the project.

Two thousand workers lose their jobs. The union struggles to gain recognition from the new owner. Conditions of work and pension rights are undermined. Consumers have to pay more for services because of previously undisclosed liabilities that the owners have identified. A year after the sale, the company reports a huge profit. Some users have, 'unfortunately', had services cut or reduced because, according to the company, the government was unwilling/unable to subsidise the costs of what was really 'social equity', service provision outside of the company's obligation to provide a market return to the shareholders. The World Bank describes the whole exercise as a great success.

While this is a familiar story, how close is it to the truth? Can unions learn anything from what has actually happened?

The story is, in reality, well short of the full truth about privatisation, or (more correctly), the commercialisation of public services and goods. Too many people, including trade unions, focus only on asset sales, especially of national entities, when they think of the commercialisation of the state sector. Regional, municipal and other local governments provide a vast range of goods and services. There is much more money – and at least as many jobs – involved in contracting out at this level. The number of workers whose rights are undermined in this kind of commercialisation is far higher than in the case of national assets, where some 'good' deals have been won for workers.

While considerable debate has occurred in South Africa on the privatisation of state owned enterprises, there has been rather less discussion of commercialisation of public services and goods, its effects on workers and how they might respond. This is a major shortcoming given governments' increasing commitment to forms of commercialisation in the public service. This chapter focuses on the experiences of the Public Services International (PSI) – the international trade secretariat for the public service – and its affiliates to explore ways in which unions can address the social aspect of privatisation.

UNIONS AND PUBLIC SERVICE MODERNISATION

Trade unions need to look closely at the full range of public sector reform, structural adjustment and related policies in order to develop strategies for defending the public service and the jobs and conditions of workers.

Public sector unions have been playing precisely this role. In 1995 the European Federation of Public Service Unions (EPSU) commissioned Brendan Martin to research the modernisation of public services in the light of European integration and to highlight union proposals for change. Martin's book, *European Integration and Modernisation of Public Services*, presents case studies from Sweden, the Netherlands, Ireland, the United Kingdom (U.K.), Germany and Denmark, as well as a United States (U.S.) comparison. In all these countries, unions have either proposed programmes for the modernisation of the public service, or have responded positively to government proposals, in a manner that has both preserved union power and promoted the concept of public services. Martin provides evidence which suggests that:

> Top-down reforms tend not to succeed in both cutting costs and improving quality … approaches which centre on empowering front-line employees have not only demonstrated how the aims of increasing quality and containing costs can be reconciled, but have also successfully responded to a further pressure for change arising from the demands of employees… for more job satisfaction and a better balance of work and home life …
> A condition of mobilising the knowledge and experience of employees on which such successes have depended is that employees have security of employment, if not necessarily any guarantees about their existing posts. Another condition is that they are consulted and involved

in the process of change from start to finish and that any changes affecting their terms of employment are negotiated through their unions. (Martin, 1996: 1-2)

Most public service workers appear to support such modernisation. Their unions review and change their policies, structures and methods to respond to the changing reality of their members' lives. Union support for further changes that improve labour productivity may well be conditional, however, on commitment by governments and management to investing in improving quality services and taking effective action to tackle unemployment through the creation of jobs to meet new and growing areas of need.

This book focuses on 'public services' as opposed to 'the public sector' or 'public sector enterprises'. It is not always easy to maintain these distinctions. For example, while many countries have treated the health sector as an essential public service, the U.K. and New Zealand governments regard it as a state enterprise, which produces/sells a commodity on the basis of public investments from which it is legitimate to seek a commercial return. While most countries regard the distribution of social welfare benefits as a core public service, the U.S. government is flirting with the idea of handing them out to private firms to administer. Some governments have even contracted out tax collection.

So while this book focuses on the core public service, it would be dangerous to concentrate only on what the current South African consensus defines this to be. Neo-liberals have a gift of being able to commodify any public service. The 'innocent' contracting out of data-processing in tax collection can become a reason for the whole operation to be contracted out. One of the objectives of TNCs is to get a leg in the door of an agency or sector. There have been instances of a TNC obtaining a cleaning or computer contract in a country's internal revenue service and then purporting to have experience in tax collection when tendering for a contract in another country.

The list of priorities for privatisation and contracting out will be different in each country. In general, privateers are interested in key state enterprises, especially if they offer significant market share in the global product or service. Public utilities are high on the list. Unions need to be able to look at their country's broad public sector to identify possible 'entry points' for TNCs.

SEEKING SECURITY IN CHANGE

Unions are promoting change. At the same time, their message to governments is clear: sustainable change is only possible if the unions are on board. As the Trade Union Advisory Committee (TUAC) to the Organization for Economic Co-operation and Development (OECD) has noted, workers will either seek security in change, or security against change. Employers and governments must choose.

Case studies

In 1996, a compilation of case studies on union/employer interactions on environmental issues was published as part of a joint project between the International Confederation of Free Trade Unions (ICFTU) and certain international trade secretariats, such as the Public Services International (PSI).

Zimbabwe: Unions and government reform

The Zimbabwe case study relates to the connection between health, safety and the environment in reformed local government (ICFTU, 1996).

Two unions were involved: the Zimbabwe Urban Councils Workers' Union (ZUCWU), which has a potential membership of 35 000 workers employed in local authority health and community services, maintenance, and construction, and the Zimbabwe Local Authority and DDF Workers Union (ZLADDFWU), which has a potential membership of 80 000. Current union membership is, however, very low.

In 1990, the Zimbabwe Congress of Trade Unions (ZCTU), which has 32 affiliates, set up a health and social welfare department. The department works as a team with union health and safety officers.

Environment and sustainable development were difficult issues for the government to deal with. Constraints included:

- inequality, which results in the majority of the population being settled on land with low agricultural potential
- exclusion of local communities from planning and decision-making
- extreme poverty
- institutions which emphasise control, rather than empowerment.

While economic policy in Zimbabwe has promoted some diversity and self-sufficiency, it has also promoted a political legacy which links maximisation of production to a weak regulatory framework. The Structural Adjustment Programme (SAP) has reinforced this trend as part of the normal package of IMF 'Washington Consensus' conditionalities which countries must agree to if they want IMF funding assistance.

The ZCTU health and social welfare department started work with the ZUCWU and ZLADDFWU in 1992. Training and planning programmes were carried out with the assistance of the International Labour Organization (ILO) Project on Workers Education and the Environment. In November 1993, delegates formed research teams. Participants were sent out to gather information. Eventually, a process was developed which involved a range of participatory research techniques. Workers developed links with other groups and initiated a long-term process of discussion and action. Key environmental issues were identified for investigation.

The lessons which emerged from this exercise were that:
• unions should negotiate with the local authorities for better health and safety conditions for their members, and the community
• unions need to develop a more coherent response to SAP policies
• unions need to get more involved in housing issues
• workplace activities must be linked to community issues and organisations.

The Zimbabwe study is somewhat marginal to the central focus of this chapter. It is, however, one of the few documented African case studies of union involvement in modernisation and government reform outside of South Africa and it points to the urgent need for the sharing of information about other such projects.

Western European models: A union version of modernisation

Northern models on the involvement of trade unions in public sector modernisation and reform exist in more abundance. However, these may not be entirely appropriate to Africa. The issues are so different: in Africa, the problem is more one of supplying community services to the people, rather than cutting back on a fully developed public sector.

Nevertheless, European models do contain some useful lessons for Africa, even in Europe unions have had to struggle to get local and national governments to take a positive and imaginative approach to public sector modernisation. Martin notes that public service unions are increasingly seeking to put their stamp on quality initiatives. They insist on their own version of modernisation, rather than being defensively trapped into those of governments and management (Martin, 1996: 13).

Germany: Employee empowerment

The German union, ÖTV, is scathing in its assessment of the federal government's restructuring of local government in the new Länder of the reunified Germany:

> The Federal government, instead of pushing ahead with reforms, is intent on maintaining the established structures. By paying no more than lip service to reform of the public services, the Ministry of the Interior is actually standing in the way of modernisation. After German unification, the government had a wonderful opportunity to modernise public services in eastern Germany. It squandered the change, preferring simply to transpose the backward Western model. (ÖTV, 1995: 4)

ÖTV has advanced a positive policy of employee empowerment as a route to producing more and better with less. It has funded and backed local government experiments to show how this is done. This has not been easy in cases where there has been job loss for some members, and selective wage increases for others, but the union remains committed to the need for active promotion of change.

The U.K.: Fighting contracting out

The European Union Acquired Rights Directive (ARD) decreed that a new owner of an operation has to maintain existing pay and conditions, until new negotiations are due. This was to avoid the practice whereby a firm would slightly alter its shareholding, change its name and then disavow any obligations under the collective agreement in the 'former' operation.

The U.K. response was the Transfer of Undertakings Protection of Employment Regulations (TUPE), which had been blithely set aside when it came to contracting out and market testing in the public sector. Once it was ruled that TUPE applied retrospectively to contracting out, the number of bids from potential contractors virtually dried up. It was clear that contractors had previously won bids on the basis of cuts in pay, jobs and conditions.

Martin notes that there are other areas of European law which unions have been able to exploit when it comes to public sector reform. The British public sector union, UNISON, won a series of legal victories in its fight against the British government's compulsory competitive tendering (CCT) regime. The *Financial Times* quoted the following examples:

> School dinner ladies, who fought their local authority through the courts after privatisation cut their wages, have won an important pay victory. The 1 300 school-meals staff will receive about £1 500 each from the North Yorkshire County Council after a ruling by the House of Lords … (which) held that the women employed were victims of sex discrimination when their pay was reduced to less than that of male council employees doing work of equal value. (*Financial Times*, 7/7/1995)

It was 'no excuse', the judges said, 'for the council to argue it had to pay the women less in order for its own workforce to compete with tenders from the private sector' (Ibid.).

The judgement was one of a series of legal victories for UNISON in its fight against the British government's CCT regime. The verdict was, however, also welcomed by the private contractors, which have been the main beneficiaries of CCT, because it would make it harder for local authorities to cut their own currently low labour costs when submitting in-house bids. The private companies themselves have been limited in their ability to cut the wages and conditions of staff by the ARD. Whether this will shift the balance in terms of who wins contracts is too early to judge.

UNISON has also successfully challenged the refusal of a new employer to recognise and negotiate with the incumbent union in a privatised water company by reference to rights under the European law. Wessex Water had de-recognised UNISON. The union brought a case in which it established that the privatised company remained an 'emanation of the state' because it provides a public service, is regulated by a state authority and exercises certain statutory powers on behalf of the state. This enabled its employees to consultation through their unions, the court agreed.

The U.K.-based Public Services Privatisation Research Unit (PSPRU), owned by a number of British public sector unions, has traced virtually all contracts subject to CCT in the local government and health services sectors. It has been able to document the very high rates in different services of contracts either being terminated (for contract failure or high prices), taken back in-house or being won back by in-house bids when the contract came up for renewal.[1]

In fact, many U.K. public sector workers are routinely denied even the right to tender for their own jobs when the government decides to market test an agency or to contract it out: the government simply decrees that no in-house bids can be accepted. This is a result of the fact that in open competition with the current public sector workers, the private sector loses about 80% of the bids it puts in. This is from the protagonists of the level playing field of the free market!

Sweden: Labour rights and better services

The PSI Swedish affiliate, Kommunal, which organises municipal workers, devised a commercially successful training programme, Komanco (loosely translated as 'Come on then!'), which it sold to municipalities on the basis that they would get their money back if they did not make the agreed savings. Kommunal contracts with the municipality to train its staff so that new work methods and organisation will deliver better services, higher quality jobs and more satisfied autonomous work teams, which deliver the goods at some agreed lower price. No contracting out, no privatisation, everyone happier in their work, the public purse charged less, the union developing its strength and credibility, and all with a money-back guarantee. Not surprisingly, the municipalities are queuing up for the programme.

Eastern European experiences

In 1996, the PSI commenced a series of Briefing Notes for issues in public sector debates. One of these presents a number of case studies from Central and Eastern Europe (PSI, 1997).

The Czech Republic

Health sector reform in the Czech Republic was mapped out quite early in the transformation process in a document called 'The New System of Health Care,' although the changes in fact implemented deviated from those outlined. The first step was the dismantling of the regional structure of health service facilities, which instead became independent legal entities. The end of 1992 saw the establishment of a new system of health insurance, into which both employers and employees had to pay (the contributions of children, the elderly and the unemployed are met by the state). At the same time, formal privatisation of health care providers themselves got underway. This is a good example of the dangers of treating modernisation and reform of the state, commercialisation of the public sector and privatisation as separate issues.

The privatisation of health care facilities was done as part of the general privatisation process; medical care was treated as any similarly sized 'business'. The different mechanisms of Czech 'small privatisation' – restitution, direct sale to a new buyer, public auction, free transfer to a municipality and others – were applied to health care organisations.

One of the key roles of the Trade Union of Health Service and Social Care came to be helping members to become owners, collectively or individually, as a more preferable option than ending up as employees without any say in the development of their local service. The union campaigned for this and explored with the government the idea of health facilities becoming not-for-profit institutions, independent of the state, but with legal obligations to ensure accessibility to health care, and funded jointly by state bodies, health insurance, fees and charitable donations. Health care provided by not-for-profit institutions on the basis of democratically determined health care policy and state regulation would be a better option than services delivered through 'bureaucratic state structures,' the union argues, and would be 'more flexible, creative and competitive'. The union has urged the government to facilitate this new form of health care restructuring through tax incentives and to decentralise the state's role in overseeing and financing the system to more responsive and accountable local bodies (PSI, 1997).

Hungary

Hungary was the first of the central and eastern European countries to sell off the electricity sector. In 1995, the government offered stakes of up to 48% in fourteen utilities, the country's entire electricity service. The government based its whole fiscal policy for 1995/1996 around the likely proceeds.

Opposition to this plan was led by the Hungarian electricity workers' union, which argued that electricity should remain a publicly controlled service in order to protect the interests of consumers. 'The government turned a deaf ear to our arguments,' a union leader explained. But the government could not ignore the strike called right across the energy sector. This forced it to meet the unions. The result was an agreement which included:

> commitments that a majority of the shares would remain in state hands; consumer protection through a package of social protection measures; 5% of the privatisation proceeds to be allocated to an education and training fund for workers; a commitment to specified social, welfare, management and operational issues ands the establishment of consultation procedures. (PSI, 1997)

Privatisation in Estonia, Poland and Bulgaria

Unions in these three countries were faced with massive privatisation programmes covering electricity, gas, water, railways, health services, education, street cleaning, urban transport and others. They have adopted a number of positions, frequently trying to win the right of workers to have priority rates for discounted purchase of shares in these services. The main goal of the Association of Estonian Trade Unions is that employment guarantees should be attached to contracts and be honoured after privatisation. It is assisted by the fact that, since 1993, the country has had a tripartite system under which the Privatisation Agency is obliged to keep employers and employees informed about enterprises to be privatised and the conditions, mainly relating to employment, being negotiated with prospective buyers. This commitment is, however, coming under pressure from terms attached to International Monetary Fund (IMF) support, which specifically bar governments from either increasing unemployment benefits or the minimum wage, despite agreements with the unions that both would increase.

Some World Bank field staff are interested in promoting such national-level tripartite discussions: they find themselves involved in a privatisation project where a sensitive matter such as severance needs to be settled. If there is prior agreement among unions, employers and the government about how the whole process of state sector modernisation/reform will be handled, then the process can be more successful. 'Prior agreement' does not mean that the unions make all the concessions: it does mean that, if a privatisation is going to proceed, it will not be marred by avoidable delays and disputes which both lower the price obtained and result in a higher subsequent rate of unemployment. For many workers, it means that they will get better deals. For some enterprises, it means that the resulting costs can sway the decision in favour of state retention. There is, however, one major problem with this whole approach, as will be seen shortly: the World Bank is not prepared to promote such a policy, even though it would make life easier for its own project staff and would lower the conflicts and costs in some projects.

It is with good reason that unions insist on the centrality of the right to take industrial action over government plans for public service reforms or privatisation. This was certainly the reason behind the strong PSI campaign to stop the entry of South Korea into the OECD until public sector unions have full trade union rights. Unions internationally campaigned on this issue and convinced a majority of OECD member states that this was a matter of principle.

Events between 1997 and 1999 in Korea, subsequent to these developments and as a result of the East Asian crisis, are still too fluid to allow us to predict the outcome. It is clear, however, that the Korean government has been forced both to negotiate and to concede on matters never before treated this way in Korea. So, trade unions have taken the initiative in proposing public service reform themselves, have gone on strike to protect members' interests and those of the community and have undertaken massive international solidarity campaigns to promote or protect the rights of public service and public sector workers.

DRAWING LESSONS

The European experience shows that, forced by unions to respect the rights of workers currently doing the job, the private sector simply cannot compete. Trade unions affiliated to the PSI in many countries have gone on the offensive, pointing to the inability of big business to compete on a level playing field. They have often been successful in forcing governments to look more closely at what it is that they thought they were doing when they embarked on simplistic programmes of modernising the state.

Offensive co-operation

The PSI has produced considerable educational and analytical material for its affiliates so that they can understand what it is that governments are really trying to do when they start public sector reform programmes. Rather than waiting for what appears to be an 'innocent' corporatisation programme or a 'helpless' response to World Bank demands for structural adjustment, unions can develop their own vision of what they think the public sector should be and develop tactics for achieving that and, in the process, protect the rights, jobs and working conditions of their members.

The Danish LO education-organising programme, *Work and Development*, is built on the assumption that workers and their unions often know what restructuring and reorganisation will most effectively achieve the 'mission' of the service or utility. The programme tries to get workers and managers to identify common aims and values and to develop strategies that can achieve both the employer's and the workers' objectives. It starts from the assumption that workers want satisfying jobs and more autonomy at work, but that they also want job security and a conflict-free environment. The programme has been adopted by many municipalities and central public authorities.

It should not be assumed that working together means selling out on basic union principles: part of the approach is called *offensive co-operation*. All co-operation is contingent on the employer remaining committed to social dialogue. If this is withdrawn, the gloves come off.

While it is important to look at models or success stories, it should also be stressed that no union can carbon-copy another country's struggle. Each campaign must be designed in its own national context. Past success is no guarantee of future success. Nobody can question the effectiveness and strength of the U.K. and New Zealand public sector trade union movements over the past century. They were strong, well organised and often very successful. Yet both have proved inadequate in the face of the new challenges of globalisation and an internationally organised neo-liberal putsch. Unions must constantly reinvent themselves and revisit their roots and rationale. Scandinavian public sector unions have poured enormous resources in the last decade into going back to their members to see what they want, to redefining the relationship of the union to its members at each workplace and to inventing new methodologies in exploring how a union tries to stay in control of the modernisation effort from a trade union perspective.

In terms of the relative progressiveness of trade unions on the issue of public service reform, the ÖTV in Germany should be revisited. While the union's proposals for local public service delivery in Hagen were very popular with the citizens and had a mixed reception initially from the union's own members, the greatest hostility came from the elected politicians. What makes this intriguing is that the proposal was clearly aimed at saving money and would make life easier for citizens by establishing a number of 'one-stop-shops' where a citizen could go to transact business with a number of public agencies or to do all the paper work for a process which would normally have required visits to a number of public agencies. Such efficiency and the resulting improved morale and work satisfaction of the union's members did not sit well with the politicians' views about public sector trade unions. It worked.

Other forms of commercialisation also have to be considered in this discussion. Take corporatisation, for example. Corporatisation is used by many governments as a means of introducing private sector approaches into a public enterprise or utility, or as a stage on the road to an asset sale. A department of state, for example, the department of electricity, is converted into a wholly-owned state business. It has to operate under commercial law and must return profits to the state. Typically, it is at this stage that massive job losses take place as the new (or 'converted') managers trim the corporation down to a size that makes it attractive to potential buyers.

In New Zealand, this process went hand in hand with the decision, taken in the late 1980s, to split the new corporation, Electricorp, into five business units, each of which insisted on a separate collective agreement between it and the PSI affiliate, the New Zealand Public Service Association (NZPSA). This not only imposed extra burdens on the union, but it also saw each business unit targeting different conditions for cut-backs in the negotiations. What had been a tightly disciplined and well-organised division of the union was divided into five different sections.

If unions in OECD countries have difficulty responding to reform, the problems are even greater in Africa. In September 1996, the Commonwealth Local Government Forum (CLGF) sponsored a seminar on local government reforms in Accra, Ghana. Senior central and local policy-makers from eighteen Commonwealth countries, rich and poor, signed the Accra Declaration on Good Local Government.

Martin, who reported on the conference for the PSI, recorded the Ghanaian Minister for Local Government, Kwamena Ahwoi's, vision of local government reform:

> The main challenges ... are the ... need to create effective sub-national institutions for management of change in a democratic manner, the promotion of effective and sustained people-oriented and participatory development, and the effort to ensure peace through peoples' involvement in governance. The objectives of the reforms include the prevention and management of local conflicts which often result from people's demands to be involved in governance; promotion and protection of the basic human rights of the people through access to opportunities for self-realisation and services and to power and authority structures. (Martin, 1996a)

How much credence can be placed on the assurances about democracy and popular participation may be judged later in this chapter from the structural adjustment paper written by Ekei Etim on the basis of replies to a survey of PSI affiliated unions, most of whom felt that consultation and participation were rarely part of the game. But, after describing the usual litany of problems claimed to typify the African public sector (dictatorship, corruption, inefficiency, mismanagement, etc.), Ahwoi went on to note:

> Other reasons for reforming our local government systems include the fact that the marginalisation of local governments led to situations in which the most basic needs of the people were left unattended to. These basic needs are best determined and addressed by the local people themselves, yet denied of power, functions, resources and skills, despondency and inefficiency held sway in our local governments. (Ibid.)

Martin comments, however, that considering the reality of Ghana as seen in a field trip, most of this is rhetoric.

Responding to transnational corporations

Government is not the only player in public sector redesign. The French water multi-national, Lyonnaise des Eaux, is chasing water contracts all over the world, including South Africa. Lyonnaise does not only want the contracts, it wants a workforce (and unions) that will not be a source of conflict and disruption. It has flown South African union representatives to France and Argentina to meet 'satisfied' workers and unions in Lyonnaise operations there. In turn, the South African unions have been in contact with public sector unions around the world through the PSI, so that they get the full picture.

The involvement of the TNCs in the public sector may transform the relationship between unions in the North and those in the South. The ability of the TNCs to shift production and/or resources amongst countries means that an African union may be as central to any international campaign to deal with that TNC as any well-resourced northern union.

Lyonnaise operates, either alone or in partnership, in public services in several African countries, North, South and Central America, Asia, Australasia, Central and Eastern Europe and Western Europe. It is involved in catering, cleaning, construction projects, energy and environment services, health services, security services and prisons, and, of course, water. In some countries it has set up business with its other competitors in order to keep new entrants out. The PSPRU has noted that vast corruption often accompanies these TNCs and the extent to which they ride to success on the backs of public sector trade unionists who are not allowed to tender for the services which are their bread and butter (PSPRU, 1996).

However, the news is not always bad. In many countries, state workers have fewer collective bargaining rights than workers in the private sector. When Malaysia decided to corporatise (and eventually privatise) its electricity operations, it was able to provide attractive options for staff: guaranteed jobs for a number of years, the right to go 'back' to the state sector if people did not like the new arrangements, increased salaries, improved conditions and the right to collective bargaining. Of course, it is easy for a monopoly electricity generator and supplier to offer such conditions. If one starts at the top end of the commercialisation spectrum and works down to the less marketable, the deals become less generous. But the principle of privatisation or commercialisation will have been accepted by a lot of workers.

Although they have not been able to match some of the Malaysian 'gains' for workers, many other countries, such as Sri Lanka, have insisted on job retention guarantees for a number of years when an asset sale occurs. The question to be asked on the basis of this last set of observations is: Are there ways in which trade unions can influence the general approach to modernisation of the state? Is it possible to set up tripartite framework agreements at the national level so that commercialisation of the public sector is not done on a piece-meal basis? Such approaches pit the strongest workers against the weakest and deprive the latter of their rights and jobs.

Defending public goods

Equity has often been a hallmark of public sector employment. Equal pay, child-care facilities, parental leave, multi-cultural policies and employing people with disabilities are evidence of a conscious recognition by state employers that they should be seen to lead in this area. Such policies have often been the victims of neo-liberal versions of state reform which regard these policies as market-distorting, non-transparent or overly prescriptive in telling employers how to achieve valuable social goals (for the neo-liberals never question that these are 'good' goals – we should just allow managers to find 'right price' solutions to achieving them). A valuable critique in this regard is the review of the state sector reforms in New Zealand commissioned of Allen Schick by the New Zealand Treasury and the State Services Commission. Schick is broadly enthusiastic about the reforms from a managerial perspective, but expresses concern that the concentration on a contract-and-price mentality has seen public sector employers downgrade training, employee development, working conditions and strategic planning for the future (Schick, 1996).

Schick's report goes even further, however, in looking at the character of the public sector reforms (and he has reviewed such programmes for the OECD in Australia, France, New Zealand, Sweden and the U.K.). He is not content to look just at the very defensible new managerialism which has brought about radical (and often very positive) change in many of these countries. In the New Zealand case he notes that the concentration on the neo-liberal fascination with principal-agent and contract theories has led to developments which amount not just to a restructuring of the state, but its transformation. Set the right prices for outputs which each department will contractually deliver to its minister; you evaluate the department's chief executive on the basis of meeting those contracted obligations; pretend that there are no other parties (the government as a whole, clients, voters, citizens, other departments etc.) to the contract; pretend that outcomes are not really the concern of public sector activities; focus on money and highly technical accountability. In his most damning criticism, he says that what has happened in New Zealand is that the responsibility of the state and its managers has been inadequately replaced by technical (but very demanding) accountability. The concept of public goods of concern to the citizenry as a whole has gone out of the window, in favour of getting the market price for such goods right – chiefly for business purchasers. Much public sector reform is not reform at all: it is merely pricing public sector goods in a competitive market.

Governments (and the World Bank) are fond of justifying privatisation or contracting out by pointing to the failure of the public sector. The public sector unions' stock response – that there is nothing wrong with the public sector – is of no use. There often is and much must be changed. It is, however, legitimate to ask how much of the failure of the public sector is a result of deliberate under-resourcing by the government. Public service cutbacks may be more than attacks on the services and their workers; they are a prelude to what will become finger pointing in a year or two, when government says, 'see how ineffective the public sector is – we have to privatise it.'

RISKS OF REFORM
AND STRATEGIES FOR DEALING WITH THEM

The promotion of public sector reforms, industrial action and international solidarity all have distinct risks. Unionists are very familiar with the risks involved in strike action or solidarity work against repressive regimes like apartheid South Africa or South Korea. There are also risks in unions promoting change or managing reform. Members may accuse the union leadership of 'class collaboration', and where members stand to lose in the changes they may take independent or 'wildcat' action. Sweden, Denmark, Finland and Zimbabwe have all seen (temporary) splits in the public sector union movement, with nurses and doctors taking independent action because of a relative wage loss brought about by the reform process.

In certain cases, the impact of state sector changes on unions is more directly negative. Some countries have laws which prevent one trade union covering workers in both the public and the private sectors. Such was the case in the Solomon Islands which, being a small country, had a very small, but well-recognised union for postal and telecommunications workers, who fell under a single government ministry. When the telecommunications section was corporatised in the late 1980s it was deemed to be outside of the public service. As a result the union had to split into two, non-viable unions.

It is this threatened destruction that makes it impossible, or difficult, for unions subject to such laws to deal with privatisation or reform in any 'positive' manner. Unions that can follow their members into the private arena can participate in meaningful negotiations about reform, secure in the knowledge that they will be able to defend their members' rights. The PSI paper, *A Public Sector Alternative Strategy* (PSI, 1995), advises PSI affiliates that trade union rights must be attached to any support they give to social dialogue and social partnership.

Bargaining Strategies

Unions also come under other strains as public services modernise and restructure. In many countries, one tendency has been for collective bargaining to decentralise, sometimes at the behest of the union, more often as a result of government initiatives.

Bargaining may be decentralised, though whether this is a good or bad thing depends on the state of the economy and the unemployment rate. In New Zealand, the NZPSA opted for such an approach just before the Labour government started the public sector reform process which avalanched into corporatisation, then privatisation, and then deregulation of the labour market. The result was that the union, which until the mid-1980s negotiated only a handful of central agreements, now found itself having to negotiate hundreds. On the one hand, members identified closely with the new process, since they were intimately involved in negotiations.

On the other, the union had neither the resources which the new process required nor the time to develop them. The old geographical branches, which had been the base for organising and policy-making, collapsed, as members put their energy into departmental/corporation-based informal structures. It has taken a decade to deal with these developments, and few would argue that it was easy or well done.

Tensions can also arise between unions over where workers should find their home. There may be competing national centres, or unions may see themselves benefiting from an 'agreement' that privatised workers be 'handed over' to an existing private sector union. Public sector unions can find themselves in a defensive or negative position, where they will do everything to protect their own strength. In both the U.S. and the U.K., the decisions of public sector unions to follow their members into the private sector has had a significant impact on their strategic approach to the modernisation of the public sector.

In some instances, the 'old guard' of private sector unions has not taken kindly to the emergence of 'milk-and-water' weak public sector unions in terms of numbers and influence. The public sector unions, with their large women's membership, have introduced new and difficult issues, such as pay equity and sexual harassment, to union debates. Their approach to industrial action, moreover, has often been different to that of the private sector unions.

Apart from the change in legal status, a decision to introduce private sector industrial relations machinery into the public sector in order to deliver more market-driven results from negotiations, can impact on both worker rights and trade union strength. This can be good or bad, depending on the precise nature of the changes. Union negotiators, who have always negotiated paid rather than minimum rates, can find themselves with a divided membership when confronted at the negotiating table with new managers brought in from the private sector who are trying to establish a performance-related pay scheme. Conversely, the newly acquired right to take industrial action can strengthen the union – if it knows how to use this power.

The right to collective bargaining is normally defined fairly narrowly to focus on the collective agreement for the sector, enterprise, or workplace concerned. Yet there are two other areas where workers and their unions would see this right applied: for workers in the public sector, it is a demand, often not met, that they be involved from the outset in discussions on public sector reform, including privatisation. For all workers and their unions, it is also a right to be involved in tripartite discussions at the national level on social and economic policy matters of this kind on a consistent basis. Here, there is a need for pressure to be applied in two different directions. Governments undergoing genuine restructuring with the IMF, World Bank or bilateral 'aid' support, which are not prepared to respect internationally recognised worker and trade union rights, should be barred from such 'assistance'. In turn, the international financial institutions and donor governments must be pressurised to incorporate into their programmes and projects requirements that trade unions and other organs of civil society be able to participate in these projects as full partners.

In Central and Eastern Europe, a difficulty facing workers and unions, especially in utilities and enterprises established with commercial objectives or given so-called 'budgetary independence', is that no-one is prepared to own up to being the management. Unions want to negotiate wages, allowances, pensions, job conditions, etc., but they are shunted from pillar to post: 'No, it's still the people in the ministry who set our budgets, so go see them,' or 'Yes, the ministry is the source of the funds but you'll have to deal with the hospital head since he (and it will be a man in the new market society) has to determine line-item allocations.' End result: no improvements in pay and conditions while costs continue to spiral. Another factor is that governments often decree that corporatised (and certainly privatised and contracted-out) workers will lose their civil servant status. While civil service salaries may be low, the service remains attractive because of job security and good pension rights. The issue may divide the union membership between those with one or two years of service left, and those who have only just started work.

The Social Wage

So far, this chapter has concentrated on those workers (and their unions) within the public sector. However, it should be recognised that many of the goods and services provided in the public sector are a substantial proportion of the social wage 'paid' to all workers. Many workers would regard it as their right to have free or subsidised access to education and health and to have telecommunications, electricity and water at below-market costs. If commercialisation of the public services raises the cost of these goods and services, workers may feel that their rights have been infringed, especially if their wage negotiations do not result in an increase to cover these costs. This is why it is very important for the trade union movement, across all sectors, to display solidarity in defending public services. Unions should insist on tripartite discussions when confronted by two common positions adopted by governments: that these matters should at best be discussed only with public sector unions, since it is their employer-employee relations which are affected; or that they should not be discussed with the unions at all, since these are political decisions outside of the employer-employee relationship.

Many workers feel that a nation should own and control its own strategic resources. If asset sales or contracting out result in investment, servicing and pricing decisions being taken in New York, London or Tokyo, they believe they have lost national sovereignty rights. While this has obvious emotional appeal, it has to be questioned whether having local capitalists making the same decisions is any real advance, over and above the possibility of being able to harass them more easily.

Harry Kelber cites the potential impact on welfare beneficiaries in the U.S., where big firms are queuing up to take over state and city contracts to run welfare schemes.[2] They offer to regulate the welfare rolls, train people for jobs and find jobs for people. Under these arrangements, the big firms will actually determine eligibility standards and benefits. Kelber asks: 'Can you imagine what these companies, with their experience in down-sizing employees, will do to the welfare rolls, if the more people they lop off, the larger will be their own profit?'

UNIONS AND RESTRUCTURING IN AFRICA

It is well and good to talk about what is possible in nations where the union movement is strong and well-resourced, and in countries where governments have some minimal formal commitment to democracy and social dialogue and a strong economy. It is easier for a government to deal with its own people and trade unions when it does not fear the hot breath of the international financial institutions on its neck. But what happens in Africa? Are there any governments that can challange the World Bank or the IMF? What can they do when international or bilateral donors say that money, aid and technical assistance are conditional on the 'right path' being followed?

In 1994, the PSI commissioned a study entitled *Structural Adjustment Programmes and the Public Sector in Africa* from Ekei Etim of the Pioneer Agency for Development in Africa (PADA). The study was based in part on a survey of PSI affiliates in Africa and their experiences of Structural Adjustment Programmes (SAPs). Foreign grants, loans, investment and other forms of 'aid' have become a dominant factor in Africa's development equation. Without such aid, little seems to happen. The foreign aid syndrome – the dependency culture – is so devastating that it subverts rather than energises development. The stranglehold of debt servicing in the face of collapsing commodity prices in the 1980s offered African countries few options for attracting new resources. This led to a situation in which there was only one option: adopt the terms of the SAP or perish.

In an overview of the African debt crisis on which most SAPs were based, Etim notes:

> One of the most effective means of ensuring that poorer countries adopt SAPs was the promise of continued foreign aid. As Zambia and other indebted countries learned, non-compliance with the terms of SAPs resulted in cuts in other forms of foreign aid, and without the IMF 'seal of approval', no credits were forthcoming from international commercial banks. By 1990, sub-Saharan Africa had become a net transferor of resources to the North through interest rates and the conditions for repayment ... The architects of the SAPs see the crisis in Africa as one of production. This thesis holds that African governments have been mismanaging their economies. Also that they are not producing sufficient goods to export in order to pay for their expenditure on imports, social services and debt repayments. Thus put, the solution to the crisis is the SAPs. This would cut government spending, especially on 'unproductive' social services, privatise public sector enterprises, devalue currencies so that imports are expensive, to promote domestic investment and increase export earnings. (Etim, 1994: 3-4)

Etim found that stabilisation programmes were the first steps to reforming the economies. They addressed economic problems (such as balance of payments deficits and inflation) and set targets: the reduction of public spending, reduction of credits, devaluation of currencies and the removal of price controls and subsidies. SAPs were the second step: medium-term programmes aimed at reactivating national economies by encouraging foreign investment, relaxing financial regulations and reducing state involvement in the economy by privatising certain services and enterprises. They were meant to encourage trade through reductions in taxes on imports, competitive exchange rates and export promotion.

The proponents of privatisation argued that state enterprises in Africa were overstaffed, bureaucratic and corrupt and claimed that it would attract overseas investment into Africa and liberalise market operations. The reality of privatisation in Africa does not live up to these claims, however. Few state corporations have been privatised with African governments selling off only a small percentage of their assets. In the case of Zambia, only 11 out of 150 government companies were privatised in the first year of a five-year programme. The value of privatisation in Nigeria between 1988 and 1992 was less than 1% of that in Argentina or Mexico, even after adjusting for Nigeria's smaller gross domestic product (GDP). Most African countries lack the financial institutions and regulations to allow for the processing of shares. Only the stock exchanges in Egypt, Kenya, Morocco, Nigeria, Ivory Coast, South Africa and Zimbabwe are of sufficient size to back privatisation – that is seven out of 52 countries. In fact, the irony of privatisation and public service reform in much of the world is that it cannot proceed unless there is a competent, strong and stable state to create and manage laws, structures and institutions which will give investors security and guaranteed return on intellectual property rights. Also, a majority of the African population cannot afford to buy shares. It is mainly TNCs and African elites that engage in share dealings. Finally, in most African countries, the financial sector, despite reform efforts, is still heavily burdened by public sector demands for credit – with the central government alone absorbing more than 30% of domestic credit (Etim, 1994: 5-6).

The PADA study traces the effects of the SAPs on the public sector – all the more dramatic in African economies, where the public sector is such a central employer and standard setter. Etim notes, for example, that the public sector accounted for 54% of non-agricultural employment in Africa, compared with 36% for Asia, 27% for Latin America and 24% in industrialised countries. SAPs and their associated loans targeted public sector wage bills and public sector reform programmes; they tended to try to replace public sector workers with those from semi-autonomous agencies, to increase the financial and managerial responsibility of hospitals and schools in countries with little experience in this area and to encourage deregulation in situations where governments did not know how to deal with emerging monopolies.

In exploring the lessons for Africa from the World Bank/IMF medicine, Etim states:

> In recent times, the trade unions have been prevented from managing the policy changes by their governments. Prevention has been in the form of decrees, as in the case of Nigeria, arrests of trade union leaders, vetting of conference materials to be used by unions for press conferences and withdrawal of trade union rights such as the right to strike. Public sector employers have tried to remain competitive by cutting costs through retrenching workers, reducing remuneration and, where possible, introducing flexibility such as the employment of part-time, casual and contract workers. Also, privatisation, where it has been introduced, has led to inequality in the distribution of income and wealth. (1994: 10-11)

SAPs have caused established civil servants to lose their jobs and an increasing proportion of public service staff (in Ghana and Nigeria, for example) are on short-term and temporary contracts. African responses to the questionnaire on part-time and temporary work, prepared for the fifth session of the ILO Joint Committee on the Public Service, showed that temporary employment in the public sector had increased faster than other forms of employment. The uncertainty created in employment conditions in the public sector has led to a movement of workers to the private sector and also to migration to Europe and the U.S. The brain drain will continue to be a problem in Africa unless job security is restored and the quality of working life is improved.

A high quality of working life is a necessary precondition for high productivity, but personnel cannot experience a high quality of working life unless they see their work as productive. Unions point to the problems of less motivation and a decline in the morale of workers caused by poor working conditions, including the lack of safety at work, pollution, stress, closure of creches and playgroups. Another factor is the withdrawal of workers' rights, with the suspension of collective bargaining, harassment at the workplace, the introduction of longer working hours and increase in workloads. The withdrawal of workers' rights and the relatively high membership fees have caused unions to lose a large number of members. Workers do not feel that they are getting value for money, as the trade unions are incapable of protecting workers' interests.

The World Bank and the IMF have, for many years, promoted a model of growth and development based on the assumption that 'public is bad: private is good'. This has underpinned the enthusiasm for privatisation. In his book, Martin's concern is with the way in which the change in global relations has shaped change in the public sector. In line with many public sector trade unions, he suggests that both the state and the market should be the servants of society, the key concepts being democracy and citizenship:

> There is no more guarantee that the state services the public interest than that the market does so, as many of the world's people can testify, and therefore in considering the need for power to be restored to the state, it is necessary also to pay attention to the ways in which that power is exercised. If the state and public sectors are to contribute effectively to sustainable economic development, to social justice, to elimination of poverty and to pluralist democratic society in which power is accountable and decentralised, then these standards must be reflected in how they set out to achieve those aims. The state should command sufficient power and resources to ensure that all people can make full contributions to and derive fair benefits from the economic, social and cultural life of their communities, because the market alone cannot ensure this and left to itself tends to prevent it; the state should have only as many powers and resources as it needs for this purpose, so that the private and 'third' sectors and institutions of civil society can also perform their roles effectively. (Martin, 1993: 187)

The appearance of the World Bank's 1997 World Development Report, *The State in a Changing World*, has added a new element, which suggests that both the Bank and governments can be challenged to live up to the report's call for popular participation and effective labour-management programmes.

There is a dilemma for the international trade union movement in dealing with the problem of the international financial institutions. Some form of structural adjustment is vital for much of Africa. Continued, unequivocal support from the IMF, the World Bank or bilateral donor governments often props up dictatorial and/or corrupt governments. Workers and the communities they serve do not benefit from this and the country often gets deeper into debt as the anti-democratic forces either spend the money on military waste or use it corruptly for their cronies or megalomaniac projects. Pressure is needed to ensure that aid is conditional on real democratic reforms. Where Northern unions are involved in such pressure/campaigns, they must be seen to be working closely with trade unions in the affected country.

At a seminar for World Bank staff on the role of labour in the privatisation of public enterprises which a PSI representative addressed in June 1996, there were constant questions about when in the process unions should be involved. It was mind-boggling for some of these people to hear that unions expect to be involved in all such matters, not from any particular point in time, but as a permanent part of labour relations. To ask the Bank's staff to advise governments to involve unions in this way was just too much: this was interference in internal affairs.

A positive note was, however, struck towards the end of 1996. The non-governmental organisations (NGOs) which have been most active in lobbying the World Bank on its SAPs and calling for a change in direction, convinced the Bank's leadership that a formal exercise to evaluate SAPs should be conducted. The SAP Review Initiative (SAPRI) was funded by Bank-supported endeavours and is taking ten countries as case studies. Governments, resident Bank staff and relevant NGOs, including public sector trade unions, will examine the record of SAPs in the selected countries to look at the impact on the excluded and the 'victims', with a view to seeing whether the programme(s) should be reoriented. This is an opportunity for trade unions to see both whether they can affect the direction of changes in the public services and whether they can work with NGOs in effecting public sector reforms which benefit more of the community. This will fail totally, of course, unless governments show good faith. The governments involved have to accept that their policies, as well as those of the Bank, will need to change if the SAPRI exercise shows that SAPs have unequal negative effects.

CONCLUSION

The analysis outlined in this chapter presents a huge agenda for trade unions in South Africa and elsewhere in Africa. In most African countries it is frankly impossible in our lifetimes. The two dangers are: to pretend that it is not impossible and to try to do everything; or to give up right now on the basis that it is not possible at all. The story is told of a family that is lost. They know where they want to go, but do not know the direction. They find a 'wise counsellor', probably with good left-wing credentials, who tells them: 'Well, if that's where you want to go, I wouldn't start from here'. And that is the advice many unions receive – to start from where their advisor or donor organisation is at. It is obviously bad advice: you have to start from where you are and with what you have. If that tells you that it will take ten years to get to your destination or that you will never get there but that you can help the next generation get there, well, that is what you have to do.

Unions which want to embark on this road must engage in strategic planning to map out the road, to tally their resources, to work out where and with whom to stay on the way and to know which of the next generation should be trained to carry on the expedition. We should start out, and soon.

In summary, there are pluses and minuses in terms of the effects which the modernisation and commercialisation of the public sector has on workers and trade union rights. The devil is often in the detail and smart unions are therefore cautious about adopting a knee-jerk ideological attitude to public sector reform in general. The members will often have complex views; the union may stand to win as much as it loses; society may make some efficiency and productivity gains even as it loses universality of or accessibility to services of sometimes doubtful quality. A sound case-by-case approach is often the only way that a public sector union can serve its members' interests best and be perceived to be acting in the community's interest by promoting flexible and accountable services to the people.

For all the above reasons, PSI has placed a high priority in recent years on helping unions, especially those in the developing world, to position themselves for the future. Its educational programme on strategic planning is aimed at helping unions to work through the process of identifying their strengths and weaknesses, where they want to be in three-to-five years' time, what is on their likely agenda and how to plan to be on top of all this. Unions cannot win or protect rights that they never aim to get or to use.

4

UNIONS INSIDE THE STATE

The development of unionism in the South African public service

———— ✦ ————

Ian Macun and Christine Psoulis

Macun and Psoulis provide an extremely useful overview of unionisation trends in the public service. It was only in the 1980s that public servants gained limited representational rights, but only on a racially and occupationally divided basis. Moreover, they were not permitted to join trade unions, engage in collective bargaining or strike. With the advent of democratisation in the 1990s, the public service was brought under the ambit of the Labour Relations Act, allowing for the first time the full development of trade unions and collective bargaining.

The form of unionism has been shaped by the character of public service management, which has been centralised, bureaucratic and controlling in its impact on labour and labour relations. This has produced a high level of distrust and adversarialism that fueled militant unionising efforts by black workers in particular. It has also ironically contributed to very poorly developed capacity in industrial relations and human resource management within the public service and particularly within the civil service.

Moreover the peculiar history of the public service led to the development of a range of organisations to represent workers, with different constituencies, interests, and ways of operating. Public servants' success in winning gains will depend on finding ways to achieve greater co-operation. Despite their different histories these organisations face a number of common problems. One is adjusting to the changing structure of bargaining, and the inevitable devolution of aspects of bargaining to provincial and even institutional levels. A second issue concerns union mergers, driven by the need to maximise leverage in the central and sectoral bargaining councils. These may occur along political lines, a sectoral logic, or in a haphazard fashion to maintain viability by increasing membership. Finally, mergers may change the unions' links to their trade union federations

INTRODUCTION

In his discussion on unionisation in South Africa during the 1970s and 1980s, researcher Steven Friedman describes agricultural and domestic workers as 'workers the eighties forgot'. He might well have added public service workers. The rapid unionisation and worker militance of the 1970s and 1980s bypassed the state, whose internal industrial relations remained hidden from the public eye. Apart from a few isolated attempts by relatively unknown unions, state employees did not organise effectively until the early 1990s. By this time, the transition to democracy had begun in earnest and developments in public sector industrial relations began to resemble those of the private sector, with rapid change occurring over a short period of time.

In most countries, public service industrial relations have a distinct history from those of the private sector. There are different procedures for regulating terms and conditions of employment. Industrial conflict assumes different patterns and is dealt with in different ways. Union organisation also differs. Recently, this situation has changed. In many countries the state has become the largest employer. There is greater overlap in service provision between the public and private sectors and governments have been subjected to economic constraints that have translated into industrial relations challenges (Treu, 1987: 2).

Understanding unionisation in the public sector thus requires a sensitivity to both the particularities of industrial relations in this sector and to the way in which these have been changing in the context of economic and political developments.

This chapter will limit itself to an examination of three major issues:
• firstly, it will distinguish the particular nature of labour relations within the state
• secondly, it will describe the development of unionisation in the 1980s and 1990s

- finally, it will outline the character of employee organisations that developed during this period.

The focus is mainly on the civil service – that is, the agencies and workers who are directly employed in the running of government departments. Developments in the broader public service (which includes those involved in service delivery – educators, health personnel and the police) will be dealt with in more general terms, and mainly for the 1990s.

THE NATURE OF LABOUR RELATIONS

Both management structure and job structure affect the nature of relations between employers and employees, especially given the historical complications of the South African public sector. (See Chapter 2 by Posel for a description of this history.)

Management structure

The formal management and co-ordination of labour relations within the South African state began with the formation of the Public Service Commission (PSC) in 1912, two years after the creation of an independent national state. Its purpose was to depoliticise personnel relations and to develop an efficient and competent administration.

The PSC remained virtually unchanged over the years. Renamed the Commission for Administration (CFA) in 1984 and granted wider responsibilities, in 1993 it once again became known as the PSC.

The PSC was responsible to Parliament. It could make recommendations, but these had to be approved by Parliament or a Cabinet Minister. Its major function was to co-ordinate and regulate employment in the different state departments. It also played an important planning and policy function with regard to employment issues and was responsible for all aspects of the employer-employee relationship. These included:

- bargaining with workers around conditions of service
- disciplinary action not resolved at departmental level
- the resolution of grievances between the state and individual employees.

Although departments were responsible for day-to-day labour relations issues through the PSC, management was highly centralised. This tendency increased over time. The PSC became an extremely bureaucratic form of management, based on a complex web of rules and regulations contained in various legislative measures, such as the Personnel Administration Standard (PAS) and, in particular, the Public Service Act. These legislative measures were reviewed after 1994 and some of the functions of the PSC were incorporated into the Department of Public Service and Administration (DPSA) when it was created in 1995.

As in the private sector, the style of management in the public service has been slow to change. Management techniques were intended to enforce strict control over employees. The PSC, for example, had an Organisation and Work Study Directorate, staffed by inspectors who supervised the activities of departments, almost all of whom had work study officers. The work of these officers involved 'examining methods and procedures in minute detail and determining what has to be done, why it has to be done, how it is done and how that which must of necessity be done, can be done better'. It was only in the early 1990s that new techniques, that had been in widespread use in other countries from the 1980s such as quality circles, were experimented with in the South Africa public service. De Bruyn points out the effects of such a system:

> (These) forms of work organisation ... do not maximise the creative and innovative potential of workers. Instead they maximise employer control. This is epitomised in the excessive layers of supervision and layers of hierarchy. (1996: 201)

Jobs were constructed on the basis of tightly specified job descriptions that accentuated divisions between mental and manual work, tied workers to narrow areas of responsibility, and thus militated against the development of meaningful career paths.

Job Structure

Public service jobs are fragmented and poorly remunerated relative to the private sector. The job structure is highly complex and characterised by 'an extraordinary number of job categories and a correspondingly complex system of wages and wage differentials' (Standing et al., 1996: 216). By the early 1990s the number of occupational classes had been reduced from 520 to 340, but salary differentials remained marked. Low wages for unskilled workers and for those involved in service delivery, notably nurses and police, persisted.

In all the occupational groups, wage rates and conditions of employment have varied significantly by race and gender. De Bruyn notes that the hierarchy is: 'white men, white women, African men and, at the bottom, African women'. With the exception of nursing and educational work, occupational differentiation has persisted, with Africans and women being concentrated in the lesser-skilled categories of work.

Until the late 1980s, this was exacerbated by the categorisation of employees into officers (with permanent status), temporary, and contract workers. Permanent officers received increased benefits during the 1980s as part of the state's rationalisation efforts, but these were not matched for other categories. Steps were also taken to address discriminatory practices against women, although white women were the main beneficiaries. The category of temporary employee was also abolished (De Bruyn, 1996: 188-196).

Despite these attempts, differentiation and discrimination have persisted. The state's ability to address these problems is constrained by a prior commitment to reducing the wage bill as a proportion of public service consumption expenditure. Employment relations continue to provide ample grounds for grievances on the part of public service employees and, theoretically, for sustained collective organisation.

THE DEVELOPMENT OF UNIONISATION

Bounded consultation

The Public Servants Association (PSA), was formed in 1920, shortly after the Public Service Act provided for the recognition of staff associations. Recognition was based on majority representation of 'officers' – permanent employees in the various divisions of the public service. It also required that staff associations be representative of certain 'interest groups', which translated into representation along racial lines. The PSA therefore represented white, permanent civil servants.

With recognition came formal consultation through the Public Service Joint Advisory Council, a body established by the Public Service Commission (PSC). The council was a purely advisory body with which the PSC consulted on labour relations issues. It was composed of equal representation of the PSA and the PSC. Until the 1980s the PSA remained the only organisation within the public service recognised by the apartheid state. While there were other bodies in existence, such as the Medical Association of South Africa (MASA), these played no significant role with regard to labour relations. From the early 1980s, the number of bodies expanded and by 1985, the Commission for Administration (CFA), as the PSC was briefly known, had granted recognition to the Public Service League (PSL), the Public Service Union (PSU) and the Institute of Public Servants (IPS), all of which were represented in the advisory council.

All the organisations active within the state up until the 1990s could be classified as staff associations. Their role was either purely advisory, or involved some form of consultation. They did not conceive of themselves as trade unions: they had limited independence from their employer and the pursuit of industrial action did not feature prominently in their mode of operation. These associations were all racially based and, with the exception of the PSL, whose membership included substantial numbers of temporary workers, they represented mainly permanent employees (Golding, 1985: 48r).[1]

The leadership of these organisations has been described as 'conservative and bureaucratic'. It was only in the PSL that there were internal battles 'over the direction of the union and over forms of representation' (Ibid.). Their interaction with the state as employer was of a purely consultative nature and was bounded by bureaucratic, managerial control, diverse employment strategies and divided organisational identities. This is not to suggest that these associations were completely ineffective. They were able to raise a number of concerns and they did so regularly, particularly regarding wages and other conditions of employment. The PSA, in particular, played a key role in improving the pension benefits of civil servants in the early 1970s, and it continued lobbying for the introduction of collective bargaining during the 1980s. In the absence of any effective collective bargaining, however, employees were bound by their employer's unilateral determination of wages and conditions of employment.

Transition

From the late 1980s, the public service entered a period of turmoil, which set in motion a process of profound change in labour relations. The origins of this process lay in the Wiehahn Commission which, in 1979, had already recommended the extension of union recognition and collective bargaining to the public service. The commission noted that a number of advantages would follow the extension of workers' rights to public servants. These included, among other things, that:

- it would give such personnel a greater degree of involvement in decisions affecting their terms and conditions of service, which in turn affects their daily lives and those of their families
- decisions by the state on such matters would be more readily accepted by public servants if they had some sense of participation, however limited, in such decisions
- the image of the public service in the eyes of the private sector and the country as a whole could be enhanced (Wiehahn Commission, 1982: 528).

The commission went on to recommend the inclusion of the public service under the old Labour Relations Act of 1981. These recommendations were not politically acceptable to the government of the time, and the fact that the public service did not fall within the terms of reference of the Commission offered a ready-made excuse for ignoring its recommendations. However, the rapid development of unionisation in the private sector after 1980 undoubtedly had a demonstrative effect on public sector workers.

Political pressure from within Parliament and from the private sector, which had become more vociferous in its criticisms of the increasingly ineffective and costly public service, were an added source of pressure on the state to restructure itself internally (Golding, 1985: 45). Political developments within the National Party (NP) added to this impetus, albeit for different reasons, and after PW Botha assumed leadership of the party in 1979, one of the first measures announced was the rationalisation of the public service. This entailed streamlining state departments (the number of departments was reduced from 39 to 22), improving the image of the state and re-evaluating and reorganising employment practices. It also involved a process of centralisation of power within the state and the removal of obstacles, including personnel, who would obstruct the new direction that the state was taking under Botha's leadership. From 1981 a process of occupational differentiation was begun, which was ostensibly aimed at improving the system of personnel administration and its efficiency (CFA, 1982/1983: 18). Another view of its objectives was that it was aimed at:

> winning over civil servants to the state's new political orientation through improved material benefits and opportunities. It meant substantial salary restructuring and a general package of improved housing subsidies and loans, pension provisions and other perks. (Golding, 1985: 46)

Restructuring the state also involved, from the mid-1980s, a process of 'commercialisation' of state enterprises, which entailed retrenchments, a freeze on new employment (employment continued, nonetheless, to expand during the 1980s), attempts to reduce real wages and a drive to privatise large parts of the public sector (Community Resource and Information Centre, 1990). Opposition from various quarters slowed down the process of privatisation, although the commercialisation of state enterprises continued.

In 1988 the CFA submitted proposals to the Cabinet aimed at amending the Public Service Act to allow for joint determination of remuneration and conditions of service by staff associations and the CFA. In the same year, a directorate of labour relations was established by the CFA to undertake research, evaluate the state of labour relations and to liaise with staff associations to 'constitute bargaining and consulting bodies and to provide supporting services for them' (CFA, 1988: 30). Seminars in labour relations had been first introduced in 1986, and by 1988, just over 500 officers had attended these seminars.

In some respects, this flurry of activity signalled a recognition by the state of the inevitability of change. Simultaneously, it was a last ditch effort to maintain the status quo. This is well captured by the recommendation of the advisory council that the CFA:

> bring the role, place and status of the recognised staff associations pertinently to the attention of departments and administrations, in order to influence positively the perception of recognised staff associations held by officers/ employees and to counter the influence of undesirable organisations (trade unions), which do not have the interests of the public service at heart. (CFA, 1988: 57)

Strikes

These changes did little to delay the inevitable. In late 1989 and in 1990, health workers, teachers, police and prison warders embarked on a wave of strike action. Many workers were not union members and only joined unions after taking part in the strikes. In nearly all cases the underlying issues were the same: wages, union recognition, solidarity with dismissed or harassed workers and discriminatory treatment. Significantly, there were no strikes within the civil service of the South African state, although a number of the homeland administrations (such as Bophuthatswana, Venda, Gazankulu and Lebowa) were affected by strikes and stayaways.

Over the next few years, the number of trade unions organising public service workers grew rapidly. Membership of existing unions, such as the National Education, Health and Allied Workers' Union (NEHAWU), formed in 1987, and the PSA, increased dramatically. Negotiations on a new dispensation began soon after the strikes, culminating in the passage of the Public Service Labour Relations Act (PSLRA) in 1993, which put in place a labour relations system in line with that governing the private sector.

The Public Service Labour Relations Act

The PSLRA was a key moment in the transition of public service labour relations and highlighted a controversial issue: whether the public service should be governed by a separate dispensation or be incorporated under the Labour Relations Act (LRA). Before 1994, there was much debate on this issue, with African National Congress (ANC) Members of Parliament supporting the extension of the LRA to the public sector. A key criticism of the Public Service Labour Relations Bill related to its dispute-resolution procedures and the extent to which these favoured of the state. According to the ANC MP, J.H. Momberg (who crossed from the Democratic Party to the ANC before the 1994 elections):

> The Bill draws on sections from the LRA, but fails to maintain the balance between employer and employee interests found in the LRA. Once these checks and balances are jettisoned, the legitimacy of the legislation and its workability are compromised. (Debates of Parliament, 1993/1994: 42 (10692))

The Act was passed in 1993, but it was short-lived. In late 1996, the public service was included in a revised LRA, albeit with certain transitional measures. The transition in public service labour relations was formally complete, but in many respects the real challenges of transformation were only beginning (see Chapter 6, Patel and Chapter 7, Baskin).

Representation

During the transitional period, a number of crucial institutional and political changes occurred, shifting the nature of labour relations from consultation to interaction between the state and representative organisations. The first of these changes was the creation of new collective bargaining structures consisting of a central chamber, provincial councils and departmental structures (see Chapter 5, Adair and Albertyn). In the education sector, a separate bargaining structure, the Education Labour Relations Council (ELRC) was set up; a negotiation forum was also established for the police (see Chapter 6, Patel, Chapter 9, Garson and Chapter 10, Marks).

Secondly, labour relations were transferred from the PSC to the newly established office of the Minister for the Public Service and Administration. A process of negotiation, which had been started in the early 1990s, was formalised within this structure, although the primary emphasis appeared to be on Central Chamber negotiations.

The third major change was the statutory recognition of trade unions, first under the PSLRA, and then in terms of the LRA. This established a permanent foothold for the unions that had been struggling to gain a presence since the 1980s. It also opened the door to new unions and increased competition between unions. By 1995, 19 unions and staff associations were meeting with government representatives in the Chamber; by 1996 there were 22 (see Chapter 6, Patel).

The ANC's election victory also led to changes in the orientation of certain organisations towards the government. The two largest COSATU affiliated unions, NEHAWU and the South African Democratic Teachers' Union (SADTU), were more wary of taking action against the new government. 'We are negotiating with a democratic government, and not the National Party,' a representative explained. 'We must remember that there is a difference between the two' (1997: confidential telephonic interview). On the other hand, a newly-formed independent union, the

South African Health and Public Service Workers Union (SAHPSWU) claimed to be 'the only militant union' in the Chamber. Whether these changes in orientation will have a real effect on the functioning and character of such organisations remains to be seen. The industrial action organised by COSATU unions and those from the Federation of Unions of South Africa (FEDUSA) during the 1999 wage negotiations, suggests a more complex relation between unions, as representatives of public service workers, and as organisations which share a common political perspective to that of their employer.

Growth

One of the most striking features of public service unionism has been the rapid growth in union membership and the number of unions. In the early 1980s the PSA was the largest organisation, with approximately 80 000 members. By 1999 there were nearly 20 organisations representing more than 980 000 employees, a union density of approximately 96% (PSCBC, 1999). In the 1980s, Japan registered 67%, West Germany 75%, and Britain 80%. In relation to these countries and to the local manufacturing industry, South Africa's rate was extremely high. (For a breakdown of union membership in 1999, see Appendix 4.1.)

Although there is an absence of data for the different branches of the public service, it would be safe to assume that there is significant variation and that this is likely to be further affected by the rationalisation, or 'right-sizing', programme currently underway. Union density is probably highest within the health and education sectors and lowest within the central and provincial administrations. Local government has long been unionised and has been regulated by the LRA.

The late development of public service unionisation in South Africa can largely be explained by the nature of management and employment relations which has been outlined here. These have discouraged organisation and have attempted to incorporate workers vital to the state, such as the permanent officials, to ensure control over the remaining employees (see Chapter 2, Posel). Repressive labour relations were supplemented by legal restrictions. All of these factors retarded the process of collective representation, but also provided the basis for the explosion of militance in the early 1990s and the rapid increase in unionisation within a short space of time.

UNION CHARACTER

Unionisation is frequently treated as an undifferentiated process, in which a union movement becomes a homogenous entity with few differences between organisations' behaviour, attitudes, structure or style. This approach does not go very far in understanding the dynamics of unionisation, particularly in the public service, where quite different types of organisations operate.

The notion of 'union character' may assist in making sense of the ways in which unionisation has occurred and in evaluating the prospects for further union growth in the public service. There are two ways in which this term has been used which can help in understanding the public service.[2] The first is the argument by Blackburn (1967) that the performance of a union as a bargaining agent is a function of its level of workplace organisation and its position on the spectrum of what he calls 'unionateness'. This is a measure of an organisation's commitment to the general ideology and principles of trade unionism which involves:

- regarding collective bargaining and the protection of members' interests as its main function, rather than professional activities or welfare schemes
- independence from employers for purposes of negotiation
- militance, using all forms of action which may be effective
- declaring itself to be a trade union
- registering itself as a trade union
- affiliation to a larger association of unions, such as a federation
- affiliation to a political party.

The first five elements are concerned with the function and behaviour of organisations, while the last two are measures of the level of identification with the wider labour movement. Undy et al. (1981) use the term 'union character' to refer to the strategies and tactics used in the process of job regulation. They argue that unions change particularly with regard to political action and a growth in militancy. For some unions, this entails development along well-established lines, whereas for others it may involve more qualitative change.

As Beaumont points out in both these treatments, organisational change involves increasing militance and an increased integration and sense of identity with the larger mainstream union movement. In the case of public sector unions organising white-collar workers, 'it is contended that such unions become increasingly similar (along these two basic dimensions), from the late 1960s, to blue-collar unions in both the public and private sectors' (Beaumont, 1992: 53). An important reason for the change in union character has been the operation of income policies, which have led to dissatisfaction with pay amongst public service employees resulting in a push for their organisations to affiliate with union federations in order to gain access to government decision-making.

While the South African situation differs in important respects from the international one, this approach to union character is useful in highlighting a number of features that can be used to assess changes in South African public service unions: the extent to which they operate as unions, their relationship to collective bargaining, their approach to and use of industrial action and their relation to the wider labour movement. Moreover, both the approaches suggest ways of evaluating the changes that have been occurring in many of these unions.

Classification of organisations

The organisations representing workers in the public service differ in significant respects. Indeed, to refer to the 'unionisation' of the public service is something of a misnomer. Three types of organisation can be identified.

Staff associations

Staff associations are involved in advisory forums, consultation and full-scale negotiations. Their preparedness to take industrial action is not always easy to determine and their degree of independence from the employer may vary. Staff associations tend to represent workers in the more skilled occupations and offer a fairly wide range of benefits to their members. Examples of such organisations in the South African public service include the Public and Allied Workers' Union of South Africa (PAWUSA), the United National Public Servants' Association of South Africa (UNIPSA), the PSA and the PSU.

Professional associations

Professional associations represent the interests of highly skilled personnel. They may also play a role in the regulation of entry into professions through certification procedures and training requirements. Examples include the South African Medical Association (SAMA, formerly the Medical Association of South Africa, MASA) and the Democratic Nursing Organisation of South Africa (DENOSA). Organisations such as SADTU and the Hospital Personnel Trade Union of South Africa (HOSPERSA) are concerned with particular features of professional and semi-professional groupings, such as educators and nurses, leading to certain organisational dynamics which distinguish these organisations from those oriented primarily to blue-collar workers. Organisations that do not have the membership size to qualify for access to the Public Service Co-ordinating Bargaining Council (PSCBC) are the Society of State Advocates of South Africa and the Association of State Attorneys.

Trade unions

Trade unions express a clear commitment to negotiation on behalf of members, backed if necessary, by the use of sanctions. They are generally independent of employers and tend to adopt a more member-centred approach in their organisational structure and functioning. Examples include NEHAWU, SADTU, and the South African Police Union (SAPU).

Characteristics of organisations

The organisations party to the PSCBC exhibit a number of characteristics which distinguish them from their private sector counterparts and which illustrate their different backgrounds and organisational development.[3] The majority are not affiliated to any of the country's major federations and express a clear commitment to independence and political neutrality. With the exception of SAPU, these are all staff or professional associations. The relatively low level of identification with the wider labour movement is related to the concern with bread-and-butter issues and with the interests of members as distinct occupational groups, rather than as members of broad social classes. It is possible that, in dealing with the state, these associations opt for political neutrality as the easiest way to navigate between potentially competing or compromising political interests between members and the state as employer.

The two major federations to which the remaining organisations are affiliated are COSATU – three affiliates – and the Federation of Unions of South Africa (FEDUSA) – three affiliates. COSATU and its affiliates are well known for their relatively high level of commitment to working class interests and to left-of-centre politics. FEDUSA has expressed a commitment to independence and political neutrality. Despite the fact that these federations have relatively few affiliates amongst the organisations represented in the Chamber, they represent the largest number of organised workers and tend to operate as two powerful blocs to which the other organisations align themselves.

All the organisations present in the PSCBC engage in collective bargaining on behalf of their members around remuneration and conditions of service. This is a post-1994 development which has led to significant changes in the character of those organisations that did not previously engage in bargaining activity. The move to collective bargaining has been accompanied by an increase in militance, with some staff associations engaging in strike action since 1994. For the unions, such as SADTU and NEHAWU, industrial action was more common during the early 1990s, when they were trying to gain access to bargaining.

With the exception of the IPS and the Police and Prisons Civil Rights Union (POPCRU), all organisations reported steady increases in membership – and for some, such as the PSA, SADTU, SAPU and NEHAWU, membership growth was extremely rapid over a relatively short period of time in the 1990s, and was not dependent on mergers. There have only been three mergers during the 1990s. The old PSL is now incorporated into PAWUSA. The PSAAWU merged with the PSA, and DENOSA and the South African Nursing Association (SANA) merged to form the new DENOSA in the second half of 1996. There is, however, a considerable degree of overlapping membership between organisations, a feature not found amongst private sector organisations. Nurses, for example, may belong to both HOSPERSA, which offers an indemnity scheme, as well as NEHAWU, which offers a militant and predominantly black working class orientation.

Employee organisations in the public service are relatively more heterogenous in terms of racial and gender composition when compared to private sector unions. This feature relates to the fact that the service employs a high proportion of women. There is also a more even representation of the different racial groups. Many of the staff associations represent a wide spread of occupational groupings, from management to unskilled workers.

While most organisations claim to practice decentralised decision-making, this is complicated by the fact that they have relatively few branches compared to unions of similar size in the private sector. The high degree of centralisation of collective bargaining complicates these efforts. A decentralised structure would, however, be in keeping with recent moves towards decentralised decision-making within the structures and departments of the state in general (see Chapter 5, Adair and Albertyn). A number of organisations are regionally based (for example the HWU in the Western Cape and the National Public Servants' Association (NAPSA) in KwaZulu-Natal), or have their origins in the former homelands.

Despite the differences, there has clearly been a growing convergence between many public service unions and their private sector counterparts. The largest and most influential unions have either directly engaged in industrial action or have shown a greater willingness to countenance militant action. There has also been a growing identification with the wider labour movement and this has been particularly marked through the growth of the COSATU-affiliated unions and the formation of FEDUSA in March 1997.

The Federation of Unions of South Africa

FEDUSA arose from a merger between the old Federation of SA Labour (FEDSAL) and the Federation of Organisations Representing Civil Employees (FORCE). FORCE had been established in 1995 to co-ordinate the activities of some of the larger public service organisations such as the PSA and PAWUSA, but began merger talks with FEDSAL quite soon after its formation. At its formation, FEDUSA brought together 25 affiliates representing a membership in excess of 515 000, including over 200 000 public service workers. Although FEDUSA combines unions in both private and public sectors, it represents the most recent attempt at realignment and co-ordination amongst some of the public service organisations. This process assumed increased significance when the new threshold of 20 000 members for access to the PSCBC took effect in 1998, which threatened the position of many small staff associations.

CONCLUSIONS

The consequences of the 15-year delay in modernising public service labour relations have been inherited by the new state. Government's vision for the public service includes: 'an ethos of service, committed to the provision of services of an excellent quality to all South Africans in an unbiased and impartial manner; geared towards development and the reduction of poverty based upon the maintenance of fair labour practices for all public service workers irrespective of race, gender, disability or class' (DPSA, 1995: 14). Attaining such a vision would be difficult enough even if state policies and services were grounded in stable, efficient and productive labour relations. The fact that the state has to grapple with the transformation of its own labour relations while simultaneously creating a new public service presents a formidable challenge.

The new state does not have a well-developed relationship with its own employees and, as a consequence, it lacks a stable bargaining partner. The unions have to cope with rapid change and the degree of fragmentation and competition amongst unions is relatively high. Organisational resources are placed under pressure and internal procedures and structures remain undeveloped.

The employer side is marked by a lack of experience of industrial relations and, particularly, of bargaining. Management is under pressure to improve its processes of mandating and interacting with the parliamentary process. It has to devolve greater managerial responsibility and take collective bargaining processes to lower levels of government (see Chapter 5, Adair and Albertyn, Chapter 6, Patel and Chapter 7, Baskin).

Both labour and management within the public service thus face formidable challenges, and they do so within an environment characterised by greater economic constraints and increased job insecurity. Bringing about change in a way that accommodates both the interests of employers and employees, as well as those of the public (in the form of more equitable and effective service by government) will require labour relations that are simultaneously stable and dynamic. To achieve this will require paying attention to the distinctive needs, tasks and history of public service labour relations. It may also require recognising the limitations of collective bargaining. In a situation where there are not only two competing interests in the bargaining arena, but three (taking the public, or 'national,' interest into account), creative approaches to labour relations and collective bargaining will be needed. These might involve:

- subjecting wage changes for certain occupational groups to an independent review process
- maintaining the centralised structure of bargaining, but with an increased emphasis on co-determination at lower levels of government
- ensuring more effective and judicious dispute resolution procedures.

The success of transformation in public service labour relations will undoubtedly demand a high level of innovation by both management and labour. The fact that so much has already been achieved within such a short space of time gives cause for cautious optimism as far as the future is concerned.

APPENDIX 4.1:

Trade Unions in the Public Service Co-ordinating Bargaining Council, 1999

DENOSA	47 862
HOSPERSA	49 836
IPS	7 192
NAPTOSA	78 987
NEHAWU	155 019
NPSWU	16 517
NUPSAW	28 191
PAWUSA	24 939
POPCRU	57 402
PSA	185 803
PSAAWU	2 941
PUSEMO	6 267
SADNU	7 065
SADTU	204 686
SAMA	7 814
SAOU	26 554
SAPSAWU	12 077
SAPU	58 801
UNIPSA	3 863
Total	891 816

(Source: PSCBC, 1999)

5

RESTRUCTURING MANAGEMENT IN THE PUBLIC SERVICE

Implications for new legislation

———— ✦ ————

Barbara Adair and Sue Albertyn

While massive changes have occurred in the public service labour movement, similar transformations have occurred on the management side, as surveyed in this chapter by Adair and Albertyn. The new government has undertaken a radical restructuring of the public service to overcome the legacy of the apartheid state and to avoid a fiscal crisis. The changes have emphasised decentralisation by creating autonomous managers at all levels.

But amendments to public service legislation have been piece-meal and create many unintended problems. National Ministers and Members of the Executive Committees at provincial level have been accorded original managerial powers with regard to the organisation of their departments and employment and dismissal of employees. However, the legal framework governing the public service in fact profoundly disempowers managers and workers alike. Managerial power has only been decentralised in relation to human resource management, and even these powers are limited. Managers do not, in terms of the amendment laws, have the power to determine pay and other conditions of service, or to retrench surplus employees. They must still organise their departments within a nationally determined grading system, which is inflexible and does not take account of sectoral needs and differences.

Within the departments all decisions have to be made by the highest authority, which does not readily delegate powers to the appropriate level of management. Decision-making remains highly hierarchical and does not foster accountability and responsibility, or a focus on service delivery.

New legislation, regulations, and collective agreements must ensure that heads of departments remain responsible for the overall organisation of their departments, while providing for the delegation of powers to the most appropriate level. They should avoid attempting to micro-manage labour relations for the public service as a whole, but should specify minimum standards within framework agreements. While ensuring equality of standards throughout the public service, these would simultaneously allow for greater managerial flexibility.

INTRODUCTION

In the 1970s and the 1980s the public services in the developed world were swept up in the general wave of global economic restructuring. In this restructuring the role of the state, especially in relation to the provision of services (for instance welfare, health and education), provoked heated debates and analysis. Neoliberal literature in the 1980s focused on issues such as the 'overloaded state', 'fiscal crisis' and 'crowding out' by the public service of the wealth-generating private service (Ferner, 1993: 52). Questions raised included whether or not the state should be the foremost service provider, whether in fact it had the capacity to provide these services, or whether it should direct others towards providing the services as a more appropriate method of organising the public service. In addition to this, the economies of the developed world faced a fiscal crisis, which compelled them to cut back on state expenditure. The obvious place to cut back was what appeared to be an unproductive public service.

The resultant restructuring of the state internationally has generally taken two forms:
- redefining what government should legitimately be providing in the form of services
- restructuring the way in which the public service is managed, in that a more entrepreneurial private sector style of management has been introduced.

In the developed nations, the strengthening of the public service managers' right to manage has been addressed by radically devolving powers to managers at the local level and coupling public service managerial contracts of employment with individual performance incentives. Public service managers no longer have their management practices prescribed to them by a central authority; they are now required to develop management styles and practices appropriate to the particular markets that their department is required to service. The post-bureaucratic state has emerged (Schick, 1996; Hoggett, 1996; Fredman and Morris, 1990).

This transformation of the public service started in South Africa in 1994, following the election of the first democratic government. After the elections the state faced the overwhelming task of delivering services to 40 million people, instead of the 8 million who had been served by the apartheid government.

The state was also faced with a fiscal crisis. The deficit was large, taking up valuable state revenue and the public service now had to pay for the delivery of services to the whole population, where the base for service delivery was frequently non-existent. A radical restructuring of the public service was necessary. The numerous policy documents developed by the state on public service transformation have emphasised the need for the public service to decentralise radically, create autonomous managers who have the power to manage their own departments and where possible, to divest themselves of the actual provision of some services through privatisation, according to the White Paper on the Transformation of the Public Service (1995).[1]

These policy proposals on the transformation of managerial authority draw directly from the models that have been implemented elsewhere in the developed world. They are, however, being implemented slowly. The state has not yet recognised that legislation is the foundation for any reform of the public service. Numerous policy documents on public service transformation, more particularly transformation of public service human resources, have been generated, but a legislative base to effect these changes has not accompanied these proposals.

For example, in 1997 a Public Service Management Bill was drafted by the Department of Public Service and Administration setting out how legislation could give effect to the policy proposals on human resource management that had been developed. It was accepted in principle by Cabinet at the end of 1997, but was never published in the Government Gazette nor submitted to Parliament for adoption. This draft bill was never passed and discussions as well as the development of further policy proposals have continued.

THE SOUTH AFRICAN PUBLIC SERVICE

The public service legislative framework includes:
* the Public Service Act and regulations passed in terms of that Act
* the Employment of Educators Act and regulations passed in terms of that Act
* the South African Police Services Act and regulations passed in terms of that Act.[2]

The legislation in the public service is characterised by:
* centralised management, with top-down hierarchical management structures
* a rule-bound, rather than a goal-oriented culture, which results in poor service-delivery
* management that is unskilled and unproductive.

The extension of modern labour legislation to the public service as a result of the passage of the Labour Relations Act in 1995 has caused tensions between the archaic, prescriptive and inflexible public service legislative framework and the LRA's emphasis on equity and self-regulation.[3] This tension undermines the efficiency of work processes in the public service, in that managers are forced to manage within conflicting paradigms. This is especially apparent in the way disputes are resolved and human resources are managed.

The process outlined in the 1995 White Paper on the Transformation of the Public Service has already led to significant changes in the operation of the service in that there have been a number of amendments to public service legislation.[4] However these amendments are piece-meal and to a large degree create more difficulties than was originally anticipated.

The Public Service Act covers those employees employed in the 'traditional' public service and regulates their conditions of service. Section 8 of the Public Service Act states that persons employed in the public service include all employees employed in both national departments and provincial administrations, but excluding educators and police. The public service consists of the national departments and the provincial administrations, as set out in the Schedules to the Public Service Act. Schedule 2 of the Public Service Act lists the national departments and the provincial administrations. The provincial administrations are established in the constitution as relatively autonomous political entities that not only have administrative and executive powers, but to a limited degree can develop legislation in accordance with their own needs. The provincial administrations, however, do not have legislative powers in relation to employment.[5] Only the Minister for Public Service and Administration has legislative power in relation to employment in terms of the Public Service Act.[6]

The national departments and the provincial administrations deliver a variety of public services, including health services. The national departments are a defined entity in that each one has to deliver a specific coherent service. There is for instance a national Department of Finance and a national Department of Safety and Security. The provincial administrations are, however, not coherent structures. They are made up of a number of different departments, each performing and delivering a different service. The number of departments in each provincial administration varies; the only similarity between the nine provincial administrations is that they have the power to create departments which deliver services, if these fall within their power of authority as determined by the Constitution.[7] Prior to amendments to the Public Service Act in 1999, the provincial departments were not seen as autonomous from the provincial administration. The provincial administrations and not the provincial departments, in terms of employment and managerial authority, were viewed in the same way as a national department. The status of the provincial administration equalled that of a national department, despite the differences in the number of employees employed, the type of work that they did and the fact that the provincial administrations were made up of a variety of different departments.

In the education sector, with regard to educators or teachers employed in the provincial administrations, the Minister of Education is vested with the power to determine terms and conditions of employment and other aspects of human resource development for teachers.[8] The non-teacher employees in the Departments of Education, at both the national level and in the provincial administrations, are employed in terms of the Public Service Act.

In the police sector, with regard to police in the national Department of Safety and Security (there are no police employed in the provincial administrations), the Minister of Safety and Security is vested with the power to determine terms and conditions of employment and other aspects of human resource development for police.[9] The employees in administrative or management positions in the Department of Safety and Security, excluding the employees in the Safety and Security Secretariat, are employed in terms of the Public Service Act.

Prior to 1998, management authority in the public service was vested in the Public Service Commission (PSC). Section 3 of the Public Service Act, prior to its amendment in 1997, gave the PSC responsibility for determining the human resources framework for the public service as a whole, including the determination of terms and conditions of employment. The PSC had the power to make recommendations on all aspects of human resource development. These included terms and conditions of employment for both national departments and provincial administrations.

In 1996 the Public Service Amendment Laws reconfigured managerial power in an attempt to transform the public service. The amendments accorded the Minister for Public Service and Adminis-tration all those powers previously vested in the PSC. The national Ministers and the provincial Members of the Executive Committees (MECs) were also accorded original powers with regard to the organisation of their departments, employment and dismissal of employees.[10]

In a further amendment to the Public Service Act, the Public Service Laws Amendment Act No. 86 of 1998, the provincial administrations, which have the status of a national department in terms of the Act, are divided into provincial departments. Each provincial department mirrors the structures of the national departments.

This means that where a provincial administration has the legislative competence in terms of the constitution for instance in education and health, the MECs in these newly created provincial departments now have the managerial authority to organise their departments and hire and dismiss employees.[11] Autonomous departments within provincial administrations have therefore been created.

In addition, the rigid provisions regulating the management of disciplining public service employees have been repealed and replaced by a collective agreement of the Public Service Co-ordinating Bargaining Council (PSCBC). The collective agreement ensures that discipline will be managed in a flexible way and removes the need for the restrictive legislative provisions that previously existed.[12]

On 1 July 1999 the new Public Service Regulations came into effect.[13] These regulations amplify the powers conferred on executing authorities in terms of the legislative amendments to the Public Service Acts of 1997 and 1998. The regulations repeal the lengthy provisions on human resources management contained in the Public Service Staff Code. Those areas of the Public Service Staff Code that deal with terms and conditions of employment were incorporated into a collective agreement of the PSCBC, called the Collective Agreement on Remunerative Allowances and Benefits.[14] The new regulations and the collective agreement emphasise the decentralisation of managerial powers.

The new Public Service Regulations and the Agreement on Remunerative Allowances and Benefits, although drafted in plain English, are ambiguous and may lead to legal challenges. In essence they merely summarise the core provisions of the old Public Service Staff Code without changing or amending the substance of these provisions. It is unclear whether the old Staff Code may be relied upon if the regulations or the agreement are silent on an issue, although the fact that both documents are essentially a summarised version of the old Public Service Staff Code suggests that this may happen.

Furthermore, the regulations are not clear as to what powers the Minister for Public Service and Administration will retain, in that there are still many prescriptive rules established at national level which bind the national and provincial departments. For instance the Personnel Administrative Standard (PAS) which was deemed to be a collective agreement in terms of the old Public Service Labour Relations Act, Proclamation No. 105 of 1994, continues to exist despite the repeal of this Act.

Management authority in the public service from 1 July 1999 is therefore no longer as centrally organised as it was under the previous legislative framework. However, managerial power has only been decentralised in relation to human resources management, and even these powers are limited.

Managers do not have the power to determine pay and other conditions of service for their employees in their departments or provincial administrations. The authority to determine pay and other conditions of service is vested in the Minister for Public Service and Administration, the Minister of Education and the Minister of Safety and Security at the national level.

WHY NEW PUBLIC SERVICE MANAGEMENT LEGISLATION IS NECESSARY

The White Paper on the Transformation of the Public Service lists the following problems in the public service, as it is managed at present:

- lack of service delivery
- centralised control and top-down management
- lack of accountability and transparency
- absence of effective management and low productivity and
- persistence of a rule-bound, rather than a goal-oriented culture.

The legal framework governing the public service is largely responsible for these problems, in that it profoundly disempowers managers and workers alike. Despite recent amendments, the Public Service Act, the Employment of Educators Act and the South African Police Services Act, as described above, perpetuate this scenario.

Control is still highly centralised. Managers in different departments, institutions and provinces have little or no autonomy or responsibility to make decisions that affect their specific departmental needs. For example, executing authorities may determine their own organisational structure, however, they may not retrench surplus employees and they must organise their department within the prescribed nationally determined grading system, which is inflexible and does not take account of sectoral needs and differences. Even within the departments and institutions, all decisions, no matter what they are, have to be made by the highest authority, the executing authority. Executing authorities do not readily delegate their powers to the appropriate level of management in the department. Decision-making thus remains highly hierarchical with senior and middle management having very little decision-making power. Accountability and responsibility for decision-making is not fostered by these practices. Managers do not 'manage', but are responsible for ensuring that employees abide by a complex set of rules and regulations, rather than concentrating on output and service delivery. Managers tend to place more emphasis on whether they abide by a rule, such as ensuring that their staff have completed the necessary leave forms, rather than on whether their staff member has performed. Within the regulations there are no provisions for effectively monitoring performance or assessing merit, nor are there provisions for appropriate human resource development programmes.

Clearly legislation that determines the limits of management power needs to be replaced by new legislation. A number of proposals in this regard are set out in the 1996 Green Paper entitled 'A new law for a new public service'. The Green Paper raises a number of policy issues that will have to be dealt with if the public service is to transform and makes proposals for the development of new public service legislation. Rather than legislation being a set of rules, it recommends that legislation should contain a set of procedures setting out how power or authority is to be devolved. The Green Paper recommends that legislation should be enabling, rather than regulatory. Departments and provincial administrations should have relative autonomy to determine their own management systems, collective bargaining practices and, in the statutorily defined bargaining councils, their own dispute-resolution mechanisms.

The need for legislative change is not unique to South Africa. It is one that has been recognised by those countries which have substantially changed the structures of their public services. The change in the law must be the starting point for all transformation, in that public service managers can act only in accordance with the law that creates them. If the law is not synchronised with policy proposals, managers lack the power to implement policy proposals as their power and authority is derived from legislation. In a report on legislative change for the Australian public service it was stated that:

> a very substantial cultural change is needed in the Australian public sector to make substantial improvements in program delivery involving a fundamentally simplified public sector employment framework ... the current highly centralised, inflexible public sector employment provisions do not meet the diverse needs of a modern public sector and represent a significant impediment to efficient program delivery. (National Commission of Audit, 1996)

Should new legislation be adopted in South Africa it must be enabling legislation which creates flexibility and empowers managers rather than merely regulating them. Such legislation needs to ensure the following:
• mechanisms for the creation of broad policy by a national authority, which may set parameters within which managers can operate

- a decentralised management system, in which the responsibility to make decisions is delegated to the most appropriate management level
- appropriate collective bargaining structures
- an accountable system, in which performance indicators are institutionalised
- mechanisms whereby the public can address issues relating to service delivery and through which public response to such delivery can be measured.

In Australia this approach was adopted. Legislation was drafted which set out:
- public service standards and ethical values and how they should be applied
- the framework for public accountability
- employment principles, covering such areas as merit selection, equity, recognition of family responsibilities, participative work practices and fair decision-making
- the basis upon which employment powers are vested in agency heads. (National Commission of Audit, 1996)

PROPOSALS FOR NEW PUBLIC SERVICE MANAGEMENT LEGISLATION

New legislation must set out new rules for the organisation and management of the public service. The legislation must also give effect to provisions contained in the South African Constitution. These include:
- the promotion of professional ethics
- the economic and efficient use of resources
- co-operative governance
- accountability and transparency
- good human resource management
- employees who are broadly representative of the South African people.[15]

The first question that needs to be addressed is whether or not all sectors should be covered by one statute, or whether each sector should have separate legislation. To a certain degree this policy decision is answered in the Constitution, which stipulates that there is one public service.

Therefore it would be appropriate that all sectors be covered by one statute. This statute should not be prescriptive. In order to create maximum flexibility it should be enabling, with a responsible minister being able to set only certain minimum standards in order to ensure that uniformity of service delivery and the distribution of resources are harmonised.

Legislation needs to set out the powers and duties of a central authority, which may be the Minister for Public Service and Administration, other Cabinet Ministers and Members of Executive Committee (who are referred to as 'executing authorities') and heads of department.

The responsibilities of executing authorities must include taking any actions, or delegating this power, to ensure that the state is administered and managed in accordance with the Constitution and government policies. An executing authority should also have the power to appoint a head of department, evaluate the specific organ of state for which the executing authority is responsible and appoint advisors, including political advisors. The policy issue that needs to be resolved is whether or not politicians should be responsible for the management of departments, or whether this should be the domain of heads of department and managers only. Currently the Public Service Act as amended and the Employment of Educators Act provide that politicians are responsible for the management of their departments. The question is essentially whether the role of politicians is to manage, or whether their role is to ensure that their managers manage and implement policy that they develop.

This question was addressed in both Australia and New Zealand. The states in both countries evolved, as has the South African state, from the British public service system in which executive powers were exercised by political heads. Any powers exercised by administrators or managers were all delegated from the political heads of departments (Fredman and Morris, 1990: 14). The Australian government recognised that 'agency heads', or what in South Africa would be termed heads of department, should be appointed on the basis of their management skills to manage departments. The legislation made agency heads independent and not subject to a minister in relation to human resources or staffing decisions. While the Public Service Commissioner set standards, the manner in which these standards were to be implemented was not prescribed. Agency heads were therefore encouraged to develop systems and structures best suited to the needs of their own particular department, with the Public Service Commissioner providing guidance (National Commission of Audit, 1996).

The New Zealand government introduced this same system in 1996. In New Zealand it was recognised that this approach would entail a great deal of political risk in that heads of department, who are not elected but appointed, would be responsible for the day-to-day management of departments. Ministers would be excluded from this process with their only responsibility in this arena being policy guidance, the provision of resources, monitoring performance and enforcing accountability (Schick, 1996).

New Zealand took the concept of managerial accountability to political heads a step further than their Australian counterparts, however. Ministers play an extensive role in the appointment of their managerial heads, rather than these appointments being effected by a collective or more neutral body, like the Public Service Commissioner in Australia, or in South Africa the Cabinet or Executive Committees.[16]

For departments to deliver a cost effective and efficient service they must be properly managed. In line with international precedents, therefore, it is proposed that new legislation in South Africa should ensure that the head of department is responsible for the overall management and organisation of the organ of state. In fulfilling this function, the head of department must have regard to the Constitution, the Public Finance Management Act and government policies. This would represent a fundamental shift from any previous legislation in the public service, in that original powers would be accorded to an administrator, not a politician. This proposal will empower public service managers to respond to the market and the needs of their department, which response may be politically driven, but need not be.

Any new legislation would also need to accord with the Public Finance Management Act No. 1 of 1999, amended by Act No. 29 of 1999. This Act states that heads of department are the accounting officers for their department. Clearly if a person is responsible for the finances of a department this person must also be able to manage the department and use these finances as they deem appropriate.

It is further recommended that in any new legislation the head of department should be directly accountable to the executing authority when fulfilling his or her functions. The head of department must consult with the executing authority on the management and administration of the particular organ of state. This will ensure that, while an administrator may have original powers to manage a particular national or provincial department, the administrator is ultimately responsible to the political head of the department. In this way, politicians will at all times be informed, thus making managers politically, as well as administratively, accountable.

The head of department should have the power to appoint and dismiss employees, create appropriate positions, appoint executive officers and manage collective bargaining. This would allow heads of department to appoint their senior managers on fixed-term, performance-based contracts of employment. Senior managers would be appointed or dismissed by the head of department in consultation with the executing authority. In other words, the executing authority and the head of department must agree on the appointment or dismissal of senior managers. Fixed-term, performance-related contracts have been introduced in those countries that have initiated these types of reforms, with the objective of making senior managers directly accountable for the performance of their department, and thus improving service delivery. This would also dispose of a current difficult issue in the public sector, namely that senior managers are presently accommodated in the collective bargaining structures of the public sector. This is unique to the public sector. In the private sector, senior managers are not part of collective bargaining structures but negotiate their salary and terms and conditions of employment directly with their employer. Fixed-term, performance-based contracts for senior managers in the public sector would allow the remuneration of senior managers to be varied and differentially structured as determined by the executing authority and head of department with the senior manager.

Performance contracts for senior management have been introduced in most developed states where substantial public service reform has taken place. It is widely recognised in the private sector that performance contracts are appropriate for senior management in that they are evaluated in accordance with specific performance targets, which are generally linked to the profitability of the enterprise. However, performance-related targets in the public service are less tangible and more difficult to measure, as public service managers do not work to increase productivity for increased profits. A political evaluation of performance may be different to a managerial evaluation of the same performance. Performance management systems may be a powerful way of shaping culture, in that outputs are evaluated rather than inputs. What must be cautioned against is the situation where senior managers are unable to meet their performance targets because they have no control over the political process or policy formulation, which is the terrain of the legislature and the responsible minister or MEC. Caution must be exercised in not creating managerial scapegoats whose contracts are terminated for non-performance, whereas in reality any manager could not realistically meet the policies and targets developed by the politicians (Hoggett, 1996).

Any new legislation on human resource management must provide for delegation of powers, with specific directives for the head of department to delegate certain managerial powers to the most appropriate level. Despite the new Public Service Regulations there is little delegation of power by heads of department – power and authority continue to be highly centralised – a situation which does not foster accountability by senior management and that is both inefficient and disempowering.

It is recommended that in new legislation the Minister for Public Service and Administration should remain responsible for the overall effective administration of the public service. The Minister should retain the power to pass regulations, formulate managerial guidelines and manage collective bargaining on behalf of the state as employer in the PSCBC. However, instead of collective agreements in the PSCBC attempting to micro-manage labour relations for the public service as a whole, the collective agreements of the PSCBC should be in the form of minimum standards and framework agreements. This would ensure equality of standards throughout the public service, but would simultaneously allow for greater managerial flexibility in the different sectors of the public service. Regulations passed by the Minister for Public Service and Administration should also serve the purpose of providing a framework to guide managers in formulating actual policies in their particular departments. The important role of a central institution to set frameworks and standards has been recognised in all reforms of the public service that have been developed internationally. Even in the most far-reaching reform processes, for instance in Australia and New Zealand, it was recognised that a central institution or body to set standards is imperative to ensure accountability and coherence in the public service. In both Australia and New Zealand the Public Service Commissioner and the State Services Commission play this role respectively (Schick, 1996; National Commission of Audit, 1996).

It is proposed that this role should be split in South Africa between the Public Service Commission and the Minister for Public Service and Administration. The Public Service Commission has a constitutional mandate to monitor the evolution of management in the public service.[17] The Public Service Commission has, to date, failed in this mandate. It needs to be revived as an institution and restructured to be able to fulfil its constitutional mandate of ensuring that standards and management expertise are not compromised in the public service. The Minister for Public Service and Administration can, and has, set the standards for the management of human resources in the public service.[18] This process needs to be continued.

CONCLUSION

It is clear that if the various policy documents on public service reform and transformation are to have any effect, there is a need for a new statute on public service human resources management. Legislation is the necessary enabling tool to effect change in the public service. Any new legislation would need to be premised on the uniqueness of the public service. Unlike the private sector, which can chose to whom, how and whether to deliver a particular service, the public service is constitutionally bound to provide equal services to its citizens. It may not be cost-effective to provide water to a small farming community in an outlying area of a province, but this is not a valid criterion for failure to deliver the service. Legislation needs to take this into account and must allow sufficient management flexibility to ensure accountable and output-oriented service delivery. Outputs, however, cannot only be measured by cost-saving mechanisms; performance must be evaluated economically and socially.

Instead of being a series of rules and prescriptive operating practices, any new Public Service Act needs to provide a framework within which managers are able to exercise their powers. Differential standards and practices may well emerge but these need to be based on clear social policy decisions, not arbitrary economic ones. For instance differential salaries may emerge for heads of department and senior managers in different departments depending upon the nature of the service delivered by the particular department. Policy decisions will need to be made on whether senior managers and heads of department are remunerated at private sector rates or whether the public service continues to remunerate at lower rates.

In a phase, real public service transformation depends upon a new Public Service Act which *empowers rather than merely regulates.*

6

GROWING PAINS

Collective bargaining in the public service

————— ✦ —————

Imraan Patel

Collective bargaining is an extremely new phenomenon in the public service, dating from the birth of the Public Service Bargaining Council in 1993. Though the South African public service has developed a pioneering system of collective bargaining, the system has come under significant stress and should experience further change in coming years. Patel assesses the origins of the new system and identifies the most pressing challenges facing it.

The most important is the unfolding process of budget reform. This now occurs over a three-year cycle, and increasing power has been given to the provinces. There is thus pressure to devolve bargaining on the same lines. There will be an interesting dynamic between collective bargaining, budget reform processes and administrative reform as public service transformation progresses. Collective bargaining will inevitably change to accommodate these other transformations.

But there is not yet a shared understanding between government and unions, or indeed within either camp of the future direction for collective bargaining. Key questions include: at what level it should occur; what issues are appropriate to be on a particular table (or indeed subject to bargaining at all); whether bargaining should be occupationally or functionally delineated; whether bargaining should aim at producing frameworks or detailed implementation strategies; and what the division of power should be between the central Public Service Co-ordinating Bargaining Council and sectoral councils.

INTRODUCTION

South African labour relations were radically altered by the Labour Relations Act (LRA) of 1995. For the first time, the public service was covered by the same provisions as the broader workforce. Section 36 of the Act entrenches the right of state workers to bargain collectively with their employer (the state). The Act makes provision for a Public Service Co-ordinating Bargaining Council (PSCBC), sectoral bargaining councils and bargaining councils for provinces and departments.

The extension of general labour relations legislation to the public service is the result of a decade-long struggle to introduce a modern and progressive labour relations framework in this sector. At the core of this framework is the use of collective bargaining as the preferred method of wage determination.

Elements of collective bargaining in the public service were introduced in the late 1980s and formalised in 1993, in the form of two separate pieces of legislation: the Public Service Labour Relations Act (PSLRA) for workers employed under the Public Service Act of 1994, and the Education Labour Relations Act (ELRA) for public service educators. In terms of the LRA of 1995, the key bargaining structure is the PSCBC. With a coverage of 1,016 million workers it is the largest bargaining forum in South Africa. The LRA of 1995 replaced the 1981 LRA which excluded the public service from its scope. In addition to directly determining the working conditions of more than 15% of employees in South Africa, PSCBC agreements and processes will influence outcomes within the broader labour market, and have significant implications for the ability of the public service to deliver.

Collective bargaining in the public service is, however, still in its infancy. The next decade will shape the structures, processes, culture, and nature of bargaining. The fragile and developing process will be under tremendous strain. The current bargaining environment is influenced by constraining macro-economic policies; conservative attitudes on the roles and responsibilities of the state; constitutionally-driven reforms aimed at fundamentally changing the governance, organisation and management of public service institutions; fiscal federalism; increasing privatisation and contracting-out; and greater expectations by communities for increased service delivery with the same or reduced resources.

Internationally, the system of collective bargaining for public service workers is not about to be discarded, but it is also under tremendous strain. International lessons will need to be analysed to ensure the sustainability, integrity and effectiveness of public service collective bargaining in South Africa into the next century.

This chapter examines the past, present and future of collective bargaining in the public service. The discussion is divided into three sections:

- section one traces the history of public service collective bargaining
- section two reviews the international experience
- the final section considers collective bargaining challenges confronting unions and government into the future.

HISTORY OF PUBLIC SERVICE COLLECTIVE BARGAINING

Constructing the history of collective bargaining in South Africa is made difficult by the lack of secondary material. Studies prior to 1990 on public service labour relations were few and far between, sketchy and mainly carried in the *South African Journal of Labour Relations* and the *South African Labour Bulletin*. This chapter was developed largely from interviews, primary documents, and personal experience.

Collective bargaining has been defined as the continuing institutional relationship between an employer entity (in this case, government) and labour organisations (trade union or staff associations) exclusively representing a defined group of employees (the bargaining unit). It is concerned with the negotiation, administration, interpretation, and enforcement of written agreements covering wages and salaries, rates of pay, hours of work, and other conditions of employment. The collective bargaining relationship between employer and union is a continuous one, involving contract administration as well as contract negotiation (Davey et al., 1982: 2). Collective bargaining, therefore, covers two basic subject matters – the price of labour and the system of industrial jurisprudence (Ibid.: 6).

From unilateral determination to collective bargaining

Public service collective bargaining in South Africa is woven into the general political and labour relations fabric of the country. In common with the private sector, the determination of terms and conditions of service has shifted from unilateral employer determination to fully-fledged collective bargaining in the early 1990s, mainly as a result of struggles waged by workers and their unions in the 1970s and 1980s.

The political system of apartheid fragmented public service labour relations. Prior to 1994, South Africa was divided into 11 governments and 4 provincial administrations. In addition to the former Republic of South Africa (RSA), there were four 'independent states' (the former TBVC states) and six self-governing territories (SGTs).[1] Each had its own body of statutes and laws regulating matters within its legal competence, including labour relations (Public Service Commission, 1997: 3).

South Africa's public administration system was modelled on the highly centralised system of personnel management practised by the British civil service. The powerful and independent Public Service Commission (PSC) – later the Commission for Administration (CFA) – was key to this system.[2]

Collective bargaining underwent significant changes as a result of the 1995 LRA. The new Act facilitated greater co-ordination of bargaining through the creation of the PSCBC, which includes within its scope educators, uniformed personnel employed in the South African Police Services (SAPS), as well as workers employed in national departments, provincial administrations, and a number of organisational components of government. It excludes members of the National Defence Force, the National Intelligence Agency, and the South African Secret Service.

The LRA provided for separate bargaining councils for police and educators and for the creation of additional sectoral councils. It entrenched the existing bargaining arrangement by converting departmental and provincial bargaining chambers and councils into fully-fledged bargaining councils. Finally, it facilitated the possible participation of the public service in bargaining councils in the wider labour market.

The 1995 creation of the PSCBC and sectoral councils is the most significant development to date in public service labour relations. The setting up and operation of the new bargaining arrangements will dominate these relations for the foreseeable future. The PSCBC was preceded by four separate, but interlinked processes:

- the establishment of a Public Service Bargaining Council (PSBC) for workers employed under the Public Service Act, excluding educators
- the development of the Education Labour Relations Council (ELRC)

for educators employed under the National Policy for General Education Affairs Act 76 of 1984
* the development of the National Negotiating Forum (NNF) for uniformed personnel in the SAPS
* the general development of labour relations (or lack of it) in the former 'homelands'.

The Public Service Bargaining Council

The need to involve employee representatives in the determination of wages and working conditions in the public service was raised as far back as 1922. However, as Posel shows in Chapter 2 in this collection, no public servants were allowed to form registered unions or to bargain collectively. Efforts by public servants through their recognised staff association, the Public Servants Association of South Africa (PSA), for the setting up of a formal bargaining mechanism began in 1979, in the context of the Wiehahn reforms to labour legislation.

The mid-1980s witnessed militant struggles by organisations such as the National Education, Health and Allied Workers' Union (NEHAWU) and the Health Workers Union (HWU), for recognition and fully-fledged collective bargaining. While the apartheid government sought to expand the role of employee organisations, only racially-based staff associations were granted recognition and were allowed to participate in consultative structures. The limited nature of these structures and the exclusion of progressive unions, rendered them ineffective.

After several years of consultation and growing pressure from the wide range of employee organisations, the government committed itself to collective bargaining in 1988. Altogether, it took more than five years – and the impending transition to democracy – to translate government's broad commitment to collective bargaining into legislation. In 1993, the PSLRA and the ELRA were passed.

During the initial period (1990-1993) the government, represented by the CFA, still viewed unions as a challenge to managerial prerogative and to the CFA's constitutional right to determine wages and employment terms and conditions within the existing wage policy of government. Government representatives also lacked basic knowledge of labour relations and negotiating skills.

Inexperience was evident on the employee side as well. This was particularly true of unions which had not been involved in the old structures. Due to the different histories and ideological perspectives of the employee organisations, they were unable to present a united front. In essence, employee organisations were divided into two major blocs, the first composed of recognised staff associations led by the PSA, and the second a progressive union bloc led by NEHAWU. The weaknesses of both parties, coupled with divisions.within the employee side, entrenched adversarialism in the bargaining process. This was further strained by the impending change in government in 1994.

The PSBC and the Government of National Unity

The election year 1994 was a crucial time for public sector bargaining. In just twelve months, the participants moved from adversarial bargaining – resulting in a wage deadlock – to the joint exploration and determination of options. The incoming Government of National Unity (GNU), which took office in May 1994, had to deal with two bargaining rounds in its first year of office. The PSBC had to finalise improvements to the minimum wage that came into effect in April and a general salary adjustment that came into effect in July 1994. The process of negotiating for improvements for 1995 also began. A critical issue that was highlighted in these initial rounds of bargaining was the relationship between the budgetary and collective bargaining processes – which remains a fundamental issue of public service bargaining.

The creation of a single public service through the Interim Constitution introduced its own set of pressures into the bargaining process, the most important of which was the need to achieve parity in the conditions of service for workers employed in the eleven different governments that existed prior to April 1994. This was an issue of particular concern to workers from the former TBVC states (further discussed in a later section of this chapter).

By 1994, the number of employee organisations represented in the Central Chamber had risen from the initial 11 to 18, mainly as a result of the inclusion of employee organisations operating as crisis committees in the former homelands (PSBC, 1995: 2).

On the government side, the Cabinet remained the final authority on conditions of service. In terms of the executive, a ministerial post was created for Public Service and Administration. The Interim Constitution transformed the CFA into the Public Service Commission (PSC) and as part of the process of creating provincial governments, provided for the establishment of Provincial Service Commissions. These developments clouded the allocation of responsibility for collective bargaining on the employer side. This issue was only fully resolved with the adoption of a new model for state administration by the Cabinet on 21 February 1996.

The new model granted greater managerial autonomy to departments and provinces within centrally determined policy frameworks. The responsibility for defining these frameworks was transferred to the Minister for Public Service and Administration via the creation of a Department of Public Service and Administration (DPSA). The PSC was converted into an advisory and monitoring body directly accountable to the National Assembly.

The current shape of bargaining was influenced by two major factors during this time. Firstly, the election of the democratic government raised expectations, particularly from workers in the lower echelons, for significant wage improvements. Expectations were further fuelled by the high salaries granted to elected members of national and provincial governments. A demand for a minimum wage of R1 500 (championed by NEHAWU) was merged with a demand for a 15% general salary increase (mainly championed by the established staff associations).

Government accepted the need for a minimum wage, a narrowing of the wage gap, the introduction of a skills-based grading system and the need to pay market-related salaries. To meet these multiple objectives, a radical restructuring of the wage system was required. Bargaining was not confined to salary scales, but was geared towards fundamentally changing the salary and grading system. The 1995 wage negotiations saw a complete revision of the old grading system (see Chapter 7, Baskin).

Secondly, the presence of leading former unionists in the Cabinet, Parliament, and within the PSC was clearly evident in the way in which the bargaining process unfolded in 1994. Tense and unproductive negotiations ended in deadlock on 22 September. On the basis of advice and strategies formulated by several former unionists, including Alec Erwin (at the time Deputy Minister of Finance), John Erentzen (then Special Adviser to the Minister for Public Service and Administration), and other unionists in the cabinet, the Minister and both Deputy Presidents Thabo Mbeki and FW de Klerk intervened in the bargaining process.

It was agreed to set up task teams to establish short-, medium- and long-term strategies for addressing the needs of public servants in respect of salaries and other conditions of service as well as general labour relations matters (PSBC, 1995: 2). The aim was to get away from adversarialism and embark upon joint problem-solving. It was hoped that bargaining would also focus on major structural change, rather than adjustments.

One of the specific objectives of the task teams was the development of a medium-term (three-year) wage improvement plan. It was expected that the task teams would also propose fundamental changes to the wage system.

The teams became operational in early 1995. Due to considerable logistical problems, the immense task at hand, and the learning curve that the employee representatives had to undergo, they were unable to deliver a three-year plan. However, they did reach agreement on wage increases for the 1995/1996 financial year. The teams reiterated the need for fundamental change to address key structural weaknesses in the salary system. The problems included an inadequate minimum wage, unjustifiable differences between comparable public servants, the wage gap, as well as specific problems experienced by a variety of occupational groupings. The long-awaited changes were finally introduced in 1995, with a proposal to the Central Chamber for a new 16-band grading system to be introduced over three years, starting in July 1996 (see Chapter 7, Baskin).

The three-year plan was developed and agreed to prior to the adoption of government's restrictive macro-economic strategy (the Growth, Employment and Redistribution strategy, known as GEAR, one of the key objectives of which is controlling the public service wage bill), which politicised future bargaining.

The new grading system was positively received by all employee organisations. However, unionists have suggested that the state effectively bypassed the task teams in introducing the new system. But as the proposal was generally favourable, it was not contested by the unions.

Education

The education sector roughly mirrors the public service process. Until the establishment of the white Teachers' Federal Council (TFC) in 1987, the CFA was largely responsible for improvements in the wages and working conditions of educators. Because of the large numbers of educators, however, Ministers of Education were able to influence the wage determination process through the Cabinet and the CFA. White teacher organisations had considerable political influence, which they used to lobby for the appointment of ministers (see Chapter 9, Garson). The CFA treated educators as a specific sector and provided for specific improvement strategies for these workers playing off these increases against the rest of the public service and vice versa.

As with the public service in general, fully-fledged bargaining was preceded by consultation. In the early 1990s, the state set up a Research Committee on Education Structures (RECES), which was a loose, consultative body. It was initially boycotted by progressive organisations, but in the early 1990s it became an important site where key labour policy decisions were made, with all organisations on board.

The structure of the ELRC was similar to that of the PSBC, with a central chamber and chambers at the provincial level. The central chamber was, once again, the important bargaining site, with provincial chambers playing a negligible role.

Other similarities with the PSBC process include the establishment of joint research committees in 1995 (similar to the PSBC's task teams) to develop proposals and strategies for consideration in the ELRC. Finally, the education sector was characterised by the presence of two major employee blocs: the South African Democratic Teachers' Union (SADTU) and the National Professional Teachers' Organisation of South Africa (NAPTOSA). The relationship between the two organisations was initially antagonistic, but there has been a gradual shift in attitudes and greater co-operation between them.

Unlike the PSBC, the ELRC has facilitated the adoption of agreements that extend beyond conditions of service into the realm of policy-making (see Chapter 9, Garson). It was able to play this dual role more successfully because its scope is limited to a single occupation within a single industrial sector.

The National Negotiating Forum

The police sector has a shorter collective bargaining history. Before the introduction of the PSLRA in 1993, police personnel grievances, whether 'collective' or 'personal', were dealt with on an individual basis by higher-ranking police officials and strict limits were placed on unionisation. In September 1995, the National Negotiating Forum (NNF) was established separately from the PSBC, consisting of employer and recognised employee organisations. The NNF did not deal with individual concerns, but issues of mutual concern to employee and employer bodies (Marks, 1997: 2 and Chapter 10 in this collection).

The move from consultation to collective bargaining is also evident in this sector. A forum for consultation was established by the South African Police Labour Regulations promulgated in November 1993. However, it did not enjoy significant powers until the adoption of the revised regulations in 1995, which set up the NNF.

Unlike the ELRC, the NNF was more directly tied into PSBC processes, particularly with respect to wage matters. This is because police salary scales are based on general public service scales. As such, the NNF was in many respects a junior bargaining partner. In common with the education sector, however, the NNF was able to deal with bargaining and engage in consultation and negotiation on policy issues. Employee organisations in this sector were also divided into two blocs – the Police and Prisons Civil Rights Union (POPCRU) and the South African Police Union (SAPU).

The TBVC states

Although the CFA had no direct authority over personnel in the SGTs and the TBVC states, it maintained a significant influence over pay and personnel administration. The influence was greater in the case of the SGTs, whose administrations generally followed standards applicable to the RSA and where improvements in conditions of service were financed by a central budget vote.

In the TBVC states, the CFA wielded influence under the guise of multilateral co-operation. A number of standing committees were created with representatives from the CFA and TBVC states. Through these forums, the CFA was able to exert significant influence with respect to personnel, government organisation and conditions of service for workers in these areas. The forums were established in 1985 and continued to function until 1993.

The PSLRA introduced a new era in labour relations. The Act extended labour rights to public servants in certain TBVC states and SGTs who did not previously enjoy such rights (PSBC, 1995: 8). The history of the 'homelands' stops at this point in time, as workers were integrated into one of the three processes already described, depending on their occupational group. Workers employed in public utilities (such as telecommunications) who were part of the homeland public service were amalgamated with the utilities that existed in South Africa.

The three main bargaining structures that existed prior to the 1995 LRA all share a similar development – from unilateral employer determination to fully-fledged collective bargaining and from highly adversarial bargaining to one of greater co-operation. However, the NNF and ELRC differ in one important respect from the PSBC. Because these structures covered a single occupation within a single industry, their bargaining agenda was more focused and included elements of policy formulation. There is no doubt, however, that the PSBC was the senior partner and set the bargaining agendas on the crucial issues of wages, benefits and employment in the other two sectors.

INTERNATIONAL EXPERIENCE

Procedures for determining public service wages can be extremely complex. There are almost as many detailed systems as there are members of the International Labour Organisation (ILO, 1986: 73). Three published comparative studies – on public service pay determination mechanisms and pay systems in 21 Organisation for Economic Co-operation and Development (OECD) countries, public service labour relations in Europe, and such relations in Southern Africa – provide useful lessons for South Africa.

The OECD experience

The OECD survey reveals an enormous variety of pay systems and pay determination methods in public services.[3] There do not seem to be any moves towards a common model, despite some similar changes and common challe1nges (OECD, 1994).

Collective bargaining as a method of fixing wages remains strong in many countries. Free employer determination is a minority procedure, except for management, particularly higher management. In a number of countries, there have been moves to bring the conditions of management more in line with the private sector. These changes should be seen in the context of major changes in the style and structure of public service management (Ibid.: 7).

In several countries, the public sector has come to represent one of the remaining bastions of union strength. Public service employers are effectively constrained in their choice of policies by the expectations of employees and their unions and by what those outside of the service regard as appropriate (Ibid.: 7). Common features of the public service, such as centralised control and the personnel policies that accompany this, are also seen as obstacles to increased efficiency.

Within OECD countries, there have been two broad reform strategies. The first emphasises the need for greater cost control and efficiency. It involves maintaining relatively centralised systems of pay determination and administration, but exploring flexibility through changes in grading systems and pay scales, greater use of allowances, and changes in working time arrangements. The second seeks to break up large employment units into smaller ones, and to devolve management and pay decisions to individual departments and agencies. Performance-related pay systems are linked to this strategy (Ibid.: 10). While the first strategy runs the risk of stifling flexibility, the second raises the problem of cost control, since decentralised managers are mostly not supplying competitive markets.

The study also makes useful observations on the relationship between the budget and the collective bargaining process. Public sector pay is a major component of government spending and therefore has an impact on the macro-economic balance of an economy. When control over public sector pay is shared, some control over its budgetary impact is lost (Ibid.: 8).

A problem identified with national salary scales is that of adaptation to regional labour market pressures. A uniform national pay scale leads to pay rates that are unattractive either for recruitment or retention in tight labour markets, or where living costs are high (Ibid.: 19). It is also difficult to update national scales in line with general market and other economic conditions and to satisfy the needs and aspirations of different occupational groups (Ibid.: 20). The maintenance of a single public service pay system also tends to be more fragile than under unilateral action.

The European experience

The European study was commissioned by the European Public Services Committee (EPSC) of the European Trade Union Congress (ETUC) and was published by the FAFO Institute for Applied Social Science. The publication is divided into two sections, country reports and content issues. Based on reports from over 140 European trade unions, it reveals that public sector restructuring is blurring the distinction between the public and private sectors (Olsen, 1996: 7). The right to bargain is not legally entrenched in most of these countries, but because of the long-standing relationship between the parties and the trust that has developed, agreements are normally effected into law.

All European countries have a central administration, the core element of which is the civil service. While regional and local administrations exist with varying degrees of responsibility, there is a significant level of centralisation in wage determination.

Centralisation has been facilitated by a significant degree of voluntarism on the side of employer and employee organisations. Compared to South Africa, there is a smaller number of trade unions, which have established *ad hoc* structures to negotiate on their behalf. While negotiations on behalf of the state are usually handled by the Ministry of Finance, there is specific acknowledgement that no single ministry can act without the agreement of other departments – an association which improves the bargaining process. Greater centralisation of bargaining is facilitated by the negotiation of framework agreements, rather than actual wage rates, which are dealt with at other levels.

The southern Africa study

The southern Africa study was part of a conference sponsored by the Friedrich Ebert Stiftung (FES) and the Institute of Development and Labour Law (University of Cape Town), held in Harare, Zimbabwe, in July 1996. Country reports (from Angola, Botswana, Lesotho, Malawi, Mauritius, Mozambique, South Africa, Namibia, Tanzania, Zambia and Zimbabwe) indicate that public sector workers in southern Africa generally have access to collective bargaining for all or parts of their sector. In most countries, general labour legislation governs bargaining in both private and public sectors.

There are, however, significant variations and restrictions on collective bargaining in the region. In Malawi, the right to bargain is provided for in the 1996 Constitution, but there is no specific legislation to establish bargaining structures. In Botswana, only blue-collar workers have the right to collective bargaining. In Zimbabwe, the central public service does not have access to bargaining. In Mozambique, terms and conditions of service are determined through a Pay Review Council system, to which unions can make representations.

It is difficult to map the future path for public service collective bargaining in Southern Africa. While countries like Malawi and Namibia are moving towards collective bargaining as a result of more open constitutions, others, such as Botswana and Lesotho, are attempting to curtail the rights of public servants. Future trends will be significantly influenced by the level and quality of unionisation.

COLLECTIVE BARGAINING IN THE DEMOCRATIC SOUTH AFRICA

The bargaining structure established by the LRA for the South African public service – the PSCBC – includes all employee associations that were members of the central chambers of the PSBC, the ELRC and the NNF. The following matters fall within the ambit of the PSCBC:
- matters that are regulated by uniform rules, norms and standards that apply across the public service
- matters that apply to conditions and terms of service that apply to two or more sectors
- matters that are assigned to the state as employer in terms of the entire public service and not assigned to the state in any particular sector.

The LRA also provides for the establishment of sectors of the public service. The ELRC and the NNF, as well as departmental and provincial chambers of the PSBC are all deemed to be sectoral bargaining councils. Existing provincial chambers of the ELRC will be incorporated into the provincial bargaining council. The President is empowered to designate further sectors after consultation with the PSCBC. The Act does not provide a clear definition of a sector within the public service. In fact, the draft negotiating document simply entrenched the status quo, by making provision for both a PSBC and an ELRC. The provision of the PSBC was a result of eleventh-hour lobbying by public service unions and others involved in public service labour relations,[4] and the PSCBC constitution was finalised with the assistance of the Commission for Conciliation, Mediation and Arbitration (CCMA). The constitution improved bargaining by reducing the number of unions through increasing the threshold for membership from 1 000 to 20 000. It also helped to establish the PSCBC as an entity in its own right.

A key issue that was not fully resolved was the precise division of powers and functions between sectoral chambers and the PSCBC. This will remain a contentious issue for many years to come, with greater divisions within employee organisations than between the organisations and the employer.

The structure and functioning of collective bargaining

Collective bargaining arrangements are subordinate to the Constitution and legislation concerned with the organisation of the state and the distribution of powers and responsibilities within government. For example, if the law grants operational autonomy to a particular government agency, such as the South African Revenue Services (SARS), then collective bargaining for employees within this agency will fall outside public service bargaining arrangements. Fiscal authority also plays a role in determining the type of bargaining arrangements that are set up.

One of the most significant changes affecting collective bargaining was the 1997 amendment of the Public Service Act. Executing authorities (Ministers and provincial Members of Executive Committees (MECs)) were given greater powers over work organisation and aspects of personnel management, such as hiring and firing. These changes will lead to an ongoing battle between centralised and decentralised negotiations.

The education and police sector studies in this book identify the division of responsibilities between the sectoral chambers and the PSCBC as cause for concern. In general, based on the advances that have been made in these sectors, police and education unions and employers believe that the PSCBC should deal with as few issues as possible, and that key negotiations should take place at the sectoral level. On the other hand, unions outside the education and police sectors and DPSA seek greater powers for the PSCBC. This issue may remain a key bone of contention in the years to come. In anticipation of possible disputes, Section 38 of the LRA provides for the establishment of a dispute resolution committee under the auspices of the CCMA. (See Garson, Chapter 9, and Marks, Chapter 10, for more details.)

It is now generally accepted that the drafters of the LRA were not entirely familiar with the dynamics of public service bargaining. While the Act defined the PSCBC as a co-ordinating structure, it does not support the creation of a new structure, but rather envisages the reconstruction of the PSBC into the PSCBC. This is borne out by the fact that the LRA did not provide for a sectoral council for the PSBC.

However, the 'public service' bargaining council must differ substantially from the council for educators and police. These councils cover single occupations in single industries, whereas the 'public service' council would cover a multitude of occupations spread over many industries. Maintaining the integrity of a single bargaining unit for the entire public service, with the ability to meet the needs of the various groupings, can be achieved. However, to do so calls for creativity in the nature of bargaining, including an effective division between the various structures that make up the public service. In addition, it may call for the use of special measures such as allowances, and may even require the use of alternative wage determination methods to complement the bargaining process. Agreement has been reached for the creation of a sectoral council for health and another that covers the rest of the public service, the General Public Administration Council.

The division of responsibilities has an impact on the development of further sectoral councils. If sectors are significantly empowered to deal with terms and conditions of service, there will be considerable pressure to demarcate further sectors.

NEHAWU has also raised the presence of senior management in the bargaining council as a problem, because of the conflict of interest that arises when managers, in effect, negotiate with themselves over their own salaries and working conditions. The DPSA has been exploring ways in which this can be overcome without affecting the constitutional rights of senior management. In 1998 increases for senior managers (which included all directors and higher) in the public service were dependent on signing an individual performance agreement. It is hoped that this will improve accountability and performance of senior managers. However it will take at least five years for such a system to work effectively.

One of the key problems identified by the established and bigger unions in the PSBC was the poor management of the bargaining process. Preparing for collective bargaining requires a range of predetermined planning activities (Rayworth, 1992: 27). There have been instances where even though meetings were held over a week, they were unable to cover all the agenda items. A reduction in the number of employee organisations, establishment of a year planner of meetings and the appointment of fulltime officials in the PSCBC should resolve this issue and strengthen bargaining. A difficult issue to resolve, but one which would significantly improve bargaining, is to ensure that broad agreement is reached before the budget is made public. The non-implementation of agreements was a key weakness in the PSBC and the ELRC. The perceived failure of the initial education 'right-sizing' programme has been blamed on poor implementation. In the public service, there are examples of agreements signed in 1994 not having been implemented, or being implemented incorrectly. The adoption of dispute resolution processes and increased capacity to deal with disputes should address the problems.

The necessity of employer organisation

Beaumont notes that the public sector in most parliamentary democracies is characterised by a diffusion of management responsibility that arises from constitutional divisions. These, in turn, reflect assumptions about the value of checks and balances, political versus non-political decision-making, local versus central control, and the multiple funding sources of many public sector organisations. The result is that formal and actual responsibility often differs – a situation which holds a number of consequences for collective bargaining (Beaumont, 1992: 68). Most importantly, it results in employers who do not pay and paymasters who do not employ (Ibid.: 70).

The dynamics of management organisation are evident from a detailed case study carried out on the 1992 health workers' strike (Adair and Nyembe, 1994: 359). The study highlights the following problems which persist today, albeit in a slightly different form:

- The CFA was unable to negotiate effectively, as the amount available for increases was pre-determined in the budget. Unions did not understand this, and assumed bad faith bargaining on the part of the CFA.
- The communication that existed between the representatives of the state as employer, namely the CFA, and the direct employer of public service workers, namely the Transvaal Provincial Administration (TPA), was totally inadequate. Furthermore, the TPA was unable to resolve any disputes that arose as a result of the negotiations.
- Within the state, the ministries that were large employing agencies were unwilling to get involved in settling the dispute, as a result of the power of the CFA and a lack of expertise.

The employer's inability to settle quickly often produces higher-priced final settlements (Saran and Sheldrake, 1988: 14). Shared management responsibility demands appropriate employer organisation. Effective management organisation is not only crucial to the finalisation of a collective agreement, but in large, complex government units, is also crucial for administering the agreement (Aaron et al., 1988: 114).

The Minister for Public Service and Administration is responsible for determining who represents the state in the Central Chamber of the PSBC. In the sectoral council of the ELRC, the Minister of Education determines representation, while the National Commissioner of Police, rather than the Minister for Safety and Security, performs these functions in the NNF. However, the designated representatives in each bargaining forum receive mandates from the same source: the Mandating Ministers Forum (MMF).

In this way, the Cabinet maintains control over the bargaining process, and mediates between different ministers' interests. This process arose because improvements to conditions of service are regulated by a single budget vote under the control of the Minister for Public Service and Administration. Parliament has no direct influence on the collective bargaining process.

The composition of the MMF is not fixed. However, it usually comprises ministers responsible for large numbers of public servants (Education, Health, and Safety and Security), the Minister of Finance, the Minister for Public Service and Administration and 'ministers that understand unions and how they operate,' according to a former senior offical in the PSC. A major weakness, particularly with the increase in powers being given to the provinces, is the exclusion of premiers. Provinces were included in the bargaining chamber in 1995, though the premiers were present as representatives of the Minister for Public Service and Administration. In view of the problems experienced in implementing agreements, the inclusion of the provinces is positive. In early 1997, provincial representatives organised themselves into an inter-provincial labour relations forum to explore ways of improving their participation in the bargaining process.

With budgetary reforms geared towards fiscal federalism and global budgets to departments (and possibly to institutions), the appropriateness of the mandating process is called into question. Ministers may not be in the most appropriate position to define mandates that both satisfy employee demands, and ensure that structures of government are able to recruit and retain sufficient numbers of the personnel required for effective service delivery. The process and outcome of collective bargaining is crucial for the effective functioning of all government departments and provinces. The co-operative governance model that lies at the heart of the Constitution needs to be applied to the collective bargaining process. This must ensure the effective participation of institutional management, as well as provincial and departmental managers. Such a model is crucial for two reasons: because of their practical day-to-day experience, these managers will facilitate better agreements, and participation will ensure ownership amongst managers, in turn leading to improved implementation. The application of co-operative governance to the bargaining process will require better management of this process, as well as a more effective communication strategy within government.

In many countries, the finance ministry co-ordinates negotiations on the employer side. The danger of such an approach during a period of transition is that cost considerations may override considerations of equity, development and justice. Over the next few years it is vital to ensure a balance between the finance and human resource wings of government in influencing the outcome of the bargaining process.

Managing the bargaining process

Effective communication is central to successful negotiations. Unions have, in general, displayed much greater capacity to inform and brief their leaders and members at institutional level. The process of communication within government is much slower, mainly as a result of the channels that have to be followed. The DPSA, for example, will send a circular to a province, which sends it to a sub-region, from whence it is sent to the institutional manager, who then makes it available to the appropriate person in that institution. This cumbersome method of communication is particularly ill-suited to the period of transformation, in which fundamental changes are being made. Government needs to create effective and rapid communication capacity at all levels.

Alternative pay determination

Small, but crucial occupations have fought to be removed from the scope of the PSCBC since they are unable to win concessions within the overall bargaining arrangements. Unions have rejected such suggestions because they fear that this would eat away at the integrity of the bargaining process and lead to fragmentation.

There are ways of addressing the fears of such groups without fragmenting the PSCBC or sectoral councils. The first strategy requires government to champion the needs of these groups. It could make special funds available to meet their needs. It will, however, be difficult to assess objectively their demands, and it may be necessary to use some form of independent pay review.

A number of public service unions in the United Kingdom have recently demanded pay commissions in place of collective bargaining. The pressure for such arrangements is particularly strong in areas where industrial action hurts the consumer, rather than the government. Independent review bodies remove negotiating rights, but they avert the rivalry and procrastination between parties. If pay review bodies are to be accepted, their terms of reference and power will have to be clearly defined. Such bodies should propose settlement rates for particular constituencies, taking into account both government's wage policy as well as service delivery considerations, rather than the political power and strength of the occupational groups being reviewed.

CONCLUSION

The move towards new and effective bargaining structures, coupled with changes ushered in by the Constitution on the administration and budget process, raises more questions than answers. The upcoming period is crucial, as it will lay the foundation for the development of collective bargaining and, by extension, public service labour relations as a whole for the foreseeable future. The issues facing South Africa are in many ways similar to those faced elsewhere in the world. South Africa is favourably poised to assume the role of world pioneer. Being an effective pioneer will, however, require clarity of vision, a common purpose and the ability to introduce new and innovative solutions.

7

PUBLIC SERVICE BARGAINING

An assessment of the three-year wage agreement

———— ✦ ————

Jeremy Baskin

The 1996 three-year agreement between government and trade unions was a landmark in public service labour relations. Not only did it provide major salary increases, but these were to be financed through an ambitious program that located remuneration issues in the context of public service transformation. Baskin's chapter is the first systematic analysis of the agreement, the changes it fostered over the three-year period, and its implications for the future.

Public servants received substantial wage increases in 1996 and increases closer to inflation in 1997 and 1998. At the same time the size of the public service declined by more than 13%. These losses dramatically decreased the proportion of low-paid, unskilled public servants, yet the anticipated savings from 'right-sizing' have not materialised. Between 1996 and 1998 personnel expenditure rose from 46,6% to 50,1% of total expenditure, and the state's salary bill rose by an average of 12,2% per annum.

Creative solutions need to be developed to link bargaining and the budget: government must improve its internal processes and its method of allocating funds for improvements to conditions while unions need to find ways of balancing inevitable differences which will arise within the union bloc. The LRA needs to be re-examined so that its dispute procedures will stand the test of a genuine bargaining confrontation. The retrenchment moratorium has largely been a Phyrric victory for unions as down-sizing has occurred in any event; there is a need to focus more on the question of right-sizing (the appropriate and affordable size of the public service). There are deep weaknesses in the grading system which make it inappropriate and unaffordable in the medium-term as a system of pay progression. There is also a need to deal with a number of problems related to pay and grading in the different sub-sectors of the public service. But it will be a challenge to do this without losing the general framework established in centralised bargaining.

INTRODUCTION

During March 1996 a three-year agreement was concluded between the state (as employer) and public sector unions.[1] This agreement covered a range of issues, from wages to restructuring of the grading system, and governed conditions in the public service from 1 July 1996 until the end of June 1999. It was an important step in the reform of employment conditions and human resource management in the public service. The public service agreement covers all public servants, other than those in the Defence Force and Intelligence Services,[2] and covers substantially more employees than any other collective agreement.

This chapter assesses the three-year agreement.[3] It begins by outlining the main features of the agreement and the expectations of the parties at the time it was concluded in 1996. Section two then examines the actual changes – in conditions, expenditure, employee numbers, voluntary severance packages (VSPs) and so on – that have occurred over the three years. Finally, the paper looks at a number of issues which are relevant to the future of collective bargaining in the public sector. In short the chapter compares the situation in the public service before, during and at the end of the three-year period.

KEY FEATURES OF THE THREE-YEAR AGREEMENT

The three-year agreement concluded at the central Public Service Bargaining Council provided for:

- 'right-sizing' the public service
- voluntary severance packages (VSPs)
- restructuring of pension benefits
- improving pay and conditions of service.

Right-sizing

'Right-sizing' the public service – though key mechanisms were left for future negotiations – established the principle that the size of the public service be related to 'available financial resources'. The application of this aspect remains contested, with government stressing fiscal constraints and unions stressing that job cuts will damage service delivery. The parties have agreed on the need for right-sizing and that service delivery should be paramount, but they still have different views on what this means and how it should be achieved. In the 1996 agreement the unions 'took note' of the measures government intended to introduce.[4]

One of the Government's goals – 'a leaner and more cost-effective service' – explicitly involved reducing the wage bill as a proportion of public consumption expenditure. This was 'not merely to save money, but also to release resources for productive investment in Reconstruction and Development Programme (RDP) related initiatives'. Whatever the motivation, the intention was clear – to reduce the number of public servants, to 'right-size' by 'down-sizing'.[5] But, importantly, the government also agreed to put employer-initiated retrenchments on hold and, at the time of writing, this agreement remains in place. According to the agreement the specific measures to be used included:

- Annual targets being set by Cabinet regarding the size of the public service, and its size in each function/department.
- The Department of Public Service and Administration (DPSA) establishing a comprehensive database to provide a clear picture of where each public servant was deployed.
- Departments compiling a right-sizing management plan.
- Reductions in staff numbers being achieved by (i) abolishing funded vacancies[6] (ii) allowing officials to leave voluntarily[7] and providing an assistance programme for them and (iii) attrition. In reducing numbers there should be a balance between lower- and higher-graded posts. Only if these steps failed to deliver the required numbers should retrenchment of supernumerary officials[8] be considered, and then only after every possible attempt to redeploy them within the public service, making use of the DPSA's database.
- Departments avoiding filling vacancies, and filling vacancies with supernumeraries or abolishing vacant posts where possible.

Voluntary Severence Packages

Voluntary severance packages (VSPs) had the official aim of reducing the size of the public service and the unofficial aim of creating room for new appointments by encouraging 'old guard' public servants to leave. VSPs came into operation from 1 May 1996. The agreement[9] allowed public officials to volunteer for severance packages; the savings generated were intended to boost wage increases in subsequent years.

To encourage applications a generous package was offered, especially for those with over ten years of service. While the head of a department was entitled to turn down any application, the agreement contained contradictory elements and an impression was created that all VSP applicants were entitled to receive the special severance package, or to have the effective date postponed for 18 months.[10]

The severance component of the VSPs was to be paid out of departmental budgets. Among the benefits were several elements to be paid for outside the state's personnel budget, most notably:
- a generous pension package for those with long service, to be paid for by the Government Employees Pension Fund (GEPF)
- provision for continuing medical assistance – essentially subsidised medical aid – to be reimbursed to the GEPF directly by the fiscus.

Restructuring of pension benefits

The restructuring of pension benefits had the purpose of making it more attractive for existing public servants to take early retirement, resign or apply for voluntary severance, and of reducing the state's contribution to the pension fund. The details were left to subsequent negotiations although the agreements reached[11] provided for a number of things, including:
- Early retirements – those retiring at 60 years would suffer no loss of pension benefits, and those retiring at 55 years and upwards would suffer pension reductions of 4% for each year below 60 years of age.
- Enhanced cash resignation benefits – normal benefits would be increased by 10% for each full year of service between 5 and 15 years.
- Transfer of accrued pension benefits to other approved funds – the full value of dormant benefits could be transferred to another approved retirement fund.

- The definition of 'final salary', crucial in determining the actual monthly pension of retiring public servants, was in future to be based on the retiring official's average salary over the previous 24 months rather than on his or her last salary. This was to deal with a past practice where some officials received last minute promotions and salary increases with the aim of boosting their final salary for pension purposes. However, the agreement explicitly made a concession for those about to retire by stating that they would not be worse off than if the amendment had not been agreed.
- Reduction of the state's contribution – the employer's contribution rate was reduced from 18% to 17% of pensionable salary. This was based on an assessment of the funding/underfunding levels of the GEPF, and amounted to a significant saving to the fiscus; approximately half a billion rand for every 1% reduction. In April 1998 it was agreed that the state's contribution would be further reduced to 15%.

Improving pay and conditions of service

Improving pay and conditions of service had the following effects: improving the minimum wage rate significantly (bringing it up to R17 100 per annum from R13 200), increasing basic salaries substantially with effect from 1 July 1996,[12] introducing a new and simplified 16-band grading system, and establishing the rules for calculating salary increases in years 2 and 3 of the agreement based on anticipated fiscal allocations and savings generated through right-sizing. In the first year no employee got an increase of less than 7,5% on their personal salary.

The 1996 agreement also made provision for consolidating and reducing the number of special allowances. A range of allowances were scrapped, affecting some categories (such as medical officers) negatively. 'Danger' and 'special danger' allowances, valued at R200 per month and R500 per month[13] respectively, were introduced – the former basically targeted at police (but also including others) and the latter targeted at the more limited category of special force units in the police and correctional services. A consolidated night-shift allowance worth R1,33 per hour was also introduced, largely benefiting hospital personnel and others working regular night-shifts.

The 1997 agreement provided for a minimum 7,5% adjustment in personal salary for those below director level, a salary increase of 5% and

3% (in grades 13 and 14 respectively) and a salary freeze for those in senior management. In practice most employees received more than 7,5% as minimum rates were generally adjusted by between 7,7% and 11,1%.

The 1998 agreement made no provision for a guaranteed minimum increase to personal salaries. It introduced differentiated increases on the minimum rate ranging from 10,5% at the bottom to 8,5% in grade 2; 7% in grades 3 to 8; and dropping to below inflation in the higher grades. Again, senior management salary minimums were frozen.

In general base increases in year one were substantial, while the increases in the subsequent two years were slightly above or close to inflation. In year one, when employee salaries were translated from the old grading system to the new 16-band system, a significant number of employees (such as nurses and police) received substantial additional increases as their posts were placed at a higher level than previously. In short, some categories of employees benefited in year one from effectively having their posts re-graded.

Employees at the very lowest level received a 29,5% increase in the minimum rate in year one, followed by virtually automatic rank promotion for those with three years of service – effectively moving from grade 1 to grade 2 and receiving salary adjustments on account of re-grading. In practice the adjustments did not always happen on 1 July 1996. And any evaluation of the size of these increases must be offset against the decline in salaries associated with the scrapping of a number of allowances which previously existed.

The changes introduced to the grading system were far-reaching. The old system of automatic notch increases was abolished and replaced with performance-related notch increases. In addition, rank and leg promotions[14] were also introduced, again based on performance assessments.

Each post in the public service was associated with one of the 16 grades – with grade 1 covering the least-skilled labourer and grade 16 covering directors-general.[15] The salary grades each comprised a salary range, typically with three salary notches.

The aim was to move to a perhaps too orderly scheme involving a 4,5% gap between notches and a 20,4% gap between grades, and no overlapping.[16] The reality does not yet match this system and there are indications that government wants to review the gaps between grades, increase the number of notches and create more, and smaller, increases.

The context of the three-year agreement

It is hard not to see the three-year agreement as a major gain for public service unions. At the time there were significant pressures for wage increases, especially from nurses and police. Isolated strikes were occurring and the new government faced the real threat of the entire public service going on strike.

Add to this a desire on the part of the new government to be seen to be more generous, and the obvious need for a fundamental overhaul of the grading and personnel management system. Government negotiators (some with union backgrounds) were familiar with the drive towards a simplified, coherent and broad-banded grading system, such as in the auto sector. The result was a deal which simplified the grading system and raised minimum rates significantly. It should also be remembered that the agreement was struck before the Growth, Employment and Redistribution strategy (GEAR) made the fiscal constraints explicit. The threat of industrial action faded.

Finalisation of the three-year agreement occurred as much outside the bargaining chamber as inside it. There were, reportedly, numerous high-level talks between senior politicians and union leadership (especially Congress of South African Trade Unions (COSATU) affiliates). It is hard to avoid the conclusion that government made a number of mistakes in the process. It clearly miscalculated the cost of the deal, especially in relation to grading and promotions, and while it expected the VSPs to generate net savings, in reality they did not. The actual design of the VSPs seemed to differ from the original intentions and mainly ended up benefiting older, established, senior public servants. Further, the revised grading system has generated as many problems (in terms of both equity and the fiscus) as it hoped to solve. Moves to new grading systems are generally more costly and time-consuming than the three-year agreement anticipated.

CHANGES OVER THE THREE-YEAR PERIOD

We now turn to examine some of the actual trends in the public service over the three-year period. It is obviously important to see what has and has not changed. Although the three-year agreement alone cannot be credited with (or blamed for) all the changes, it has undoubtedly played a role.

Much of the following analysis relies on information contained in the annual Exchequer Report (contained within the DPSA's Annual Report) and on other information kindly made available by the DPSA.[17]

The size of the public service

Figure 7.1 summarises the overall picture with the public service divided into three categories – national departments, provinces, and the services (police, defence and correctional services). It shows a 13,3% decline in total public service employment – from 1,27 million to 1,1 million – in just over three years.[18] This is a significant decline by any standards, especially since it occurred without any employer-based retrenchments and at a time when there was significant recruitment of new civil servants, especially in national departments, in provincial education and at more senior levels.

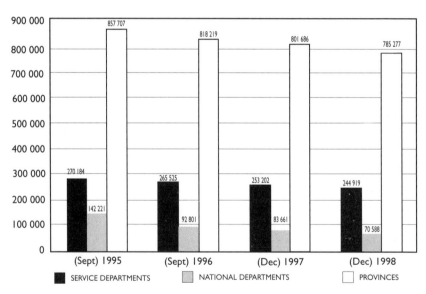

Figure 7.1: Number of public servants (national, provincial, services), 1995-1998
Source: DPSA

A similar pattern prevails with regard to race. Table 7.1 indicates the changing percentage of whites by broad-banded job grades. It reveals a dramatic fall-off in the white share of lower-graded employment. It also shows that whites remain heavily over-represented, especially in the three highest bands, although the situation has been improving slightly. Because of the relatively small number of employees in these grades these disparities do not show up in the overall public service employment figures.

Table 7.1: PERCENTAGE OF WHITE INCUMBENTS BY GRADE, 1996-1998

	1996 (Sept)	1997 (Dec)	1998 (Dec)
Lower skilled	7,3	3,5	2,3
Skilled	24,2	19,1	15,8
High-skilled production	28,8	24,3	22,3
High-skilled supervision	56,6	50,9	49,6
Management	66,2	59,7	56,9
Senior management	43,6	42,9	37,9
Total	**23,4**	**19,6**	**17,7**

(Source: DPSA)

The down-sizing seems to have occurred largely through attrition – essentially resignations, retirements and special retirements (VSPs).[19] If new recruits are added to the equation (unfortunately figures were not available for this), and if it is remembered that dismissals are extremely rare, then it indicates there is presently a high turnover rate within the public service. Presumably, given the scarcity of jobs, this high rate is partly a function of uncertainty and 'churning' caused by the post-apartheid transition, as well as the departure (with VSPs) of those who believe they possess more marketable skills. The high turnover rate can be expected to decrease as the transition stabilises.

Some of the 'down-sizing' was not really down-sizing and occurred as a result of outsourcing of functions to autonomous agencies. The most notable example of this was the transfer of approximately 11 000 employees to the new SA Revenue Services (SARS). However this does not substantially alter the overall picture, namely a significant decline in the absolute size of the public service.

National and service departments
The national departments bore the brunt of the decline in percentage terms. But this was less extreme than a superficial reading of the figures suggests.

The sharp decline in numbers between 1995 and 1996 was largely a function of statistically re-allocating employees to the appropriate province. If one analyses the figures between 1996 and 1998 and takes into account the outsourcing of SARS then the size of national departments has declined by roughly 12,1%, compared to a decline of 5,5% for the public service as a whole over the same period. The service departments declined in numbers by 7,8% over this period, with the biggest cuts coming from Defence, and with Correctional Services actually growing slightly in numbers employed.

Provincial administrations

The smallest percentage decline was in the provincial administrations where employment levels declined by 4% (1996-1998) and by 8,4% over the longer 1995-1998 period. But in terms of absolute numbers the decline was marked, with a net loss in the provinces of 72 430 jobs. Importantly this sharp drop took place without an employer-initiated retrenchment instrument. Perhaps the most notable aspect of the provincial picture is the marked distinction between the provinces, summarised in Figure 7.2 covering the two year 1996-1998 period. The figures must be treated with caution since there appears to have been some 'cleaning-up' of the statistics, with former homeland public servants being reallocated.

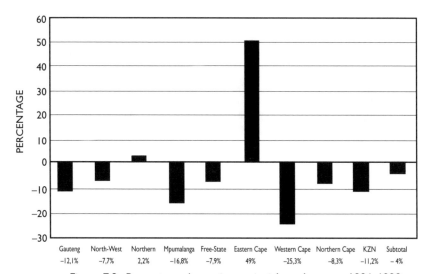

Figure 7.2 : Percentage change in provincial employment, 1996-1998
Source: DPSA

The figures strongly suggest that the lack of an employer-initiated retrenchment instrument was not a major obstacle to reducing public servant numbers. Western Cape appears to have actively worked to reduce total employee numbers, partly by encouraging VSPs. In just over three years numbers declined by over 25%, although some of this decline may have come from transferring employees to the Northern Cape administration. Free State and KZN also down-sized, although to a lesser extent, over both measured periods. At the other extreme is the Eastern Cape, although the sharp swing in numbers from 1995 to 1996 suggests unreliable data and makes analysis difficult.[20] The figures suggest that most provinces made attempts to down-size during the 1996-1998 period, largely in the face of fiscal pressures. Only Northern Province appears not to have made moves in this direction.

Changed grading profile

Perhaps the most startling change regards the changed distribution of public service employment.[21] Figure 7.3 indicates that in slightly over two

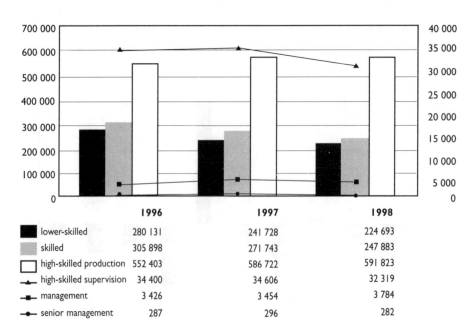

	1996	1997	1998
■ lower-skilled	280 131	241 728	224 693
▨ skilled	305 898	271 743	247 883
☐ high-skilled production	552 403	586 722	591 823
▲ high-skilled supervision	34 400	34 606	32 319
■ management	3 426	3 454	3 784
● senior management	287	296	282

Figure 7.3 : Employment trends by skill category, 1996-1998

Source: DPSA, 1996 (end September), 1997-1998 (end December)

years, while overall employment has declined by 6,4%, the bulk of the down-sizing has occurred at the bottom end. The total number of jobs in grades 1 to 5 has declined by over 19%. By contrast the middle category (grades 6 to 9) has increased by over 7%. Of the three remaining broad-bands, two have declined and one (essentially directors and chief directors) has increased, although the numbers involved are too small to affect the big picture.

The implications of this change are fairly startling. Put another way, in 1996 five out of ten public servants were in grades 1 to 5, while today the figure is closer to four in every ten. This is a dramatic change in the space of a little over two years. It is also a difficult change to explain. It does not seem to involve a significant change in gender composition; the decline in employment in the lower grades has been distributed fairly equally between men and women. And it is also hard to discover a racial pattern. Although the drop in white numbers in these grades has been particularly sharp (with only half the number of white employees in grades 1 to 5 at end-1998 as there were in Sept 1996),[22] the relatively small numbers involved cannot explain the whole story.

It may be that, following the relatively high wage increases at the bottom end, there is a tendency to shed these jobs and outsource them to cheaper contractors. It may also be that work processes and technology have changed and there is now less need for blue-collar and lower-end white-collar employees. Then again it may be that the various rank and leg promotions have resulted in upward movement or grade shifting, although it is hard to see why this should mean movement between broad-banded grades (although it is possible that the broad-bands themselves are inaccurate and need revisiting).

In the absence of hard evidence it is difficult to explain such a big change in so short a time, especially in the absence of an explicit policy intention aimed at moving in this direction. The conclusion is extremely tentative, but it is possible that there are three separate changes taking place.

The first is job-shedding at the blue-collar end (grades 1 and 2), driven by the cost impact of both the relatively high minimum rate increases, their moving from 'casual' to permanent status with attendant knock-on costs, and the rank promotions which moved most general assistants to grade 2. Three other factors may also have pushed numbers downwards: a number of 'casuals' were not taken onto the payroll and their services were dropped or contracted-out; the re-grading of police constables pushed them out of the lowest broad-band and into the next broad-band (although this band has also dropped sharply); and there may be some statistical adjustments arising from sessional part-timers having been wrongly classified as lower-grade in previous years because of their lower annual income.

Second, the impact of changed work-practices may have led to some job-shedding in grades 3 to 5. Simply put there is less emphasis on some of the lower level typing and clerical jobs, with provinces and departments wanting a smaller, more skilled, public service. The decline in numbers in the second broad-band can also, perhaps, be attributed to a drop in total police numbers (as many police left the service while, at the same time, a moratorium on new hires was in place).

Third, the new grading system meant many employees, when having their jobs translated into the new system, appear to have moved up a level and are now classified as high-skilled production (grades 6 to 9). This would explain why the decline in numbers in the 'skilled' category (over 58 000), corresponds to some extent to the increase in numbers (up by almost 40 000) in the next 'high-skilled production' band. During 1996 and 1997 a significant number of new teachers and nurses were placed on the payroll.

The changed grading spread suggests there is a need to explore the wage-employment trade-off at the lower end, and to revisit the design of the grading and broad-banding system. One effect of this changed profile is to increase the fiscal pressures being felt. Simply put, the savings resulting from the drop in lower-grade numbers does not counteract the cost of an increase in medium and higher-grade numbers. The three-year agreement provided that, in the event of employer-initiated retrenchments, down-sizing would be spread across grades. The figures indicate that down-sizing occurred for a range of reasons, as a result of unintended consequences of the agreement rather than an active policy of retrenchments.

Race and gender patterns

There has been significant progress since 1996 with regard to affirmative action (the 1995 figures are not relied on). Figure 7.4 summarises the position. While there is still over-representation of whites in the public service, the percentages for all racial groups are rapidly approaching the relative shares of both the economically active population (EAP) and even of the population as a whole. Looking at the public service as a whole, the over-representation of whites and under-representation of coloureds is relatively small in relation to the EAP. In some provinces there is, if anything, an under-representation of whites, while in national departments the opposite is generally the case. In the case of coloured public servants the relative decline in employment share from 9,4% in 1996 to 8,5% in 1998 largely reflects the fact that the Western Cape provincial administration has been the most active in down-sizing.

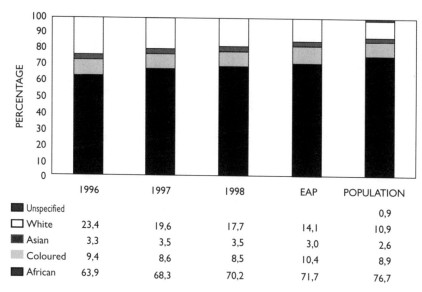

	1996	1997	1998	EAP	POPULATION
■ Unspecified					0,9
☐ White	23,4	19,6	17,7	14,1	10,9
■ Asian	3,3	3,5	3,5	3,0	2,6
Coloured	9,4	8,6	8,5	10,4	8,9
■ African	63,9	68,3	70,2	71,7	76,7

Figure 7.4 : Racial composition, 1996-1998
Source: DPSA

The overall gender pattern is similar. Women comprised 48,7% of public servants in 1996, their share increasing to 50,3% by the end of 1998. This is still below, but close to, their share of the total population, and above their share of the EAP.

While the overall level of progress is excellent, the pattern is less impressive if the position is analysed by grade. As Figure 7.5 shows, women remain heavily under-represented in the higher grades. In this the public service closely parallels, if anything is slightly ahead of, the situation in the private sector.

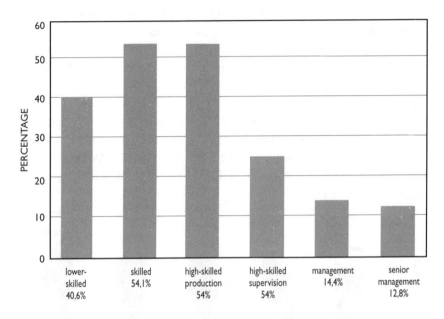

Figure 7.5 : Percentage share of women by grade, 1998
Source: DPSA, December 1998

There have been active attempts to improve the racial profile, especially at management and senior management levels. In the space of five years the senior management level (basically director-general and deputy director-general posts) has changed from being almost entirely white to being under 40% white. But progress has proved more difficult at the next two levels. It appears that the major obstacle remains the apartheid legacy that the available skills pool at the managerial and professional levels remains heavily distorted in favour of whites and males.

In short, with regard to race and gender composition the overall picture is fairly balanced, but serious imbalances remain at the more senior professional and managerial levels.

Wage trends, the wage bill and fiscal pressures

At the level of individual employees the 1996 agreement undoubtedly resulted in significant increases. The case study that follows, based on a NALEDI research project, shows the longer-term trends for some key jobs.

The changing pattern of pay (1989-1997)

A 1997 unpublished NALEDI study examined the longer-term position experienced by workers in a range of job categories. It looked at the situation immediately after the increases of 1989, 1993 and 1997 and assessed basic salary notch, allowances and bonuses before arriving at an estimate of total remuneration. Certain benefits (such as the management car allowance) were not included. The study further differentiated between those at entry level, and with three years' and ten years' service respectively.

Looking at the four-year period between 1 August 1993 and 1 August 1997, and taking a person with three years' service as a benchmark, the following observations can be made. (It should be remembered that during this time the consumer price index rose substantially, by 37,7%.)

Civil servants – with two exceptions (directors-general and administrative officers)[23] civil servants received increases above the inflation rate over this period, in some cases slightly above inflation (such as administrative clerks with a matriculation and typists) and in other cases significantly above. In the case of general assistants wages rose dramatically (by over 145%), partly as a result of increases in the minimum rate and partly as a result of rank promotions. Figure 7.6A provides a graphic representation of the trends.

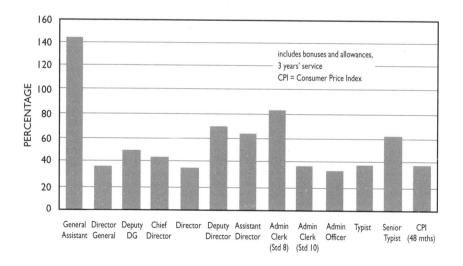

Figure 7.6A : Civil servants: four-year wage trends, 1993-1997

Source: NALEDI analysis of DPSA data

Educators – over the period teachers received significant real increases. As with civil servants the highest percentage increases generally went to those at the bottom of the pay scale, either those with lower qualifications or those with shorter service. A teacher with matric and three years' service saw his or her pay rise by almost 135% over the measured four year period – or 97% after taking inflation into account. More qualified or longer service teachers received smaller increases, but still over 50%. Figure 7.6B graphically represents the situation in three measured educator categories.

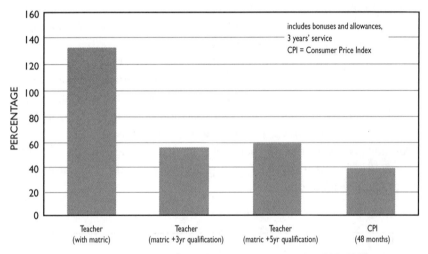

Figure 7.6B: Teachers: four-year wage trends, 1993-1997

Source: NALEDI analysis of DPSA data

Health workers – the most consistently favourable increases were experienced by nurses, as Figure 7.6C indicates. The three-year agreement, it must be remembered, was concluded against a backdrop of labour unrest in hospitals and deep dissatisfaction among nurses. Nurses, from senior to junior level, generally saw increases of around 80% (or 42% after inflation), even after a number of allowances were scrapped/simplified. Other health professionals also experienced significant increases. However the salaries of medical officers (doctors) barely kept pace with inflation. In 1993 the ratio of earnings between a pupil nurse and a medical officer was 5,3:1. In 1997 it was 3,3:1. In short, the relative pay between various occupations in the health sector has changed significantly, largely as a consequence of the three-year agreement.[24]

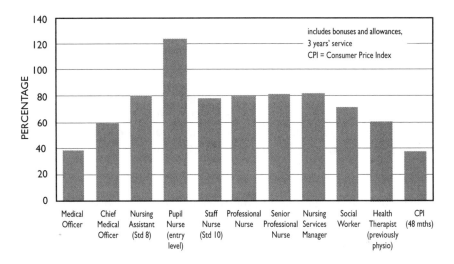

Figure 7.6C: Health workers: four-year wage trends, 1993-1997

Source: NALEDI analysis of DPSA data

Police – the SAPS also saw a fairly consistent upgrading in salaries of between 45% and 60%, at least for the occupations examined. Figure 7.6D presents the overall picture. It is unclear if these figures accommodate the danger and special danger allowances brought in under the 1996 agreement.

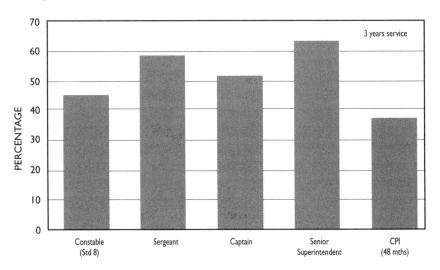

Figure 7.6D: Police: four-year wage trends, 1993-1997

Source: NALEDI analysis of DPSA data

In summary the changes over four years involved raising the minimum rates substantially (especially in the lower-paid occupations), and changing the relative pay within sectors. It must however be remembered that public service bargaining typically has more extreme settlements than in the private sector – higher than average one year and lower than average another. It will be useful to re-analyse the data after 2000 to get a longer-term view. This will undoubtedly reveal lower real increases over a longer period, than over the four year period analysed here.

One study argued that the minimum wage had increased from 75% of the Household Subsistence Level in 1991, to 125% in 1997/1998.[25] Another unpublished study argued that between 1993 and 1997, the minimum salary increased in real terms by 14% a year, compared to an average of 5% for the rest of the public service. And the DPSA data upon which the NALEDI study above is based suggests that the minimum rate increased in real terms by over 26% per annum over this period. It also appears to be the case that, in general, lower-end public service wages are above market levels, despite a KPMG finding partially indicating the contrary.[26] However, looked at from another angle, the percentage increases to salary grade minimums was, at least in years two and three, not substantially above inflation.

The most commonly cited problem in relation to public service pay is that personnel costs are a high and rising proportion of total expenditure, and that this is squeezing out service delivery and public investment. This message is contained in numerous government documents and in speeches delivered by political leaders. It is generally accompanied by calls to cut the number of public servants. The most extensive available information on this issue is contained in the DPSA's annual Exchequer Report, in the Department of Finance's annual Budget Review, and in unpublished studies which form part of the Medium-Term Expenditure Review.

Table 7.2 indicates the proportion of total budget spent on personnel. Total personnel expenditure now stands at just under 40% of total expenditure, and at slightly over 50% if interest repayments (on the debt) are excluded.[27] The situation is more extreme in the provinces with personnel spending constituting 53% of provincial budgets in the financial year 1995/1996, rising to over 59% in financial year 1998/1999.[28]

Table 7.2: PERSONNEL COSTS IN RELATION TO BUDGET
            (Millions of rands)

	outcome	estimate	medium-term exp. est.				
	FY95/96	FY98/99	FY99/00	FY00/01	FY01/02	avg. growth 95/96 - 98/99	avg. predicted growth
Personnel	57 891	81 811	86 489	90 693	94 967	12,2%	5,1%
Total expenditure	154 837	206 996	219 602	233 685	250 347	10,2%	6,5%
Interest expenditure	30 661	43 813	48 522	50 070	52 789	12,6%	6,4%
Total exp. (after interest)	124 176	163 183	171 080	183 615	197 558	10,5%	5,2%
Personnel % of total	37,4%	39,5%	39,4%	38,8%	37,9%		
Personnel % (non-interest)	46,6%	50,1%	50,6%	49,4%	48,1%		

(Source: Department of Finance, 1996a: 136)

The impact of this has undoubtedly been serious, especially at the provincial level. There has been a sharp decline in public investment and infrastructure maintenance. Problems regarding the provision of textbooks, the building of roads and classrooms, and the supply of medicines in clinics are simply the most well-publicised. Part of the problem stems from the fact that the annual Improvement in Conditions of Service budget only covers basic increases. Other costs (such as VSPs, notch increases and rank promotions) must be funded by departments from within their existing budgets.

The increase in personnel costs of 12,2% per annum over the three-year period to the end of March 1999, must be analysed in conjunction with the decline in the number of public servants (a drop of about 167 000 or 13%) over roughly the same period. In short, a larger pie is being divided among a smaller number of employees. If one divides the personnel expenditure for FY95/96 by the number of public servants at about this time (1 270 112) then the average annual salary including benefits was R45 579. A comparable calculation three years later generates an average annual salary of R74 320.[29] This represents an increase of 63% compared to a Consumer Price Index increase of approximately 25% over the same period. These increases followed a period when wage increases in the public service had lagged behind. One study argues that in 1996 average pay in the public service increased by 19% in real terms, but only by 7% in real terms in comparison to 1990.[30]

By this measure the three-year agreement marked a significant gain for unions and their members, as well as a structural shift towards a better-paid and relatively more skilled public service. However these gains have partly been achieved at the expense of employment numbers (especially at the lower end) and partly by reducing the absolute and relative share of other expenditure items. In the medium-term the effect of the three-year agreement will limit the extent of future increases and impel government towards further down-sizing, especially at the provincial level. This poses difficult challenges and trade-offs.

The impact is likely to differ from province to province, but all provinces will be under pressure to down-size. Figure 7.7 compares the number of public servants per 1 000 of population in each province. This suggests that down-sizing pressures will be most intense in the Northern Province, Free State, Eastern Cape, and North West.

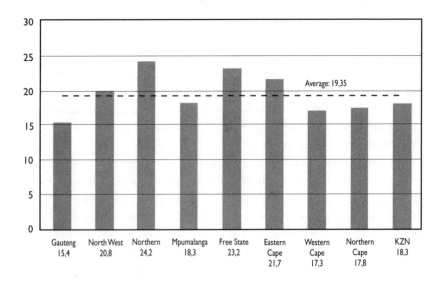

Figure 7.7: Public Servants: per 1 000 of population
Source: DPSA, December 1998

However, different provinces have different poverty and age profiles and different requirements to deliver, say, education or water. The 'equitable share' formula is an attempt to capture this. Table 7.3 presents the data in more detail and lists each province's share of population (final census data); its 'equitable share' excluding conditional grants; its revised 'equitable share' to be reached by 2003; the number of public servants per 1000 of population as of the end of December 1998; its number and share of provincial employees; and its share of the provincial salary bill.

Table 7.3: PUBLIC SERVICE BY PROVINCE

	% population	% 'equitable share' (FY98/99)	% 'equitable share' (target)	public servants per 1 000 population	no. of public servants	% share of provincial employees	% share of provincial salary bill
Gauteng	18,1	14,8	15,7	15,4	112 851	14,4	15,3
North West	8,3	8,6	8,2	20,0	67 169	8,6	8,2
Northern	12,1	13,2	13,5	24,2	119 465	15,2	15,0
Mpumalanga	6,9	6,6	7,1	18,3	51 355	6,5	6,5
Free State	6,5	6,9	6,6	23,2	61 054	7,8	7,3
Eastern Cape	15,5	17,8	16,8	21,7	136 935	17,4	17,4
Western Cape	9,7	10,1	8,9	17,2	67 940	8,7	9,4
Northern Cape	2,1	2,5	2,4	17,6	14 821	1,9	1,9
KZN	20,7	19,6	20,7	18,3	153 687	19,6	19,0
Totals	100			19,35	785 277	100	100

(Source: Statistics SA, 1998 DPSA and Department of Finance, 1999a)

Where there is a disparity between existing share of provincial employees and current/target 'equitable share' then we can expect greatest pressure to down-size. On this measure Northern Province and Free State are likely to see the largest cuts, relatively speaking.

Non-wage benefits

The state's salary bill comprises a basic pensionable salary component (which is what the minimum pay rates reflect) and non-wage components. The latter currently make up approximately one-third of the total salary bill. Non-wage benefits do not form part of pensionable salary, the key figure on which both employer and employee contributions to the pension fund are based.

At national level basic salaries (i.e. normal pay processed via PERSAL) make up 66,4% of the total bill, with other benefits (most notably state pension contributions) making up the 33,6% balance. Non-wage benefits make up a smaller proportion of the salary bill in the provinces – ranging from 33,6% in Western Cape to 26,9% in Northern Province.[31]

Figure 7.8 – using data supplied by the DPSA, and derived from financial data (i.e. actual payments) – shows how the one-third benefits portion of the state's salary bill is divided up from a fiscal point of view.[32] The figures show that the key items are:

- state's pension contribution (which has dropped from 18% to 15% over the course of the three-year agreement)
- service bonus (effectively a 13th cheque)
- medical aid subsidies to incumbent public servants
- housing subsidy for home-owners
- overtime payments.

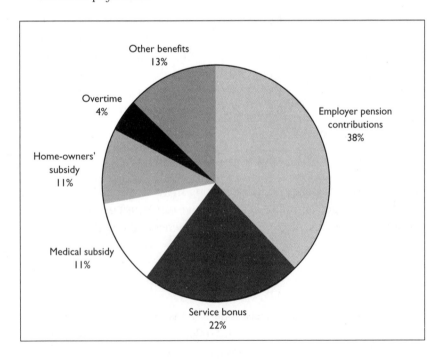

Figure 7.8: Relative share of employer non-wage costs
Source: DPSA and DSE, December 1998

These five items alone make up 87% of the state's total non-wage salary bill. The remaining 13% is made up of 31 different items none of which, on its own, is very significant in fiscal terms. For example, the motor allowance (for senior public servants), while costing well over R100 million and significant from an equity perspective, currently only comprises 0,87% of the non-wage salary bill.

The non-wage component has increased as a percentage since the early 1990s, probably as a result of the extension of benefits to all public servants. Many categories of public servant were previously ineligible for many benefits. For example women were previously unable to access housing benefits, and most black general assistants and many other employees (including some teachers) were regarded as casual and ineligible for benefits. In other cases employees were simply not informed that the benefit existed.

Equalisation of the rules has now largely happened and the proportion of non-wage costs is unlikely to increase further. Indeed there are pressures to reduce the wage bill by reducing a number of these items. However issues such as increased overtime requirements in terms of the Basic Condition of Employment Act (BCEA) remain to be dealt with, and may place upward pressure on non-wage costs. This will depend on the actual collective agreements reached within the 18-month window period which the public service has before being required to implement the BCEA. While the rules are equal the impact is not. It can be argued that the structure of the rules favours:

- civil servants and security force members, rather than other components of the public service
- higher-income earners, rather than those in grades 1 to 9
- male, rather than female public servants
- more senior employees (especially at management level), rather than those below director level.

The three-year agreement resulted in significant simplification of the benefit system. Some benefits, such as the 'danger' allowances, apply to specific posts. Others are clearly targeted at specific occupations – directly, in the case of the 'qualification bonus' paid to educators who acquire a further qualification, and indirectly in the case of 'stand-by allowances' which are generally accessed only by certain types of personnel (such as doctors). Yet other benefits, most notably the car allowance (basically a car purchase subsidy), are only available to those at director level or above.[33]

The two main benefits – pension and 13th cheque – are universal and not analysed further in this chapter. However, a number of key benefits (notably medical aid and home-owner subsidies) discriminate in practice against lower-paid employees. To access the housing benefit one must *first* buy a house and secure a bond, and then apply for the subsidy; the maximum subsidy is R1 100 per month. It is notoriously difficult for low-income earners to get bonds from financial institutions, and only middle-income housing (or a bond of around R70 000) accesses the full subsidy. Not surprisingly, the DPSA estimates that only 18% of employees get the subsidy and that the bulk of monies paid out go to better-off public servants.

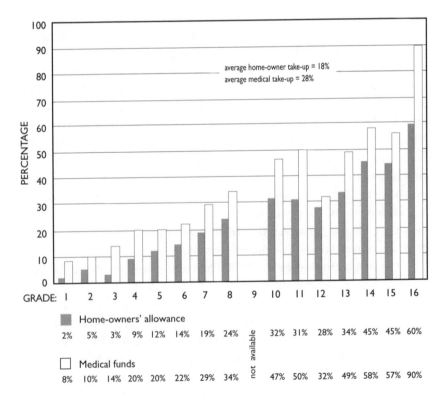

Figure 7.9: Percentage employees using medical and home-owner benefits
Source: DPSA

The medical aid subsidy operates similarly. The benefit comprises a subsidy of two-thirds of one's medical aid subscription, up to a maximum of R600 per month. This means one must be on a private medical aid to qualify, and have a monthly subscription of R900 to access the maximum benefit. Only a minority of public servants can afford medical aid subscriptions and most rely on public health care. Further, to get the full subsidy one must be on one of the more comprehensive schemes, and only higher income-earners can afford schemes with monthly subscriptions above the R900 per month mark.

Analysing figures supplied by DPSA it appears that medical and housing benefits add an average of 5,7% to the package of a grade 1 employee. The benefit then rises in both absolute and relative terms – for grades 4 to 10 it adds, on average, between 9,5% and 12,7% to an employee's package. The relative value of these two benefits then declines in the highest categories – the maximum caps placed on benefits, and the fact that higher basic salaries are earned, means they form a smaller percentage of senior employees' packages. More revealing are the take-up rates. Figure 7.9 indicates that these two key benefits clearly suit or can be afforded by some grades more than others.

Voluntary severance packages

Voluntary severance packages (VSPs) were introduced with the primary aim of cutting the number of public servants. The savings generated were to be used to improve the conditions of service in years two and three. The VSPs were especially attractive to older public servants with extensive service, since the most generous component involved improving the pension benefit.

Table 7.4 lists details of severance packages granted. As of May 1999 very few applications for VSPs were being granted. In short about 81 000 packages have been granted, with teachers and SANDF members making up significant proportions of the total.

VSP use differed dramatically from province to province. In Western Cape the number of packages granted was as high as 28% of the 1997 employment total. At the opposite extreme the Northern Province figure was a mere 1% of the 1997 total (although it may be that this province has not reported all VSPs granted); while Mpumalanga and Eastern Cape ratios are similarly low.

Table 7.4: NUMBER OF VOLUNTARY SEVERANCE PACKAGES
        GRANTED

Dept./Province	Non-educators	Educators	Total
Police	3 365	—	3 365
Defence	12 580	—	12 580
Correctional Services	957	—	957
Sub-total: service depts	**16 902**	**—**	**16 902**
Water & Forestry	2 681	—	2 681
Public Works	1 162	—	1 162
Land	147	—	147
Labour	77	—	77
Justice	50	—	50
Home Affairs	883	—	883
Health	160	—	160
Foreign Affairs	300	—	300
Environment & Tourism	223	—	223
Agriculture	413	—	413
Transport	254	—	254
SA Revenue Services	1 558	—	1 558
Other national	1 178	—	1 178
Sub-total: national depts	**7 487**	**—**	**7 487**
Gauteng	5 616	3 550	9 166
North West	2 367	1 659	4 026
Northern	960	170	1 130
Mpumalanga	821	47	868
Free State	1 655	1 087	2 742
Eastern Cape	3 642	1 780	5 422
Western Cape	9 500	11 067	20 567
Northern Cape	1 011	605	1 616
KZN	7 024	4 237	11 261
Subtotal: provinces	**32 596**	**24 202**	**56 798**
GRAND TOTAL	**56 985**	**24 202**	**81 187**

(Sources: DPSA and Dept. of Education)[34]

Working out the cost of the packages is extremely difficult, and any attempt to work out the 'savings' envisaged in the three-year agreement is effectively impossible. But it is possible to outline what is known, although the figures quoted should be interpreted as costs rather than savings.

The VSPs contained a number of elements. The first was a severance component dependent on last salary and years of service, and including a six-month continuation of any home-owner's allowance. This package was paid from the relevant department's budget and so information on this is decentralised.[35] Informed observers estimate that these packages were, on average, equivalent to seven months' salary. For those provinces where it has information (the majority), the national Department of Education says that provinces paid out an average of R51 246 per educator – or R1,24 billion for the over 24 000 educators granted the package. Minister Zola Skweyiya reported in February 1999 that packages (excluding educators and SANDF members) had cost a total of R856 million. However this figure seems extremely low – it amounts to an average severance package of R19 277 for non-SANDF, non-educator VSP recipients – and may be incomplete or reflect only one financial year's costs. The second element was a continuing medical aid subsidy to be paid by the Government Employees' Pension Fund (GEPF) and refunded to the GEPF by the fiscus. It was impossible, in the limited time available, to get information on the cost of this. The GEPF's medical aid subsidy bill has escalated in recent years but VSP recipients comprise only a small proportion of beneficiaries and the rise is probably linked mainly to the general increase in medical aid costs.

Enhanced pension benefits were the real 'carrot' to encourage VSP applicants. The deal involved enhanced benefits dependent on the individual's service record. Those between 50 and 55 years of age could choose either a lump-sum payout or a gratuity plus monthly pension; those aged 55 years and above received a gratuity and a monthly pension. These benefits were paid out by the GEPF. In some cases lump-sum payments were extremely high, apparently as high as R2,7 million. Informed sources suggest that VSP pension payments currently amount to R350 million per annum[36] and that, to date, lump-sum and gratuity payments have totalled R10,88 billion. It is hard to work out the effective cost since lump-sum payments also reduce the GEPF's long-term pension obligations; and the pensions of early retirees have been reduced pro rata.

The real figure would involve calculating the difference between what has been paid and what would otherwise have been paid in the absence of VSPs. What is undeniable is that the amounts paid by the GEPF reduced the value of the fund. In effect this means that remaining GEPF members subsidised the enhanced packages of members departing with VSPs. To some extent government shares this cost in the long-run by guaranteeing that the GEPF operates within actuarially-acceptable funding levels.

The following consequences of the VSP deal may be outlined. Whether they are negative or positive depends a great deal on whether one is looking at the issues from a union, developmental, employer or fiscal perspective.

Large numbers of public servants applied for the deal with, to date, over 81 000 packages being granted. This reduced the size of the public service. Anecdotal evidence suggests that applicants fell into three categories – 'old guard' public servants who wanted to leave anyway, more skilled and experienced public servants attracted by the size of the package and confident of the marketability of their skills, and experienced public servants over age 55 attracted by the prospect of early retirement without major reductions in their benefits. In short, those who left included many whom the state could least afford to lose, notably experienced teachers. And many who took the package would probably have left without it.

For newly-arrived public service managers the VSPs provided a way of encouraging certain established managers to leave. This made the transformation process easier and allowed for more new appointments at senior level and for easier implementation of affirmative action.

The VSPs contributed to a degree of demoralisation within the public service since not all applications were granted. This caused tensions and a number of disputes were declared against various departments. Further, the VSPs, combined with the moratorium on retrenchment, may have reduced efforts towards more creative approaches to genuine 'right-sizing'. The cost of the VSPs was high, especially if one includes the time associated with processing the problems associated with it, and the costs borne by the GEPF. Not surprisingly the government believes that it lacks an affordable retrenchment instrument. Most importantly it is hard to disagree with the anecdotal evidence that the bulk of the benefits were captured by 'old guard' public servants, especially those in the higher grades.

FUTURE ISSUES

A number of issues emerge when examining the evidence and reflecting on the experience of the three-year agreement. There appear to be many things to learn. In this section some of these issues are examined including shortcomings in the negotiating process, retrenchments, the grading and training system, the relationship between central and sectoral bargaining, the future of non-wage benefits and the issue of a 'clean wage', and the fiscal dilemma at the heart of the bargaining process.

The bargaining process

Three elements of the bargaining process appear to be problematic. First is the government mandating problem. Government's own internal processes seem to be under-developed. Some issues, such as grading and promotion systems, require a level of attention to detail that appears to be difficult to achieve at Cabinet level, yet is crucial if mistakes are to be avoided. Some of the design problems in the three-year agreement's grading and progression system can be attributed to this. So too, perhaps, can the actual operations of the VSP scheme, and the wide divergence between the anticipated savings to be allocated to improvements in 1997 and 1998 and the reality. It may be that in finalising the three-year agreement the Cabinet mandating committee was not well-integrated with the state's negotiating team or simply that there was insufficient attention to detail. Clearly, for example, some of government's fiscal problems and complaints about its soaring salary bill seem to derive from the uncalculated consequences of the agreement.

A related process problem on government's side was that the individual members of the negotiating team were covered by the agreement. This will change in future, with the exclusion of management from the bargaining unit. Further, it is not clear who carries responsibility for agreements concluded. Normal management practice would be that the managers responsible for budgeting and implementing government programmes would be deeply involved. However the direct involvement in the bargaining process by departmental accounting officers (mainly directors-general) and by provinces (who employ over 71% of public servants) was, and remains, extremely limited in practice. One of the effects has been that some elements of the agreement are paid for through additional 'improvement' allocations to departmental/provincial budgets, while other elements can only be implemented from within existing budgets. This causes perverse consequences and uneven implementation with, for example, some programmes holding back on merit and other performance awards for budgetary rather than performance reasons, others having to make last-minute provision for the costs of automatic rank/leg promotions, and accounting officers (especially in the provinces) complaining of 'unfunded mandates' being imposed on them, creating pressure to divert money from other line items.

A second element of the bargaining process which may be problematic in the longer-term relates to the balance of forces within the union bloc. The three-year agreement reflected, on balance, a major gain for employees and meant that a range of internal contradictions within the employee side could be contained. A tighter bargaining situation is likely to highlight these contradictions. For example, pursuing a more equitable benefits arrangement will be resisted if it involves reducing the established benefits (especially housing and medical) of an influential and significant minority of union members. Further, there is a bias towards the civil service[37] and away from the delivery departments which can be seen in the grading system, the salary and incentive structure, as well as in the benefit arrangements and indeed, in the operations of the DPSA. Tackling this bias will be in the interests of some members/unions and not others.

A third problematic element of the process, the legal/constitutional dilemma, is more fundamental. At its heart is the relationship between bargaining, budgeting and the supremacy of Parliament. Continuing uncertainty here is likely to cause major problems for unions in future. To some extent these problems have been contained politically since there is an alliance between key public service unions and the current government. When the problem emerged during the course of the three-year agreement it was solved politically rather than through the courts or through arbitration. But this way of solving problems is unlikely to continue forever, especially if relations become more adversarial.

The problem can be summed up as follows. Labour legislation and agreements require good faith collective bargaining between the state (as employer) and its employees. However, Parliament has the constitutional right to vote the budget annually, a budget in which personnel expenditure is a key variable. This means that Parliament can overturn an increase agreed to in negotiations by not voting the amount required to implement that agreement. Now, of course, in practice the problem need not be that severe. Government's three-year expenditure cycle means that its medium-term intentions are announced in advance. And there is an implicit obligation on the executive (Cabinet), when ratifying public service collective agreements, to take into account both the fiscal implications and the need to ensure parliamentary approval.

If the executive sticks to its medium-term expenditure plans then this effectively reduces collective bargaining to a process of cutting a pre-determined cake. An emphasis on dividing up a pre-set amount will generally lead to simple majority rule at the Public Service Co-ordinating Bargaining Council (PSCBC), and this is likely to take the form of 'across-the-board' increases, or larger increases at the lower end of the salary scale. In the medium-term this will lead to erosion of the bargaining unit as lower-end employees are replaced by contracting out arrangements, and as higher-end (and special category) employees attempt to leave the bargaining unit (as is happening with prosecutors) in their efforts to obtain a better deal.

There are no easy solutions to this problem. It may be that the design of the Labour Relations Act (LRA) regarding public service collective bargaining needs to be revisited to clarify the relative roles of the parties – it is simply naïve, for example, to expect that the CCMA or the Labour Court would be able to mediate or arbitrate effectively (even during a strike) on disputes where billions of rands and the rights of Parliament are involved. It may be advisable for the union movement to press for greater involvement in the budget-making process – although it is hard to see government agreeing to more than the present levels of consultation. It may be that any bargaining conflict in the public service is inevitably 'political' with unions having, as a final resort, the right to campaign at election time for a change in the ruling party. Whatever approach is adopted a legal/constitutional conflict can be expected sooner rather than later unless the legislation is revisited.

Retrenchments

The retrenchment issue is probably the most spoken about but also the most misunderstood. The stark reality is that the number of public servants has declined significantly (by 12,5%) over the period of the three-year agreement. Those departments and provinces which have actively tried to cut numbers have succeeded in doing so. And a decline in numbers at the bottom-end has been accompanied by an increase in numbers in the middle-range categories, the major source of upward pressures on the total wage bill.

State representatives argue that there is a need for some employer-initiated retrenchments especially in situations where relocation is impossible or inappropriate or where there are too many senior management (often inherited from the apartheid system). Certainly there are some high-profile examples which exist where the state is paying salaries to people no longer performing any services. This is adding ammunition to general calls for cutting the size of the public service.

But it is hard not to see the 'moratorium issue' as a red herring. The moratorium on employer-initiated retrenchments has arguably been used as an excuse by some senior management (and many politicians) to avoid a right-sizing process. And from the union side the moratorium has been a Pyrrhic victory, since a focus on preventing forced retrenchments has concealed the fact that down-sizing has crept in through the back door. How, for example, can the 8,6% decline in police numbers be justified?

In reality the unions have to deal with two related, but strategically separate issues. The first relates to the range of instruments available if 'down-sizing' is contemplated. These include relocations, retraining, the size of the package, employer-initiated cuts, and all the usual mechanisms to first avoid and to then, if inevitable, implement retrenchments. The second issue, relates to shifting the debate from down-sizing to right-sizing and what employment numbers (and grading profiles) are appropriate and affordable. It is hard not to see the second aspect as more important than the issue of what instruments the employer can use. Indeed, it is probably the case that the attrition approach currently being used to down-size makes any later attempts to right-size more difficult.

Grading and training

The three-year agreement ushered in major changes in the grading system. The details, summarised earlier, included:

- consolidation of existing salaries into 16 grades, each having three salary notches
- regrading (generally upgrading) of a number of key occupations
- reduction in the number of job categories

- introduction of rank/leg promotions
- agreement on target percentage gaps between grades and notches.

Certainly the grading system is now clearer, simpler and cleaner although in practice the intended system has only been partly implemented. In 1997 the DPSA commissioned a major study on job evaluation, pay and grading. The report, prepared by consultants KPMG, recommended a range of changes. These have generally not been implemented but government has indicated its desire to re-negotiate aspects of the system of pay progression.

The KPMG report argued that there were too many occupational classes and that the difference in job content between post class levels was often unclear or non-existent. Job definition was characterised by bureaucratic complexity, and the rank promotion system was discriminatory and resulted in grade drift. There was too much emphasis on academic qualifications and overlap in the content of actual jobs performed. Rewards were linked to cost control rather than performance incentives, and linked to this, the salary ranges in each grade were too narrow and the number of notches too few. The report also argued in favour of excluding management from the bargaining unit, and keeping a national system of salaries (rather than allowing provincial differentials). And it argued that pay levels were below the market median at all grades. Key KPMG recommendations were:

- the need to consolidate related occupational classes and reduce the number of post levels within occupational classes
- having fewer grades and reducing the lowest 12 grades to 8 grades
- upgrading a number of post classes, including senior specialists and principal engineers at the top-end, and constables, sergeants, professional nurses and others at the middle and lower end of the grading system
- increasing the salary span within each grade to between 20% and 30%
- moving from three notches in each grade to nine
- reducing the pay gap between the top of one grade and the bottom of the next
- scrapping rank promotion and replacing it with post promotion
- linking pay progression (notch increases) to performance and scrapping merit awards.

There is clearly a need to review the existing system of pay progression. For example, with the three-notch system many current incumbents will soon reach the maximum of their grade. Most will have little chance of promotion to a higher grade and the result will be resentment and pay stagnation. The system introduced in 1996 was bold but clearly too simplistic. However, it is unclear how a change of the magnitude recommended by KPMG could be implemented so soon after the major changes of 1996. There will also be resistance to scrapping both rank promotions and merit awards.

The drive by prosecutors to opt out of the system is strongly suggestive of the need to review the specific grading structure in key sub-sectors. It should be possible to do this without losing the unifying transverse grading structure of the public service as a whole.

Centralisation and decentralisation of bargaining

Various government departments and provinces have their own bargaining chambers/forums and the LRA makes explicit provision for separate forums covering educators and police. However it is clear that although two levels of bargaining are contemplated, in practice the key negotiation forum is the central chamber – the PSCBC. This strong centralisation has had both positive and negative effects. The three-year agreement focused on transverse issues – such as introducing a common and simplified 16 grade system, changing the basis for salary advancement, upgrading certain occupations (notably nurses and police) within the system as a whole, and improving minimum rates.

However, it is also clear that the stress on common issues has left many details, especially those specific to particular sub-sectors, unaddressed. Government has expressed concern that the problems of more skilled personnel are being overlooked and that, as a result, the public service is struggling to retain scarce skills. The future exclusion of certain senior occupations from the bargaining unit partly addresses this concern, although largely in relation to the management echelon within the core civil service and not senior, non-management occupations in the public service as a whole.

Within employee ranks, certain categories of staff (such as prosecutors) are pressing to be excluded from the bargaining unit and see this as the route to higher pay. Part of their concern is that prosecutors' conditions are not integrated with those of other employees (such as magistrates) within the judicial sector. Further, many of the criticisms raised by KPMG regarding the grading system, are hard to address in a central bargaining forum. There may indeed be a case for a different grading structure in key sectors, such as education or health or justice, if service delivery is to be improved. And there is clearly a case for breaking with the dominance of the civil service within the public service (and to address anomalies whereby, for example, the managerial head of Chris Hani Baragwanath hospital is ranked as a director rather than seen as a specialist manager of a major, internationally-recognised institution).

Failure to deal with these challenges will place pressure on the central bargaining council. But, not surprisingly, there is union concern that if powers are devolved then the very principle of centralised bargaining may disappear too and that unions will be divided and competing sectoral interests will predominate. There is no theoretical answer to this problem and getting the balance right is always an issue in centralised bargaining. But it is hard to see how the key challenges related to reviewing, say, the systems of grading, training and pay progression can be done without significant decentralisation, at least temporarily.

The big challenge will be to find a way of decentralising while maintaining an integrating framework which maintains core transverse issues and standards across the public service as a whole. Simply maintaining a centralised approach will lead in practice to simple solutions and across-the-board increases, followed by attempts by particular sectors or occupations to opt out of the centralised forum. But the fear remains legitimate that decentralising could be the thin end of the wedge that undermines the PSCBC.

Benefits and the 'clean wage' debate

Non-wage benefits, as indicated earlier, make up one-third of government's salary bill. Some benefits (such as pension, 13th cheque and overtime pay) are generally universal. Others (notably medical and home-owner subsidies) are taken up unevenly. There is a case for moving to a 'clean' wage system where non-wage benefits are simple and universal. However, such a move will clearly be resisted by those employees currently benefiting from such arrangements, and a case could be made for trying to redesign such benefits so their effect is equal across grades.

But this is easier in theory than in practice. The medical aid subsidy is a good example. One option would be to insist that all employees join an approved medical aid. But this would be extremely expensive, would be a vote of no-confidence in the public health system, and would still require employee contributions which lower-paid employees would be unable to afford. Another option might be to remove the existing subsidy, and use the money saved to improve basic salaries. But spreading the benefits so thinly would translate into relatively little for each employee, whilst existing medical subsidy beneficiaries would lose a great deal (and resist the change strongly). A further option could be to remove the existing subsidy and use the money saved to improve other incentives or increase the resources devoted to training. Another might be to simply tolerate the inequity of the medical and home-owners subsidies in the interests of maintaining employee unity, but not increase the rand amount of these allowances, thereby eroding them over time. A final and more radical option might involve exploring the possibility of using available funds towards other methods of health care provision such as clinics or a benefit fund. Whatever the approach adopted it is clear that, since they make up a massive one-third of the wage bill, non-wage benefits require serious attention.

Another difficult aspect will be the pension issue, which alone makes up almost 40% of the non-wage total. The state's contribution was recently reduced from 17% to 15% and the state (as employer) is clearly committed to reducing it further. Reduced contributions are obviously seen as a way of saving the fiscus money and as a way of containing increases in the salary bill. But it would be shortsighted to simply look at the matter in fiscal terms. Rather the challenge is to find an affordable retirement arrangement and explore the redesign of the system itself – whether 'pay-as-you-go', defined contribution or defined benefit systems.

Fiscal pressures

The figures presented earlier suggest a major crisis is looming. There are enormous pressures on the state to reduce the wage bill. The slowdown in economic growth has increased these pressures, although the unexpected increase in tax revenues alleviates the situation slightly. Fiscal projections for the next three years are for an average 5,1% growth in the wage bill per annum – below the current inflation rate.[38] In short, the size of the additional slice to be negotiated from 1999 is substantially less than when the three-year agreement was negotiated in 1996.

Calculating the impact of agreements can be difficult. Agreed increases in basic rates are accommodated through a transfer to departments – the 'Improvements in Conditions of Service' vote. Other improvements, notably employer pension contributions, are paid for directly from the fiscus. Yet other items (such as promotions to higher salary levels, notch increases, merit awards and VSPs) must be paid for by the relevant department/province from its existing vote.

Such increases can bring pay increases to an individual of between 15 and 25%.[39] It has been estimated that about 10% of public servants in specific occupations obtain promotion to a higher salary level every year. This adds between 1% and 2% to the state's remuneration bill.[40] However, the impact can differ substantially from department to department. It is estimated that 18,3% of SAPS personnel qualify for rank/leg promotions during FY1999/2000, and 48,7% in FY2000/2001.[41] The fiscal impact therefore differs markedly.

Important to note is that a number of departments have commissioned studies which strongly advise wage restraint and include recommendations such as:

- holding down personnel costs and welfare transfers in the provinces in order to increase 'other' expenditure from its current level of 22% to 30% (as it was in FY1995/1996)
- increasing non-personnel expenditure in education to 15% by increasing total real expenditure on education by 1% per annum, keeping wage increases below inflation, and letting teacher numbers decline through attrition (and allowing the learner:educator ratio to rise)
- initiating retrenchments in order to increase the percentage of budget available for health, road maintenance and other expenditure.

At the macro-level union options are essentially limited to one (or a combination) of the following:

- Getting overall state expenditure increased or limiting cuts. This brings up related macro-economic issues such as the deficit, and the level of interest and tax rates. All are matters which fall outside the collective bargaining structures, and yet influence bargaining outcomes fundamentally.

- Pushing for real wage increases, or at least keeping up with inflation. But doing so may still mean conceding a reduction in the number of public service employees.
- Trading some non-wage issues (such as reduced employer pension contributions or medical/home-owner costs) for real increases in the basic salaries of public servants. But this postpones the fiscal problem rather than addresses it, in the hope that improved Gross Domestic Product (GDP) growth will eventually reduce the problem.
- Accepting below-inflation increases in exchange for a commitment to retain (and in some instances increase) the number of jobs in the public service. But this will face resistance from existing public servants.

None of these solutions will look appealing to the union movement. In reality there are no easy solutions. Further, as this chapter has indicated, a review of the grading system is needed. But re-grading exercises are always expensive[42] and may be resisted by the fiscus, even if fiscally necessary in the longer term. However, without long-term perspectives it may be hard to place conditions of service and human resource management in the public service on a sound footing.

8

DEMOCRATISING THE PUBLIC SERVICE

Co-determination, workplace democratisation and transformation

———— ✦ ————

Imraan Patel

The development of forms of worker participation in decision-making in the public service has been little studied and even less understood. Patel's chapter is the first analysis of this problem. The new forms of participation that have emerged in the South African economy – for example the Workplace Forums provisions of the Labour Relations Act – have suffered from a private sector bias and have been treated largely from an industrial relations perspective. This accounts for the main fear unionists hold: that they will undermine collective bargaining structures. What has been missed in much of the debate is the possibility that participation holds out for democratising work. Given that the public service is a highly integrated system of institutions, democratisation by definition extends beyond the actual office or workplace to higher-level structures in which these operate as well as the policy processes that determine their fate.

The public service is not included in the LRA's provisions for workplace forums. However this does not mean that institutions for worker participation are absent. Interesting institutional innovations – in the form of transformation committees – have in certain instances given unions wide-ranging effective co-determination powers at the enterprise level. These include, curiously, participation in governing committees and enterprise boards, rights which are not included in Chapter 5 of the LRA. Furthermore, centralised bargaining in the Public Service Co-ordinating Bargaining Council occurs over issues that extend well beyond wage-setting to qualitative 'non-distributive issues' such as work organisation, as well as the restructuring of the public service itself. It is unclear whether such practices will continue, particularly given fiscal austerity and the trend towards commercialising the public service. Nonetheless, the public service has produced a potentially robust version of engagement that could serve as a model for unions to pursue elsewhere in the economy.

In order to forge ahead with the processes of reconciliation, reconstruction and development, the South African public service will have a major role to play as the executive arm of government. To fulfil this role effectively, the service will need to be transformed into a coherent, representative, competent and *democratic* [emphasis added] instrument for implementing government policies and meeting the needs of all South Africans.

(Dept. of Public Service and Administration, 1995: 11)

INTRODUCTION

In the run-up to the 1994 elections in South Africa, the tripartite alliance (the African National Congress (ANC), the Congress of South African Trade Unions (COSATU) and the South African Communist Party (SACP)) stressed the central role that the public service had to play in addressing the ravages of South Africa's past. The alliance's election manifesto, the Reconstruction and Development Programme (RDP), recognised that the public service would be able to play such a role only if it underwent extensive transformation, and that democratisation was a central element of this transformation. The RDP noted that 'democratisation requires modernising the structures and functioning of government in pursuit of the objectives of efficient, effective, responsive, transparent and accountable government' (ANC, 1994: 120).

But what does democratisation mean, and what is the contribution of trade unions to an agenda of democratisation? The RDP and subsequent policy documents offer a wide definition of this concept. Democratisation is multidimensional and impacts on the development of public policy, the allocation of public resources, as well as the delivery of government services. Because of the influence of labour in the drafting of the RDP and earlier policy documents, it was envisaged that, for labour, democratisation would mean an appropriate role and its active participation in all three of the above processes.

To a significant extent, transformation of the public service meant changing its archaic labour relations framework. Such changes began with the finalisation of the Labour Relations Act (LRA) of 1995. For the first time in South African history, the public service was regulated by the same statute that governed labour relations in the rest of the economy. Workplace forums were a key experiment of the LRA. The forums were an attempt to give effect to the RDP's worker empowerment provisions which noted that 'legislation must facilitate worker participation and decision-making in the world of work' (ANC, 1994: 114).

The real challenge to democratise the public service started immediately after the election of the first democratic government in 1994. Democratisation, however, was a contested terrain between politicians, public service managers, communities and workers. Such competition has resulted in the establishment of a variety of institutional forms, which are somewhat unique to the public service. Yet, in the main, the workplace forum model set out in the LRA was not fully informed by these initiatives.

This chapter reviews efforts at democratisation in the public service in the period 1994 to 1999, and locates workplace forums within this context. It considers the possibilities and limitations of workplace forums as significant vehicles of democratisation and highlights anticipated developments over the next decade. Because of the evolving nature of public service democratisation, however, it can only draw tentative conclusions that will require further debate and research.

CONTEXT

One of the critical challenges confronting the newly-elected South African government in 1994 was the need to overhaul fundamentally existing labour policy. The first step in the reform process was the development of a new labour relations framework consistent with the objectives of the RDP. A Ministerial Legal Task Team was appointed in August 1994 to develop a new policy framework.

The Task Team's proposals were contained in an 'Explanatory memorandum accompanying the draft negotiating document in the form of a Labour Relations Bill'. The memorandum, which was released by the Minister of Labour in February 1995, formed the basis for negotiations between the parties within the National Economic Development and Labour Council (NEDLAC), the then-existing Public Service Bargaining Council (PSBC) and the Education Labour Relations Council (ELRC).

As part of the government's commitment to harmonise fragmented labour laws, the public service was included within the scope of the Bill. Initially the draft Bill entrenched the then-existing bargaining arrangements for the public service and therefore provided for a national bargaining council for the public service and one for the education sector (Ministry of Labour, 1995: 23). No specific mention was made of the public service in the provisions on workplace forums. To all intents and purposes, however, the Task Team believed that its proposals on workplace forums would be suitable for the public service.

As a result of the fragmentation of bargaining in the public service, the public service unions focused their demands on ensuring greater co-ordination of collective bargaining and the inclusion of the police within the scope of the Act. On both scores, the public service lobby (comprising both unions and representatives of the government as employer) was successful in having these demands met. The final Act made provision for a Public Service Co-ordinating Bargaining Council (PSCBC), as well as for the establishment of sectoral bargaining councils for educators and police. It provided, furthermore, for additional sectoral bargaining councils.

As far as workplace democratisation was concerned, the debates and negotiations that followed the release of the Explanatory Memorandum in February 1995, and the initial rejection (and later modification) of the workplace forum model, were largely led by private sector unions and management. Public service unions united with their private sector counterparts in rejecting workplace forums. Their objections were based on the legitimate fear that the forums had the potential to weaken militant and democratic unions (Von Holdt, 1995: 61). However, the public service unions failed to appreciate the single most significant safeguard available to them: legislated collective bargaining. In hindsight, these unions could have used the space created by the debate on workplace forums to raise the broader issue of public service transformation and the creation of structures and institutions that would ensure greater worker empowerment in public service institutions.

TRANSFORMATION

Prior to, and concurrent with the NEDLAC negotiations during 1995, the Ministry for Public Service and Administration was engaged in a process of finalising a White Paper on the Transformation of the Public Service. The White Paper's policy framework was significantly informed by the 'new public management' ideology that has dominated the process of civil service reform in developed and certain developing countries alike in the nineties.

The White Paper reaffirmed the importance of the public service and set out a vision for a transformed service. It outlined a comprehensive set of short-, medium- and long-term strategies. These included the devolution and decentralisation of managerial responsibility and accountability, and the introduction of new and participative organisational structures and human resource development (DPSA, 1995: 48). Although the White Paper did not provide a detailed model, it made a vague commitment to an effective role for workers and organised labour.

Workplace forums are dealt with separately. The White Paper anticipated 'that such forums will play an important role in improving efficiency and effectiveness, by providing workers with a say in the day-to-day matters which affect them' (DPSA, 1995: 71). However, it reaffirmed the dominant thinking that saw workplace forums purely in terms of labour relations, and failed to link them with the broader agenda of developing new forms of management and governance for public service institutions. There is no doubt that the new LRA in November 1996 heralded a new phase in public service labour relations. It is clear, however, that the public service was marginalised in the drawing up of the new legislation. It was not sufficiently integrated into the new statute, and labour relations reform was not effectively linked to the broader process of administrative reform.

The public service was specifically *excluded* from Section 80 of the LRA which sets out the guidelines for the establishment of workplace forums. Section 80(12) places the onus on the Minister for Public Service and Administration to regulate workplace forums in the public service through the promulgation of a separate schedule to the Act. The development of the schedule must be guided by Section 207(4) which states that the Minister *may* attach a schedule to the Act after consultation with the Public Service Co-ordinating Bargaining Council (PSCBC), the succesor to the PSBC.

According to Professor Halton Cheadle, there were no detailed provisions for the public service because:

> A task team was established to look at industrial relations issues in the public service ... unfortunately, when the drafting was completed, the public service task team had not completed its work. (Interview in Satgar, 2000: 65)

Ambivalence

At the time of writing (1999), almost three years since the proclamation of the LRA, the Minister has not yet promulgated a schedule to guide the establishment of workplace forums in the public service. The reason lies in the ambivalent attitude on the part of both government and the public service unions to the forums.

The decision not to issue a schedule was not made by the Minister alone, but was based on a recommendation made at a consultative workshop on workplace forums convened by the DPSA in August 1996. The workshop was attended by employer and employee parties of the PSBC, the ELRC and the National Negotiating Forum (NNF). It agreed that regulations for the functioning of workplace forums would only be agreed upon once the PSCBC had been established and was fully functional (Adair, personal communication).[1] Nor does it appear that any actor will place the issue on the agenda in the foreseeable future.

The reasons for this ambivalence can be explained by three inter-related issues: the particular nature of the public service and the differences and similarities in the policy-making process between public service institutions and private sector firms; the nature of collective bargaining in this sector; and administrative reform in the current transformation process.

THE NATURE OF THE PUBLIC SERVICE

The public service differs from private sector firms in a number of important respects. This impacts on the institutions that are created to give effect to workplace democracy and the design and operation of these structures.

Public service institutions are not geared towards the maximisation of profit through the production and distribution of goods and services. Instead, workers and management are required to implement government policy and to deliver social and economic services. In the case of basic services, the motivating force is the need to improve the delivery of these services to the community which includes workers, management and their families. It could be argued that workers have as much interest as management in ensuring that the institution delivers effectively since they also benefit from these services.

The effective implementation of government policy, however, does not rest solely on improvements at the institutional level. It also depends on the resources available to the institution and the regulatory framework governing its operations. Resources are allocated through a complex political process involving competing government interests, meshed with a variety of formal and informal pressures exerted by civil society, including the unions. In theory, Cabinet takes the final decisions on the allocation of resources, with Parliament playing the role of overseer.[2]

Take, for example, the issue of providing improved health services to communities through clinics. Service delivery at institutional level can be improved through a variety of measures which can be jointly determined by workers and management, for example, tailoring clinic times to facilitate access by communities. In many cases, however, improving access depends on a range of sectoral or national decision-making processes: achieving service improvement through the reallocation of resources which would allow the construction of clinics in under-served communities; the development of adequate transport systems; etc.

Workplace democratisation models geared towards improving the effectiveness of public service institutions therefore require co-ordination between workplace-level and co-determination structures or other forums at higher levels. Such structures have in fact been established at sectoral and national level. The National Health Consultative Forum and the Public Finance and Monetary Policy chamber of NEDLAC are examples of such structures at these levels. However, these need to be developed and made part of a wider programme of creating appropriate structures that operate in concert with each other. Although formalised, it is unclear to what extent these structures are indeed facilitating co-determination.

The most fascinating and challenging issue confronting the public service is the role of communities in the governance and management of institutions. The client base of the public service is communities, not simply customers. In private firms, the demand and supply of goods and services is an indicator of the success and relevance of the enterprise. For public services, especially those where government exercises a monopoly, communities cannot use purchasing power to indicate preferences. Forms of direct or indirect control of the institution by the community are desirable to ensure that the institution provides the service the community requires.

This understanding is guiding current government efforts to improve community control over public services. The most significant advances are to be found in education. The South African Schools Act 84 of 1996 (SASA) gives school governing bodies powers to hire teachers and set user fees to fund improvements in education. The Act not only blurs the definition of the primary employer of public servants, but also vests significant governance functions in parents. Education highlights important contradictions between democratic structures and the need to ensure redress and equity in a period of transformation.

Another difference between the public service and private sector firms is the identification of managers and owners for purposes of co-determination. In the current set-up, even senior institutional managers are considered to be workers. They lack the most basic of powers which renders any form of co-determination futile. Changes in public service regulations in 1999 and the isolation of senior management as a group (with individual performance contracts) in 1998 are beginning to address this weakness.

Notwithstanding the differences, there are also considerable similarities between public service workplaces and private sector institutions. Lessons learnt in the private sector can and should be tested in public services – and vice versa. Experiments in capacity-building and information disclosure, for example, are applicable across workplaces.

COLLECTIVE BARGAINING

Understanding collective bargaining is crucial in evaluating workplace forums and co-determination. Satgar and Summers separately conclude that the existence of legislated collective bargaining facilitates the separation of the relationship between workers and management into a collective bargaining channel and a co-determination channel (Satgar, 1997; Summers, 1995: 809).

One of labour's criticisms of the current LRA is its failure to provide for legislated collective bargaining. Instead, the Act relies on voluntarism to provide a general duty to bargain. This failure partly accounts for the scepticism and resistance of the union movement to workplace forums. Unions fear that in the absence of legislated bargaining the lines between bargaining and co-determination may blur. Public service unions, however, have less to fear. Centralised collective bargaining is entrenched through the establishment of the PSCBC. Furthermore, the establishment of workplace forums in the public service (including their powers and the scope of issues to be addressed) is dependent on agreement being reached in the PSCBC or a sectoral council.

The development of collective bargaining in the public service since 1994 has seen a widening of the bargaining agenda in the PSCBC. This is the result of both the relative strength of public service unions, as well as the government's commitment to progressive labour relations for its own employees (Patel, 1998). However, these favourable conditions for labour are not guaranteed. The collective bargaining process will be put under tremendous strain over the next few years as a result of the on-going program of public service reform and the adoption of a conservative macro-economic framework for South Africa.

In many respects, workplace forums are perceived as redundant in the public service. At the DPSA workshop on workplace forums in 1996, as well as at a series of workshops with hospital and health personnel,[3] participants reviewed Sections 84 and 86 of the LRA of 1995, which list the issues for consultation and joint decision-making in workplace forums. Participants concluded that issues such as mergers and transfers of ownership, export promotion and product development plans did not apply to the public service. Furthermore, because of the centralisation of personnel management in the public service at the time, many of the key co-determination issues listed in the LRA are subject to negotiation at the PSCBC. These include job grading, exemptions from collective agreements, merit increases and discretionary bonuses, education and training, partial or total 'plant' closures, disciplinary codes and procedures, affirmative action and employment equity. Finally, in several institutions, issues such as work scheduling and organisation of work are being considered by management committees, which include the union or workers. Participants felt, therefore, that the workplace forum provisions in the LRA would create structures that would consume tremendous resources on the side of both unions and government, with negligible benefits. However, changes in the regulatory framework towards decentralisation and in the collective bargaining systems are changing these parameters. Labour may therefore have to reconsider its position on the creation of workplace forums in the public service.

The LRA makes provision for sectoral bargaining councils. The precise demarcation of powers between sectoral councils and the PSCBC has not been fully resolved. The finalisation of the constitution of the PSCBC provides the foundation upon which sectoral powers can be more clearly defined. An analysis of the National Negotiating Forum (for police) and the ELRC (for educators) reveals significant potential for union input into policy in the sectoral bargaining councils. The PSBC, as the bargaining council for the remainder of the public service, was more limited in straddling the divide between collective bargaining and policy issues. Alternative structures of participation, however, have emerged. The widespread dissatisfaction and strike action by nurses in the wake of the wage settlement in the second half of 1995 led to the establishment of the National Consultative Health Forum (NCHF) to deal specifically with the problems in the health sector. The NCHF was described by the Minister of Health as the first step towards a 'structured co-operative relationship' to deal with the many problems in this sector (Dlamini Zuma, 1995: 4).

On paper, sectoral bargaining allows unions a voice in policy-making. To ensure that this voice is not silenced, the public service unions will need to see that sectoral bargaining councils' role in policy matters is entrenched as a part of collective agreements at the PSCBC level. This will also encourage the adoption of a common approach across sectors.

Since 1994, the nature of bargaining has shifted towards establishing appropriate frameworks in addition to bargaining about actual levels of wages and conditions of service. This will facilitate greater decision-making at sectoral and workplace levels and assist the introduction of forms of worker participation. For example, the previous grading system was managed through a system of Personnel Administration Standards (PASs). Individual PASs were developed centrally for each of the more than 300 occupations in the public service. The PAS specified in detail the measures that applied to a particular occupational group, including a detailed description of the tasks that could be performed by members of a particular occupational class. The PAS has been identified as a major obstacle to organising work for effective service delivery and human resource development. The introduction of a new 16-band grading system, and the replacement of the prescriptive PASs with an instrument that is more advisory, known as Codes of Remuneration (COREs), are recent attempts to address the problems.

It is anticipated that centrally-determined competency levels will be introduced. A common job evaluation tool has been adopted at central level. Departments, provinces and, in many cases, institutions, will then be required to develop an appropriate work organisation model and to grade individual workers. These developments will hasten the need for the development of a workplace forum – or other appropriate co-determination structures – to enable workers to intervene in, and monitor, the application of these policies.

ADMINISTRATIVE REFORM

The public service inherited by the new government was hierarchical, centralised and, as a consequence, inefficient. It was designed to cater for the needs of a white minority and a small black elite (DPSA, 1996).

The public service is currently managed by the Public Service Act (Act 111 of 1984). This prescribes that the Minister for Public Service and Administration will be responsible for developing policy on employment and conditions of service of public servants. It further demarcates the public service into departments and provinces and provides for executing authorities and heads of departments.

In 1994, the Government of National Unity (GNU) also started a process of reforming the legislative framework governing the public service. The first phase of this process concentrated on the creation of a single, unified public service and the removal of specific discriminatory clauses, for example, the distinction between officers (mainly white, high-ranking civil servants) and employees (mainly black, lower-skilled workers). The second phase was aimed at transferring executive functions from the Public Service Commission (PSC) to the Minister for Public Service and Administration and the establishment of the DPSA. The PSC now performs the role of overseeing and monitoring in the public service as a whole. The Public Service Act of 1984 was amended to give greater responsibility to executing officers (Ministers) and Heads of Departments (Directors-General). There is strong support for completely rewriting the legislation to ensure that it is more coherent and transformative. This is envisaged to be the next phase of reform (Adair and Albertyn, Chapter 5).

Progressive unions, such as the National Education Health and Allied Workers' Union (NEHAWU), support the general thrust towards decentralisation if it is geared towards greater community participation, service delivery and human resource development (COSATU, 1997).

Decentralisation will not occur overnight because of constraints on capacity and the need to develop appropriate systems. International experience shows that it can take ten to twenty years. These cases point towards a phased process of devolving authority and responsibility. Specific milestones need to be defined for the delegation of further powers. Institutions will have to meet the performance measures detailed in the preceding step, which include the existence of certain competencies as well as systems. The Department of Health has established pilot projects in a handful of major regional hospitals to test and develop the process of decentralisation.

The devolution process offers a unique opportunity to ensure workplace democratisation. Just as the existence of proper financial systems will be a requirement for decentralisation, unions should ensure that the existence of effective worker representation is also a prerequisite. Such an approach will need to be coupled with training programmes to facilitate the development of the knowledge base amongst workers.

The old PSBC was unable to deal effectively with these policy issues. The creation of appropriate structures through which unions could influence the direction of the transformation process at the macro level has been the subject of debate since early 1994, leading to a proposal by NEHAWU for the establishment of a Public Service Forum (PSF). The PSF was an attempt to create a 'separate forum to negotiate policy and restructuring issues' (Collins, 1994: 25) to curtail the power of conservative unions in the public service. The PSF would embrace unions, government departments, and community and political organisations.

According to NEHAWU, the forum was never established 'because of the resistance of the reactionary forces in the public service and political unwillingness of the Ministry for Public Service and Administration' (NEHAWU, 1996). Progress was made in October 1995 when the White

Paper proposed the setting up of a Public Service Transformation Forum (PSTF).

Concrete plans to establish such a forum were only developed by the DPSA a year later, in September 1996. However, the plans did not take into account developments since 1994, specifically the establishment and functioning of NEDLAC. However, changed conditions have rendered the need for such a forum obsolete.

The White Paper also proposed the development of Transformation Units (TUs) in departments and provinces. The TUs would not have decision-making powers but would act as facilitating organs of transformation. The DPSA specifically stated that organised labour would only be represented indirectly through unionised staff members, and not as unions per se (DPSA, 1997). These proposals were guidelines to assist departments and provinces. Initial outside evaluation of TUs shows that, in many cases, they have become parallel management structures with an undefined mandate which do not function in a focused and strategic fashion. In addition, they are also elite-driven with little or no active involvement by lower-level workers and unions (Patel, 1998).

Concurrent with the establishment of TUs, institutional managers and workers at hundreds of institutions have taken the initiative and established structures and processes. There has been no systematic assessment of the extent of such developments, of their detailed method of operation, their successes and failures, or of their impact on unions.

PUSHING THE LIMITS

Democratising a public service that employs almost 1,1 million people spread over many thousands of workplaces is no easy task. The task is further complicated by the diversity of workplaces, external political forces, and an intense transformation project. However, it offers considerable opportunities for democratising society.

Successful democratisation will need to ensure effective co-ordination between the policy process and the processes of management and governance. Furthermore, it requires co-ordination between democratisation initiatives aimed at the workplace and those aimed at sectoral and national levels.

Workers in public service workplaces are confronted by three types of structural change:

- First, the LRA facilitates co-determination through workplace forums. Some time has passed since the new Act came into operation, however, and the movement towards workplace forums has been negligible.
- Second, departments and provinces are moving towards greater decentralisation of management authority. However, some elements of decentralisation have already begun, for example, the development of institutional governing structures (such as hospital boards), as well as forums to facilitate the participation of stakeholders (such as community policing forums).
- Third, TUs and committees have been suggested to address the specific challenge of transformation. While a detailed evaluation has not been conducted, it can be reasonably concluded that neither management nor the unions has sufficient capacity to play an effective role in these structures. The creation of alternative, and possibly competing structures does not facilitate effective co-ordination.

Since government owns public services, the scope for a management model that facilitates workplace democratisation is greatest in public institutions. Satgar (2000) suggests that the workplace forum model can be used to develop autonomous self-management in South Africa. He further suggests that the public service be used as a model that can later be extended to workplaces across the economy. At the current juncture, widespread autonomous self-management may not be possible. Unions will need to explore capacity issues and assess the possibilities that will be created by changes in the regulatory framework to identify possibilities for experimenting with autonomous self-management.

Significant opportunities do exist, however, for unions to advance experiments at specific institutions, particularly those being managed by former unionists. For example, at one time the regional chairperson of the South African Democratic Teachers' Union (SADTU) in the Eastern Cape was also the principal of a school, and the general secretary of the Health Workers' Union (HWU) was the superintendent of a major regional hospital in the Western Cape. Whether or not it is 'politically correct', or in line with values nurtured during the struggle for democracy, a significant number of new managers are open to ideas of workplace democratisation and worker participation. Progressive unions should be able to build on relationships with innovative managers and use these institutions as pilots to develop new forms of managing public services.

Pilot projects need to be sufficiently resourced to improve their chances of success, and unions should be central in this process:

> Employees in single workplaces lack the expertise, capacities, and organisational strength to engage in struggles to change the workplace. Only the organisational power and resources of the union will enable workers to make a real difference.
>
> (Von Holdt, 1995: 59)

The need for capacity on both sides to service co-determination is essential. Buhlungu (1998 and 2000) notes that union capacity has four related aspects: structural and organisational; strategic; financial and administrative. Weaknesses in any of these aspects can negatively affect the initiative to democratise.

Pilot projects need to be evaluated regularly. The evolution of co-determination and other models of worker participation will require documentation, analysis and research. Public service unions need to put into place effective short-, medium- and long-term research programmes that will focus on appropriate institutional forums, the development of union capacity, the effective participation of communities, and the impact on service delivery (Kester and Pinaud, 1994).

One of the key requirements for effective democratisation of public services is the role of communities. In the former Yugoslavia, self-management had been extended since 1953 to non-economic activities such as public administration, education, health and social security services, and scientific institutions. Unlike other undertakings, users were represented alongside workers (ILO, 1981: 51). Given the existence of diverse interests within communities and the skewed distribution of power, unions need to be at the forefront in demanding the effective inclusion of previously marginalised groups.

A potential obstacle to effective worker involvement in the management of public service institutions is that of multi-unionism. Historical conflicts between unions have rendered co-operation at workplace level extremely difficult. Structures which take current realities into account will need to be crafted. At Hillbrow Hospital in Gauteng, for example, an RDP/Transformation Committee was established in 1996. It included NEHAWU, Hospital Personnel of South Africa (HOSPERSA), the South African Democratic Nurses' Union (SADNU), and several other unions, with each organisation represented by two delegates (Mazibuko, 1996: 24). In many workplaces, however, co-operation between unions may not be possible and may even heighten existing tension between unions.

Workplace democratisation is difficult to attain, and requires more discussion within the union movement. The area of greatest influence in the short-term is democratisation at the sectoral and national level. Sectoral bargaining councils offer significant opportunities for worker involvement in policy-making. Public service unions need to evaluate the successes and limitations of the ELRC and the NNF in terms of influencing the policy process. This should inform the debate on the distribution of powers between the PSCBC and sectoral bargaining councils, as well as the demarcation of further sectors as bargaining councils. Such an assessment will need to review union capacity, employer organisation and participation in sectoral bargaining councils, and the relationship of the sectoral bargaining council to the central bargaining process.

The public finance and monetary policy chamber of NEDLAC has a potentially substantial influence on the public service. This avenue is not being used effectively to advance democratisation and transformation of the public service. Workplace experiences need to be communicated effectively to union representatives at NEDLAC to ensure the necessary co-ordination between macro-level reform and workplace initiatives.

CONCLUSION

The introduction of workplace forums in the LRA places the issue of co-determination and the broader issue of worker participation on the industrial relations agenda. In the public service, co-determination can be expanded beyond the industrial relations arena into the realm of broader political power where it can encourage more inclusive and effective methods of management and governance.

The provisions of the LRA focus on the workplace and a limited co-determination agenda. Public service institutions that offer greater scope for democratisation need to be understood and developed. To succeed, 'unions first need to define what they see as worker participation, in terms of both structures and content, outside of their traditional forms of engagement with management. Then they need to develop a broad strategy that encompasses this definition (and which includes workplace forums).' (See Godfrey et al, 2000.)

Any initiatives being taken by 'progressive' and labour-friendly institutional managers to introduce alternative management models need to be supported by labour, especially at the regional and national levels of the unions. To ensure continuation beyond the term of office of the 'charismatic' leadership, workplace democratisation efforts must be formalised through agreements, entrenched by the establishment of appropriate structures, and sustained through the development of the capacity of workers and their unions.

There is an urgent need for unions to develop positions on decentralisation and ensure that workplace democratisation becomes a central element in these initiatives. Decentralisation will require a strengthening of the policy process at the sectoral and national level, for example, in the establishment of minimum central norms and standards. A clear union position on decentralisation can also feed into the process of reaching agreement at the PSCBC on workplace forums.

Finally – as researchers often argue – there is an urgent need for further research into this important area. Specific areas for immediate investigation include:

- The role and attitude of managers (senior policy-makers as well as institutional managers) on co-determination, autonomous self-management, etc., with particular emphasis on the views and opinions of managers employed during the apartheid era, as compared to the views and opinions of managers appointed after 1994;
- The role of community organisations in the functioning of public service institutions, including an evaluation of structures such as community policing forums, Parent/Teacher Associations (PTAs), Parent/Teacher/Student Associations (PTSAs) and hospital governing structures;
- The development and extent of alternative management models in the public service, a description of these models and an analysis of their strengths and weaknesses;
- The experience of Transformation Units and their potential to play a role in democratising policy formulation, resource allocation and the delivery of services in departments and provinces.

The public service has great potential to live up to the principles of democratisation expressed in the RDP and subsequent policy documents. It may play a path-breaking role in developing democratic practices more broadly in the economy. Successful democratisation will be important, not only for its own sake, but also for achieving effective transformation of the old apartheid state and for ensuring improved delivery of services to the population as a whole. Realising this potential, however, will be no easy task for unions or for managers in the public service. It will be an area to be closely monitored and further researched in years to come.

9

LABOUR RELATIONS IN EDUCATION

———— ✦ ————

Philippa Garson

The next two chapters use case studies to analyse many of the larger issues of public service labour relations. Garson surveys the rapid transformation of labour relations in education, which in the late 1980s and early 1990s was a centre of labour struggle. In the 1990s, however, the sector witnessed rapid unionisation and the establishment of formal labour rights in 1993 and the establishment of collective bargaining in the Education Labour Relations Council (ELRC).

Despite major differences between teacher unions in recent years greater co-operation has developed between the South African Democratic Teachers Union (SADTU) and the National Professional Teachers' Organisation of South Africa (NAPTOSA), as suggested by their united front and joint action in the 1999 wage negotiations.

Despite significant improvements through ELRC, neither the teacher unions nor management is satisfied with the balance between issues to be pursued in the sectoral chamber and those to be bargained in the Public Service Co-ordinating Bargaining Council (PSCBC). In the PSCBC detailed consideration of the education sector is not possible, and white employee interests are prominent due to the influence of the Public Servants Association. But by participating teacher unions are able to bargain for a bigger slice of the pie from the outset.

SADTU's relationship with the African National Congress (ANC) has brought advantages, but at the cost of its leaders becoming perceived as having a 'cosy' relationship with their 'comrades' in government. The tension in the relationship derives from the government's macro-economic policy, Growth, Employment and Redistribution (GEAR), and the impact of fiscal discipline on education.

Meanwhile transformation in the education sector is not only a matter of education policy but also affects the quality of teachers' jobs. The changes create confusion and demoralisation and threaten to sidetrack consideration of the content of education reforms. At the same time curricular changes expose inadequacies in teachers' skills, and the inability of the government to provide appropriate training. More than other sectors – save for the police – teachers have had to interrogate the legacy of militance that brought gains against the apartheid government. Transformation imposes constraints on their freedom of action in a sector that is constantly in the public spotlight.

Democratisation has thus created considerable space for union involvement in policy formulation. These possibilities, however, bring with them new responsibilities, with which the unions must come to grips. If things go wrong, fingers will be pointed in their direction.

INTRODUCTION

Until 1993, the National Party government shunned the more progressive teacher unions. The largely white, more conservative teacher organisations relied on their informal 'hotline' to the education minister's office to win concessions. The mainly black teacher unions had no way of airing their grievances – let alone of negotiating reform. All this has changed. The largest teacher union, the South African Democratic Teacher's Union (SADTU), won recognition in 1993 and the subsequent establishment of the Education Labour Relations Council (ELRC) ushered in a new era in labour relations where the progressive unions began to play a pivotal role in formulating education policies. Teachers have won significant labour rights, indicating a radical break with the oppressive workplace environment of the past.

Whereas spontaneous militancy in the early 1990s was enough to force change, informed, research-driven policy is now called for if unions are to deal effectively with the rationalisation agenda of the state. A feature of the post-apartheid era is the ongoing and rapid transition that is taking place in the broader public service. Major changes to labour relations will continue to occur for some time, with the powers and functions of structures like the Public Service Co-ordinating Bargaining Council (PSCBC) – where matters pertinent to the entire public service are bargained – still undetermined.

While the transitional period has seen greater co-operation between the different teacher unions, it has also given rise to new challenges posed by the changing relationship between government and SADTU. On the one hand, SADTU's close ties to government have been to its advantage. However, union leadership has had to confront the problem of dislocation from its grassroots support base, exacerbated by its perceived 'cosy' relationship with former 'comrades' in government.

SADTU is also having to navigate new paths in a terrain of shifting government policy. The Reconstruction and Development Programme (RDP) has been replaced by the Growth, Employment and Redistribution strategy (GEAR), which places less emphasis on redistribution and more on fiscal discipline and rationalisation. GEAR is having a direct impact on education, with redeployment of teachers increasingly translating into the freezing of posts. Furthermore, education generally is engaged in massive transition: the new curriculum, racial integration of classrooms and bigger class sizes are contributing to stressful working conditions for teachers.

This chapter looks at how the current labour dynamics came into being, how they are being played out in the ELRC and the challenges that lie ahead for the unions:

- section one charts the history of teacher struggles, culminating in the establishment of the ELRC
- section two examines the increasingly complex dynamics governing education labour relations by analysing key ELRC agreements
- section three looks at the financial constraints on education and suggests a way forward for SADTU.

THE HISTORY OF TEACHER STRUGGLES

Before 1994, teacher struggles were closely allied to the broader battles waged against the apartheid state. Protest action by teachers elicited the familiar, iron-fisted response from the government. Until the 1980s, repressive legislation effectively silenced protest: mere criticism of the government or education department by a black teacher could lead to dismissal. White teachers were also kept in line: they were compelled to register with recognised teachers' organisations and were barred from criticising any state department. According to Logan Govender, in *When the Chalks are Down*, white teachers had, however:

relatively little to complain about [regarding] working conditions and school facilities when compared with their black colleagues, a state of affairs that might account for the apparent absence of white teacher militancy. (Govender, 1996: 33)

The powerful white Teachers' Federal Council (TFC), formed in 1987, but with roots that stretch back to the 1920s, had a 'hotline' to the Minister of Education's office. Roger Falcon, executive officer of the ELRC, points out that:

Labour relations pre-1993 were not regulated in any way. It was a loose consultative process largely between predominantly white teacher organisations that took place at a political and consultative level. The TFC, the driving force behind the smaller associations, could access and lobby government at a very high level. Because of their political affiliations they had direct access to the President. (January 1997: interview)

A strong divide has always existed between those (mainly African) teachers who have pursued trade union-like, mass-action struggles, and those teachers who have defined themselves as middle-class professionals and pushed for change through negotiation and lobbying. Progressive versus moderate viewpoints continue to split the teaching corps today, although the moderates are increasingly showing a readiness to embark on industrial action, as shown by the united action in August 1999 when most unions embarked on a protest against the government's wage settlement for public servants. They have, however, traditionally been opposed to 'any action which is not in the interests of the child, the parent, the school or the country – action which can result in a tremendous wastage of desperately needed and scarce funds for education,' according to a TFC press statement in *The Citizen* in October 1990.

Progressive teachers have argued that the exploitative conditions under which black teachers have been forced to work have eroded their rights and dignity, undermined their professional status and prevented them from teaching properly. The state took full advantage of this ideological divide, strengthening the position of the moderates by granting their associations recognition and at times conceding to some of their demands, while crushing the first signs of resistance from the more radical teachers.

Organising

The 1976 Soweto uprising and exploding education crises led to the growing politicisation of black teachers and drew stronger lines between 'militant' and 'conservative' teachers. Many young, black teachers openly supported the student protests. From 1980, they began to form their own progressive teacher organisations, including the National Education Union of South Africa (NEUSA), the first non-racial teacher organisation, which affiliated to the United Democratic Front (UDF) in 1983. From 1985, when political struggle began to intensify countrywide, a string of progressive unions emerged, triggering rapid repression by the state. NEUSA was banned, other unions were placed under restriction, and many teachers were detained.

Govender argues that the repressive climate of the 1980s led to an ideological shift amongst many teachers, who began to align themselves with the working class 'which provided the mass component of the liberation struggle' (Govender, 1996: 36). Up until this time, teacher organisations, even the progressive ones, were racially-based, largely because the conditions under which they taught were vastly different. By the early 1980s, the state had set up the Research Committee on Education Structures (RECES). This was a loose, consultative body, which was initially boycotted by progressive black organisations. By the early 1990s, it had become the forum where key labour policy decisions were made, with all organisations on board.

The National Education Crisis Committee (NECC) was formed in 1985, raising the question of teacher unity. Divisions between progressive and moderate teachers remained a stumbling block and the state crackdown on progressive leaders also fragmented organisations. The signing of the Harare Accord on Teacher Unity in April 1988 paved the way for real unity. Facilitated by the Congress of South African Trade Unions (COSATU), progressive and moderate groups (barring the white teacher associations) came together in the National Teachers Unity Forum (NTUF). Some of the English-speaking associations took part in unity talks but the Afrikaans-speaking groups were strongly opposed to the idea.

The more open political climate of 1990 gave teachers the space to highlight their grievances. New unions sprang up around the country. NEUSA organised a strike in March in the Transvaal and teacher organisations – many from the traditionally moderate groups – held rallies and marches. In April 1990, the NTUF launched a national campaign for a single, non-racial, non-sexist education system. Other demands included improved conditions in schools, conditions of service like gender parity, the suspension of inspections and a Teachers' Bill of Rights (Govender, 1996: 40).

SADTU

SADTU was officially launched in October 1990, with 18 affiliates and over 100 000 members. According to former SADTU president, and now Minister of Labour, Membathisi Mdladlana, the union's main aim was to 'eradicate apartheid and vigorously strive towards a free, non-racial, non-sexist, compulsory and democratic single education system' (*The Star*, 10/1990). SADTU also stressed its commitment to upgrading teachers, maintaining high professional standards and negotiating with the Minister of National Education (and not the other departments) for a single ministry.

Cracks in this unprecedented unity soon showed, however. Moderate teacher associations pulled out in protest against the new union's alliance with the ANC, believing that teacher organisations should remain politically non-aligned. These divisions persisted, with further dispute over whether SADTU should be a federation or a unitary body. The progressive organisations believed a union that affiliated to COSATU would be far more effective in fighting against 'long working hours, low wages, job insecurity and victimisation' (Govender, 1996: 41). The moderates believed affiliation would marginalise the professional interests of teachers; they were also suspicious of SADTU's trade union-like identity and baulked at the idea of going on strike. In August 1991, the National Professional Teachers' Organisation of South Africa (NAPTOSA) was launched as a federation of the moderate organisations. It committed itself to being a non-racial, non-political body that would promote the professional interests of teachers.

Meanwhile, the comparatively professional nature of SADTU's membership posed new challenges for COSATU when affiliation finally took place in November 1993. Beforehand, COSATU's general secretary, Jay Naidoo, played down differences, pointing to the recent protests as indicative of teachers' militant stance. 'Teachers are, in any case, workers,' he said. 'Despite their professional status, African teachers in some categories are paid less than minimums that have been negotiated for labourers by COSATU unions' (*New Nation*, 29/6/1990).

From its inception, SADTU faced obstacles from the National Party government. According to Govender (1996):

> SADTU's effort in the late 1980s and early 1990s revolved around building the union and gaining recognition. The union encountered serious obstacles from government as it struggled to organise in schools.

From 1990 to 1993, protest actions by teachers exploded with spontaneous intensity. Public demonstrations, marches, rallies, strikes, picketing, occupations and the expulsion of officials were all used to highlight grievances. In 1990, prior to the launch of SADTU, most militant action was taken by relatively unknown teacher organisations. In 1991, SADTU was consolidating its structures on the ground and contending with new divisions as a result of the formation of NAPTOSA. In 1992 and 1993, protest was primarily SADTU-driven. In 1993, strikes or 'chalks down', were, for the first time, the most prevalent form of protest. Racially-based education departments (particularly the Department of Education and Training (DET)) were usually the targets. However, inspectors and principals were also at the receiving end. The main demands were improved conditions of service and conditions in schools, salaries, stopping victimisation of protesting teachers, one education department, a resolution to the education crisis and a halt to rationalisation; and recognition of SADTU (Govender, 1996: 56).

Grievances

Working long hours with low salaries in ill-equipped, over-crowded classrooms were problems African teachers had experienced for decades. Resentment had long been simmering over poor conditions of service, such as the fact that teachers were employed by the DET in temporary positions for more than ten years. Principals and department officials were regarded as autocratic and disciplinarian. Evaluations for promotion by inspectors were seen as unjust and nepotistic and were vehemently rejected, with inspectors being chased out of schools during SADTU's national defiance campaign in the 1990s. According to Ella Mokgalane, an Education Policy Unit (EPU) researcher:

> Teachers rejected any form of evaluation by inspectors, subject advisors, principals and heads of departments. In some areas … teachers went to the extent of burning their scheme books and lesson preparation files provided by the DET. Consequently the country experienced the collapse of the teacher evaluation system in almost all the provinces. To this day, there is virtually no system of teacher appraisal or evaluation in place in most black schools in the country. (Mokgalane, 1997: interview)

Low salaries and the non-payment of salaries were ongoing grievances. The Department of Education's refusal to recognise SADTU from 1990 to 1993, despite their long-standing recognition of the moderate teacher associations, was a major contributing factor. Abortive attempts at negotiations with education departments resulted in more protest. During these years of resistance, teachers involved were frequently fired, suspended or transferred.

While teacher militancy at first met with approval by others taking up issues with the state, there was also much opposition on the grounds that students, rather than the employer, suffered most. This came initially from parents and Africanist political organisations, but SADTU's own political allies soon added their voice.

A two-week long strike in August 1993 for a minimum wage, salary increases and a halt to rationalisation, sparked widespread criticism from parents, learners, political organisations and the general public. Mdladlana conceded that threatened assaults by some parents and learners on teachers were a factor in bringing the strike to an end. Many learners supported teacher strikes, but resented the lack of consultation and the random, spontaneous nature of the protest action (Govender, 1996: 65). There were also numerous reports of intimidation by SADTU members of teachers aligned to the more moderate organisations. This heady period also saw deepening divisions between SADTU and some NAPTOSA affiliates.

The National Education and Training Forum and the ELRC

The short-lived National Education and Training Forum (NETF) was established in late 1993. It comprised all major stakeholders in education and was meant to deal with immediate crises such as looming teacher retrenchments, and longer-term policy issues such as curricula change, teacher training, restructuring the education system and combining the nineteen education departments into one. The NETF did succeed in facilitating an agreement between SADTU and the House of Representatives over proposed teacher retrenchments in 1993 and the contracts of affected teachers were extended to the end of that year. It soon became redundant, however, when the Government of National Unity took over and created a single education department, with nine provincial sub-departments.

The NETF's greatest success was in regulating labour relations in the sector. SADTU was finally recognised by the DET and by the other education departments. Legislation granting basic labour rights to teachers came about when the Education Labour Relations Act (ELRA) was passed in October 1993. The Act granted teachers the right to strike after following certain procedures, and provided for the establishment of a permanent bargaining council, the Education Labour Relations Council (ELRC), to negotiate wages and working conditions, provide for dispute resolution mechanisms and advise the State President on education labour relations. The ELRC went a long way toward containing and managing conflict once it was established.

The ELRA also gave employers the right to lock-out, adopted the 'no work, no pay' principle whether a strike was legal or not and allowed teachers to strike for 30 days without being fired. This was on the condition that the teachers' industrial action complied with established industrial relations procedures: teachers were entitled to go on strike only after a deadlock had been declared in writing and 30 days had passed between declaring the deadlock and the beginning of the strike. A strike ballot was required to demonstrate that most teachers wanted to strike, and written notice of the ballot result was to be given to the employer seven days before the strike commenced (South African Institute of Race Relations (SAIRR), 1993/1994: 722).

NAPTOSA was supportive of separate labour legislation for teachers, but SADTU, in line with COSATU's position that all workers (including those in the public sector) should be brought together under the same labour law, regarded the ELRA as temporary. NAPTOSA, however, voiced strong opposition to teachers being incorporated into the public service, and even threatened strike action over this issue in July 1994.

LABOUR RELATIONS UNDER A DEMOCRATIC GOVERNMENT

In the past, teachers were primarily fighting against apartheid education and their lack of basic rights as workers. In the more complex transitional climate, labour issues are debated in the more tempered, co-operative environment of the ELRC. Nonetheless GEAR's impact on education presents new difficulties for the unions.

The Education Labour Relations Council

Since its inception in March 1994, the ELRC has functioned as the collective bargaining forum in which the state and representative teacher organisations (SADTU, NAPTOSA and some smaller unions) hammer out agreements on both conditions of service and policy issues. Between 1994 and 1996, the ELRC adopted 38 resolutions on a wide a range of issues affecting teachers (one special resolution was adopted in 1993). The ELRC was established separately from the then-existing Public Service Bargaining Council (PSBC), specifically because of the unique conditions of service facing teachers. With the promulgation of the new Labour Relations Act (LRA) in November 1996, the ELRC stopped functioning in terms of the 1993 ELRA and began operating in terms of the LRA.

Although SADTU, as a COSATU affiliate, supports the establishment of one bargaining chamber to streamline salaries and conditions of service for all public sector employees, the union has a solid 66% majority in the ELRC, and is an influential voice within that body. Along with other COSATU-aligned unions in the public service, it stands to lose this influence if it must bargain exclusively in the PSCBC against the powerful Public Servants Association.

Under the ELRA, nine provincial bargaining chambers were to have been set up to ratify agreements in the national chamber and negotiate issues pertaining to the particular provinces. By mid-June 1998, only three were up and running: in Gauteng, the Western Cape and KwaZulu-Natal.

The successes and failures, strengths and weaknesses, of the ELRC are up for discussion. Most key players in the council point to the absence of significant teacher strikes since 1993 as proof of its relative success. However, key agreements, which granted salary increases in return for equity-driven rationalisation (amounting to the redeployment of teachers from richer to poorer schools), were badly implemented by the provincial education departments. In practice, the controversial redeployment policy has translated into the rationalisation of teacher posts in the absence of any large-scale redistribution of teachers.

Right-sizing

Both SADTU and NAPTOSA have continuously expressed great dissatisfaction with the way that right-sizing of the public service is being applied to teachers. The idea that salary increases can be funded by 'right-sizing' – cutting the number of teachers – has a negative impact on the education sector. It does not ensure that teachers with the right qualifications and experience (such as mathematics and science teachers who are in short supply) are employed where they are most needed. SADTU has warned of the detrimental long-term effects of the government's macro-economic strategies on both the teaching corps and education generally and has called for a significant increase in state spending on education.

Centralised public service bargaining may not work to the advantage of teachers. While teachers make up a significant proportion of public sector workers (380 000 of 1,2 million in 1997) they may not be able to influence significantly bargaining which does not take into account the specificities of the education sector. On the other hand, they may be able to bargain for a bigger slice of the state pie from the outset, rather than having to negotiate in the ELRC from a position of an already-determined budget. It is this situation that allows state negotiators to say time and again, 'That is all we can afford.'

Improvements

It is clear that the ELRC has led to tremendous improvement for teachers. Kenny Govender, Deputy Director of Labour Relations in the national Department of Education and former SADTU official, says: 'The ELRC created a vehicle for change. It gave all role players a direct say in salary issues and other conditions of service. Now, no party can act without the necessary negotiations before implementing changes' (1997: interview).

In the early days, negotiations in the ELRC were antagonistic, exacerbated by the different approaches and levels of expertise of the two main teacher organisations. NAPTOSA had long experience in salary negotiations; SADTU negotiators were classroom-based teachers. Kenny Govender notes, however, that:

> There has been a gradual shift in terms of attitudes, which are now far less confrontational. There is more co-operation, more bilaterals take place between the teacher organisations and there seems to be more common understanding and working together. Furthermore, politics has been taken out of negotiations, which are now purely addressing teacher concerns. (Ibid.)

SADTU General Secretary, Thulas Nxesi, describes the establishment of the ELRC as:

> ... a victory for teachers. The Council introduced collective bargaining into the education arena. For the first time teacher unions were able to negotiate at a central level the issues affecting their members both individually and collectively. (1997: 32)

Rationalisation

The unions now realise that ELRC Resolution 3 of 1996, the core agreement around education rationalisation, was not entirely in teachers' interests. The resolution introduced broad-banding to teacher salary scales and the concept of performance-related pay. Broad-banding involves decreasing the number of salary 'notches' and separating salaries from the problematic 'paper chase' qualifications which led to automatic salary increases that bore no relation to the actual quality of teaching.

Given their comparatively high qualifications compared with other public sector employees, teachers were slotted into the new salary scales at a relatively high level. This led to significant wage increases for the lowest paid teachers. Kate Skinner, SADTU's former media liaison officer, noted that 'broad-banding has condensed the number of notches and benefited the bottom end by as much as a 40% salary increase, with no teacher receiving less than a 12%' (1997, interview). This 'bottom end' of mainly black teachers makes up a considerable proportion of SADTU's membership. Skinner added that 'teachers have been relatively calm because of this agreement,' which also made provision for inflationary increases for the following two years.

The state was, however, unable to honour the commitment to substantial increases set out in the three-year agreement (see Baskin, Chapter 7). SADTU, along with the National Education, Health and Allied Workers Union (NEHAWU) and the Police and Prisons Civil Rights Union (POPCRU), declared a dispute in the PSCBC around the three-year wage agreement, however this did not lead to a strike nor to any substantial concessions from government.

Furthermore, the 'trade off' part of the resolution – that better salaries would mean fewer teachers – had begun to kick in by late 1996, leading to the realisation that the state intended cutting back on teacher numbers. The teacher organisations then requested that key agreements reached at the ELRC be referred back for re-negotiation.

The state effectively overruled the policy of national norms and standards for pupil:teacher ratios in December 1997 and subsequently declared that teacher numbers would be decided by provinces according to what their budgets would allow. In a show of unprecedented unity, all unions prepared to strike in June 1998 to prevent this, with SADTU embarking on a week of go-slow action. In the face of the united teacher body, the state withdrew the controversial amendments, and all parties joined in re-negotiating new rationalisation and redeployment agreements. The new agreement saw the unions playing a much bigger part in the education budgetary process, but they did not appear to alter the financial constraints imposed on provinces by the Department of Finance. The unions' role, while intended to bring more sensitivity on the part of the government to the specific problems in education, effectively meant the unions' buy-in to government's rationalisation agenda.

The favourable aspects of the 1996 agreement – salary increases, coupled with other improvements to working conditions like the restructuring of pensions, medical aid and extending home-ownership schemes to married women teachers – convinced the teacher organisations to accept the whole agreement. The salary hikes were carrots the unions could not shun. SADTU had a somewhat different view and claimed the government breached 'the spirit of the agreement'. Union officials complained that they were 'duped' by government; they felt betrayed by the way in which rationalisation was being implemented by the provincial departments.

The unravelling of Resolution 3 signalled the end of the brief 'honeymoon' between the government and SADTU. However, the parties still showed that they were able to negotiate. Some believe that the government has become adept at using delaying tactics and predict that the same breaches of trust which occurred around the implementation of Resolution 3 of 1996 will happen again. In the future, the union needs to prepare itself better in the form of extensive, forward-looking policy research and guard against too close a relationship with the state. This may be a difficult task, in view of the fact that many former SADTU leaders have become government officials.

Redeployment

While the national Department of Education sets guidelines, the provinces – who are the actual employers – must implement rationalisation. ELRC Resolution 4 of 1995 specified a ratio of 40 pupils:1 teacher in primary schools and 35 pupils:1 teacher in secondary schools. In the face of severe budget cuts, the provinces were, according to SADTU, implementing these ratios in a random and incoherent way. New ratios were imposed without accounting for teachers who did not have classrooms of their own, and indispensable teachers were declared redundant (Skinner, 1997: interview). SADTU requested renewed negotiations around the ratios in the ELRC, and proposed that ratios be based instead on teacher workloads.

The implementation of the agreement on voluntary severance packages (VSPs), which were intended to remove excess teachers who could not be redeployed from the system, was hotly disputed by the unions and the general public. SADTU's interpretation was that VSPs were a 'privilege, not a right'. In practice, however, the packages were available to all. By 1998, more than 15 200 professionals had opted for VSPs, draining from the system some of the country's most experienced teachers, including principals, heads of department and mathematics and science teachers already in severe shortage (see Baskin, Chapter 7). In terms of the agreement, these people may not return to the public service; many have found jobs in private schools, and some may even have returned to public schools where they are now employed on a contract basis by school governing bodies.

No large-scale redeployment took place, despite the fact that the most overstaffed provinces (Western Cape, Gauteng, Free State, Mpumalanga, and Northern Cape) had declared excess teachers. Such failures raised questions about whether the government intended to stick to the equity part of the agreement – moving teachers from well-off schools to poorer ones in rural areas or townships – or whether it was simply interested in cutting back, notwithstanding President Mandela's March 1995 assurance that no teachers would be retrenched as a result of cuts to the education budget (SAIRR 1995/1996: 124). The government insisted that redeployment, though delayed, would take place in earnest before the end of 1997, and that 33 000 new posts would be created. Neither of these goals was achieved.

The redeployment strategy, described by one district official as 'the single most dramatic change in the utilisation of teachers in the history of South Africa' and by another as a scheme that will 'make us or break us', seemed to make sense. It was consistent with the government's and the unions' commitment to equity. But, as educationist Rosamund Jaff from the National Business Initiative's Edupol pointed out, redeployment may be:

> a creative strategy, but teachers don't want to be redeployed. Most of them have families. They are not mobile. They don't want to be pushed around like chess pieces. The government has gambled on the fact that in today's economy, teachers cannot afford not to go. But what was going to be redeployment is increasingly likely to become retrenchment, particularly at a time when we need the best teachers for the introduction of the new curriculum. (1997: interview)

Performance-related pay and teacher appraisal

The state was keen to implement performance-related pay policies by July 1997, with SADTU requesting more time to research the issue. SADTU and the Education Policy Unit (EPU) of the University of the Witwatersrand have successfully piloted a new appraisal system for teachers. The archaic evaluation systems of the past were used to control teachers, rather than to develop and advance them, and were a core grievance in the early 1990s. The link between teacher evaluation and merit awards caused widespread discontent.

The new appraisal system emerged through successful co-operation between SADTU and NAPTOSA, with the latter contributing to and endorsing the new development-oriented instrument. It has been introduced in all nine provinces with varying degrees of success depending on the province's capacity. Generally appraisal has been welcomed by teachers, who 'for the first time felt they could associate with a more democratic and open form of evaluation' (Masigo, 1997: interview). Teachers now play a more active role in their own appraisal. They may select a peer to participate and may choose whether the principal or a deputy principal serves on the appraisal panel. However the new appraisal strategy has not been linked to pay increases. It was agreed that the new appraisal system first be implemented successfully and that the performance-related pay (PRP) increase be revised at a later stage.

SADTU claims that international evidence suggests that PRP schemes have been used by governments as a cut-back exercise whereby a few excellent teachers are rewarded with merit payments, while the rest are overlooked. The union is also concerned that PRP systems could severely undermine collective bargaining, by 'putting individual teachers in a bargaining position with the state and pitting teachers against one another' (Skinner, 1997: interview).

The South African Council of Educators

The South African Council of Educators (SACE), the first non-racial, professional body for teachers, was officially launched in September 1995. SACE's 48-member council has 15 state representatives, 30 representatives from the organised teaching profession, two co-chairs and a chief executive officer. According to its director, Reg Brijraj, SACE was conceptualised by teachers for teachers, promoted by the desire to establish a self-regulating body. 'The state chooses to keep a low profile,' he said, 'it wants to generate the idea that decisions are teacher-driven' (1997: interview). While there are parallels between the SACE code of conduct and the Educators'

Employment Act of 1994, the former has more to do with professional issues concerning teachers' relationships with learners, colleagues and parents, while the latter relates more closely to the relationship with the employer. According to Brijaraj, SACE will concern itself with:

> whether the profession is being brought into disrepute and will consider all issues of misconduct. However it will not necessarily become involved in disciplinary issues. It is about safeguarding both the teaching profession and the public. (Ibid.)

SACE aimed to present all 380 000 teachers with a 'registration package' and register them with the body. The process was delayed because SACE was compelled to advertise its code of conduct extensively to teachers. 'We did not want the code of conduct to be seen as another imposition on top of rationalisation and redeployment,' said Brijraj (Ibid.). 'We are mindful of the new way of thinking in the country. People need to be party to whatever is going to affect them.' By the end of 1999 almost 300 000 teachers had registered with SACE, mostly from the public service.

All teachers registering with SACE had to pay a once-off fee of R20, but monthly financing comes from the ELRC which draws its funds from the monthly contributions of organised teachers. SACE has adopted a 'grandfatherly approach' in registering teachers, regardless of whether or not they meet the qualification requirements. After initial registration, however, teachers must complete a minimum of three years post-matric training to qualify for registration. 'We are trying to develop the teaching corps to higher levels,' said Brijraj (Ibid.).

The teacher unions regard the establishment of SACE as a positive development. Professional issues:

> at present being dealt with in the adversarial climate of the ELRC, are probably better dealt with by a council of professional practitioners than by a hotchpotch of players with divergent perceptions of what they are about, as has often been the case in the ELRC. (Davies, 1997: 38)

SADTU welcomed SACE as officially bringing to an end the false opposition between unionism and professionalism, which has characterised the politics of teacher organisations. But SADTU called for more input from teachers on its code of conduct and asked for more clarity on SACE's autonomy from the state. Because SACE is funded by the ELRC, itself a state structure, its autonomy may be compromised. With the new code of conduct, parents dissatisfied with teacher performance may also take up their grievances with SACE. On the one hand, this may help improve negative perceptions of the teaching profession, but, on the other, it may make individual teachers vulnerable to victimisation.

New curriculum

The Department of Education is phasing in a new outcomes-based curriculum in schools. Initially, the intention was to overhaul the entire curriculum by the year 2005. However, it is unlikely this target will be met.

The new curriculum is skills-based rather than content-based and requires a radical paradigm shift from traditional teaching methods. It is based on 'learning area programmes' outlined by eight learning area committees, comprised of 50 people each, including representatives of teacher organisations.

Those who sit on these committees are themselves grappling with the new approaches and teachers are experiencing far greater difficulties. 'The role of teachers is central to the successful implementation of the new curriculum. But if we can't take teachers along, if they feel disempowered and unable to teach the new curriculum, the whole thing will collapse,' says Mareka Monyokolo, a policy analyst with the Centre for Education Policy Development (1997: interview).

Teachers themselves feel that they are not being sufficiently prepared to deal with the new curriculum. SADTU has committed itself to greater involvement in curriculum development, but is concerned at the haste with which the system is being implemented. NAPTOSA has warned of 'widespread unhappiness and the total unpreparedness of the teaching corps in dealing with the new curriculum. They believe the process is being rushed, and while teachers know they are supposed to start teaching outcomes-based education, many don't understand what it is' (Ibid.).There are indications that the new curriculum has already had unintended consequences. It has weakened the confidence of poorly trained teachers in under-resourced schools while in better-off schools it has taken off, and has enhanced teaching and learning. Ironically it may end up widening the gap between rich and poor schools.

Stress

A consumer health survey published in 1995 by Roche Products found that 'teachers had one of the highest average stress levels of professional groups' in South Africa:

> Factors contributing to this include large and unwieldy classes, lack of motivation – especially among high school children – uncertainty associated with having to adapt to a changing multicultural teaching environment, long working hours and pressures faced by teachers without enough textbooks and teaching aids. The survey found that teachers were leaving the profession to take up jobs or start businesses in fields such as adult education and literacy training. (SAIRR, 1995/1996: 125)

Subsequent research has shown that Grade I teachers grappling with the influx of large numbers of ill-prepared children have had their stress levels increased to new heights. The hasty imposition of a new curriculum can only exacerbate this situation.

School governing bodies

In terms of the South African Schools Act (No. 84 of 1996), elected school governing bodies (SGBs) must be established in all schools. SGBs are to be made up of parents, teachers, learners (in secondary schools only), and community members, with parents in the majority. They are meant to take on significant governance functions, including determining admissions policies, language policies, curricula and school fees.

While SADTU has always supported democratic governance structures in schools, the union is concerned about the employment of teachers by SGBs, which could undermine teachers' collective bargaining rights. In terms of the Act, SGBs can employ teachers though only the well-off SGBs are able to do this. 'SADTU is not happy with the suggestion that SGBs can employ extra teachers if they find funds. It goes against standard practice that SGBs would be the employer and not the province,' says Skinner (1997: interview). SADTU has also objected to the 'inequalities between public schools in working class and middle class areas' which would inevitably result.

The Ministry of Finance has rejected the suggestion that the state continues to be the official employer while SGBs pay the extra teachers' salaries. It is unwilling to take on the financial risk of paying such salaries if the SGBs prove unable to do so; SGBs are still regarded as the official employers of extra teachers. At the time of writing, no deadlines had yet been laid down for the establishment of SGBs in schools but there was recognition of the need for training for teachers and other participants to run them effectively.

Initially, there was some talk of SGBs taking on some of the functions of workplace forums, but in terms of the LRA, an insufficient number of teachers are employed at individual schools to set up site-based workplace forums. According to the LRA, workplace forums *may* be established. None of the unions has seriously explored whether such forums are suitable for teachers.

POLITICS AND ECONOMICS

In simple terms, the government's macro-economic strategy spells bad news for education. Major increases to the education budget will be unlikely in the future. Given that teacher salaries consume at least 80% of this budget, it will be impossible for salaries to be increased without a trade-off: a significant reduction in the number of teachers. Cutbacks have already taken place. Retrenchment and job insecurity is more of a reality than large-scale redeployment. Government backtracked on its three-year commitment to salary increases only a year after the agreement was made and the Ministry of Finance has dashed hopes that right-sizing the public service will necessarily translate into salary increases. According to SADTU's Nxesi:

> The question of cutbacks is seriously undermining the transformation agenda. Any form of restructuring means more funds. The government argues that giving over 20% of the budget to education is high compared with other countries. But they have infrastructure and a well-trained

teaching corps. A country like South Africa has had no infrastructure for the majority of people. We have to build more classrooms and train thousands of teachers who are not yet up to scratch. In addition, we have to retrain teachers to cope with the challenges of the new curriculum. For macro-economic planning you can talk of pupil:teacher ratios, but pedagogic principles concern class sizes. We are arguing that with proper research we can expose and counter the government at the level of policy. (Nxesi, 1997: 32)

Some educationists warn of the dangers of a too-powerful ELRC, which could exert pressure for salary hikes at the expense of the education system in general. According to Jane Hofmeyr the director of the Independent School Council:

With the ELRC, the government has ceded significant power to the unions, which could impact negatively on education generally. Because teachers take up 80% of expenditure, salary increases will mean cutbacks on other expenditure – textbooks, learning materials, new classrooms and additional teachers. We will have fewer teachers who are paid relatively high salaries and the education system will suffer greatly as a result. And no-one is facing up to the inevitable trade-offs. (1997: interview)

In her view, the power of the smaller, conservative teacher organisations, who are advancing the interests of the more privileged teachers, has been greatly enhanced by the ELRC:

Because so many areas of government policy can be declared of 'mutual interest' and therefore put to negotiation, they can get hijacked. Yes, it's healthy if it's going to bring teachers on board, but if everything is delayed *ad infinitum*, then efficient administration and implementation of decisions is seriously hampered. Right now it may be fine, but in four years' time there will be serious problems with the size of the salary bill. (Ibid.)

The lack of significant teacher strikes has been cited by many as proof of the success of the ELRC, but by mid-1998 this period of relative harmony had clearly come to an end, with the jobs of about 40 000 temporary teachers on the line. Clearly, rationalisation placed teachers in much the same predicament as the rest of the civil service. Hofmeyr asks:

> No-one in the civil service has job security any longer. When all other departments have the sword of Damocles dangling over them because of the government's intention to reduce the national debt and cut down on the civil service, why should teachers be immune? (Ibid.)

Changing relations

The radically altered political terrain has brought new challenges to the teacher unions and substantially changed the way the organised teacher bodies see themselves and relate to each other. SADTU has moved away from protest action to more hands-on involvement with 'nitty gritty' labour issues in the ELRC, teacher professionalism and education policy and research. NAPTOSA has undergone an equally dramatic change, finding itself in a far weaker position with regard to the state. It has at times become a vociferous critic of the state. Once fiery adversaries, and still ideologically different, the two unions now co-operate successfully in the ELRC, having formed joint committees on various issues. Brijraj says: 'There is an arranged marriage between the two. They are competitive but are beginning to specialise in their own areas of expertise in a complementary fashion. You often hear people in friendly conversation saying, "Why don't you join us?"' (1997: interview).

Traditionally conservative white teachers have begun to show an interest in SADTU. 'In this day and age, political ideology counts for very little,' says Nxesi. 'Now it's a question of numbers gained. White teachers, who want protection against rationalisation, are starting to join our ranks. It is no longer a question of colour' (1997: interview). As SADTU realises the government is incapable of delivering on its demands, the union is being forced into a closer alliance with its old conservative union adversaries. In the mid-1998 confrontation with the state, all unions remarked that they 'spoke with one voice' on key issues. The state was confronted with the formidable scenario of nearly 300 000 teachers preparing to strike. In the August 1999 wage dispute co-ordinated protest action was the order of the day.

The closer relationship between NAPTOSA and SADTU was one of the reasons for the decision by four Afrikaans teacher organisations to break away from NAPTOSA in July 1996 and form the Suid Afrikaanse Onderwysunie (SAOU) (with 28 000 members). The union's chief executive officer, Pieter Martins, said, 'We felt there was a need for Afrikaans-speaking teachers to unite themselves as a grouping. We felt they were being left out of negotiations as only a small part of a bigger team.' He remained positive about the SAOU's relationship with NAPTOSA and SADTU:

> Twelve years ago there was lots of antagonism between the different groupings. We have seen this change. People have moved closer, there is less antagonism. We now hold lots of bilaterals or trilaterals before negotiations. If you can get consensus among your teacher organisations, obviously you're much stronger in the chamber. (1997: interview)

While SAOU officials admit that the past government 'looked after them well in previous years' they nevertheless described the ELRC as 'an improvement for teachers, who feel that through their unions they have a say in what will happen to educators'. But, according to the SAOU, it has had to change '… now we have had to add a labour component. SADTU had a head start' (SAOU officials, 1997: interview).

If the post-apartheid era has seen the establishment of friendly relations between some once-antagonistic teacher unions, it has also seen a shift in alliances between former comrades in government and labour. Many top officials in the Department of Education, including its director general, Thami Mseleku, come from SADTU's leadership. On the one hand, it can only help the union that people with a good understanding of teachers' problems are in strategic positions in government. On the other hand, it creates problems for the union. The once sharp lines between labour and government are now more blurred. An observer close to the union says that SADTU has:

> incredible difficulty knowing when to whack the state or befriend it. About 70% of SADTU's top officials are now in

government, mostly in labour relations. This means there is often confusion. They don't know whether they are negotiating with comrades or adversaries and there is now ongoing debate in SADTU about whether it was advisable for so many of its officials to move into government. There is also resentment among those left behind. COSATU is increasingly being seen as a stepping stone to big jobs in government. (1997, confidential interview)

Close relationships between SADTU and its former officials in government are undoubtedly fuelling perceptions on the ground that the union is 'cuddling up to government' and that the closer its officials are to the corridors of power, the less interest they have in ordinary teachers' working conditions. SADTU officials are keenly sensitive to this perception. Its teacher forums, held country-wide in February 1997, highlighted the dislocation between leadership and membership. A SADTU regional official, John Maluleka, acknowledged that 'while there is a question of loyalty in labour's support for government, the relationship is already strained and is bound to get more strained as the government pushes an economic policy directly opposed to the RDP' (1997: interview).

The short-lived ANC-led Education Alliance, launched towards the end of 1996, attempted to fill the vacuum left by the closure of the National Education Co-ordinating Committee (NECC). It aimed to create new alliances around government strategy in an apparent attempt to neutralise potential opposition from SADTU and school and university student organisations. 'When the NECC disappeared it became increasingly clear there was no longer a reference point for organisations in the education sector to rally around. Thus the idea of the alliance was born,' says national co-ordinator Sigle Moon (1997: interview). The alliance initiative subsequently lapsed, and plans to revive it were unsuccessful.

Public Service Co-ordinating Bargaining Council

It is in SADTU's interest that most bargaining occurs in the ELRC, rather than the PSCBC; NAPTOSA is also keen for the ELRC to retain its existing functions. SADTU argues that the PSCBC should be a co-ordinating body only. It points out that teacher performance is affected by factors specific to the profession, such as class sizes, workloads and availability of resources and for these reasons, wages and working conditions should be determined by the sector and not the central body. 'If this doesn't happen,' says Nxesi, 'then we will be going to the PSCBC as visitors and the other public sector organisations will dominate the whole thing' (1997: interview).

Given the specialised nature of education, analysts believed it unlikely that the ELRC would lose too many functions to the PSCBC. However, one former union official charged that the 'teacher unions were fast asleep when the LRA was being negotiated. They didn't foresee the implications of a body higher than the ELRC'. In her view, deliberations will continue in the ELRC, but crucial decisions around the 'slice of the salary pie' will take place in the PSCBC. SADTU's Maluleka says it made more economic sense for public sector unions to:

> take the employer head-on and bargain on transverse matters in the PSCBC. If the ELRC can only rubber stamp decisions made there, then it's pointless to be repeating these processes in this chamber. It has to be acknowledged that in terms of conditions of service, the Minister for Public Service and Administration is more influential than the Minister of Education and the same applies for salary increases, where the Minister of Finance, not the Minister of Education, is in the driving seat. It therefore makes no sense to have all these ministries involved in negotiations around the same issues. (1997: interview)

A positive spin-off of streamlining the functions of the ELRC to comply with the LRA would be the discarding of 'cumbersome old dispute resolution procedures as laid down by the ELRA,' says Maluleka. He adds that new mechanisms would allow for speedy resolution at district level (Ibid.).

SADTU's relationship with COSATU

Nxesi has serious concerns over COSATU's proposal to form a single public sector union. 'We understand the civil service to be a sector with different industries,' he says:

The only thing that is transverse is salaries. And even that is up for debate, given teachers' specific working conditions. We never believed in one public sector union. It would create serious problems if teachers, nurses and police were in one union. As COSATU unions we have to instead co-ordinate the issues that are transverse for us ... We have very little experience in this field. The debate has not gone down to workers and is currently only taking place among leaders. We have to bear in mind that teachers are middle-class oriented. There were fears in COSATU when the white-collar workers (teachers) joined up. If there was already such fear at the level of a federation, how much more reservation at the idea of one public sector union? SADTU is still consolidating its position of having affiliated to COSATU. (1997: interview)

A former SADTU official now in national government feels that SATDU should reconsider its relationship with COSATU:

SADTU has to look at the broader context: Where are we taking education? Do we foster a culture of resistance over things that may not be directly related to education? SADTU needs to be committed to education and learning and orient towards the new legislative mechanisms that have been established. The more teachers embark on strike action, the more this culture is developed in our children. We need to look very carefully at this. The diversity of membership within COSATU is difficult to manage. It is increasingly difficult to please everyone. (1997: confidential interview)

CONCLUSION: THE WAY FORWARD

Skinner says that the teacher forums held in February 1997 showed that 'numerically SADTU is very strong, but its structures are quite weak. It is not getting information down to grassroots and site level' (1997: interview). She continues:

The union has become more bureaucratised and relies on print media for the dissemination of information. Ironically, this has weakened the union in significant ways. Before, we had regular mass meetings and branch meetings. We relied on an oral culture, which was very strengthening. Now we distribute SADTU's newspaper, *Educators' Voice*, in a plastic packet in the post. This is not building our structures. Also teachers are not always proficient in English. They tend not to read and don't always acquaint themselves with the issues. There is definitely a realisation that we have to meet and debate more. (Ibid.)

An ex-SADTU official now in provincial government maintains that grassroots SADTU members are still locked into the defiance campaigns of 1991. 'Things haven't changed on the ground and national leadership is elite and out of touch. They speak with forked tongues, saying one thing to membership and another to government' (1997: confidential interview). Nevertheless, Skinner described the forums as:

very, very successful in getting inputs from ordinary teachers to inform mandates. We discussed a host of critical issues, including SACE, rationalisation, the education budget, the new curriculum and the South African Schools Act. We were in effect doing the provinces' work for them. (1997: interview)

SADTU, keenly aware of its need to move away from its tradition of protest towards playing a constructive, even pivotal role in the development of new education policy, recruited a full-time researcher with a view to establishing research units in each province.

In the dying days of apartheid, education was one of the most fiercely contested areas of the public service. High profile, militant strikes were the order of the day, as black workers hurried to establish unions in sectors left behind by the labour relations reforms of the 1970s and 1980s.

By 1993, with the establishment of the ELRC, proper and effective bargaining began. Since 1994, these processes have become increasingly complex as both sides attempt to achieve reconstruction within a constrained macro-economic context. Democratisation has created considerable space for union involvement in policy formulation. These possibilities, however, bring with them new responsibilities and expectations, with which the unions must come to grips.

10

LABOUR RELATIONS IN THE SOUTH AFRICAN POLICE SERVICE

———————— ✦ ————————

Monique Marks

Marks's chapter is the second of two case studies that survey the development of labour relations in a critical sector of the public service.

Worker organisation among the police developed only during the high point of the resistance to apartheid, and was boosted during the transition to democracy. The Police and Prisons Civil Rights Union (POPCRU) represented the interests of mainly black police officers. It identified itself first as a 'civil rights union', and only in the second instance as a craft-based union, and its link to the national movement has been a crucial aspect of its identity. Its self-conceptualisation, while significant, has limited its vision as a union, and has had severe consequences for POPCRU's ability to take up shop-floor issues. Its perspective has led it at times to shun a more confrontational approach with the employer. Its internal structures have been unsettled by frequent turnover of leadership, and by poor communications particularly between national, provincial and local levels.

By contrast, the South African Police Union (SAPU), formed in 1993, was perceived as a top-down creation of police management to counteract POPCRU's gains. Whatever its origins, in recent years SAPU has made significant organisational gains and is now the largest union in the sector. As it is outside COSATU, it has been less encumbered in its dealings with government. However its ability to follow through on campaigns has been limited: it is not immune from the same organisational problems that plague its rival.

The two unions separately respond to the diverse political and workplace needs of the police, which accounts for widespread double membership in the Police Service. Though there has been considerably more cooperation in their dealings with management a merger appears to be off the cards for now. Weaknesses on the union side are matched, if not exceeded by those in management. The authoritarian and militaristic ranking system is also a problem for managers who encounter difficulty dealing with their own superiors during negotiations. Moreover the quality of labour relations expertise has been extremely poor.

Notwithstanding these problems both sides have registered gains in their bargaining forum, the Safety and Security Sectoral Bargaining Council (SSSBC). There is considerable agreement between both sides on the need to maintain the integrity of SSSBC, as a separate bargaining council within the PSCBC. Both police unions and management need to acknowledge their immaturity with regard to negotiation and equip themselves to creating an institution geared toward effective crime prevention and law enforcement.

INTRODUCTION

Perhaps the most remarkable case of the development of public service labour relations is the South African Police Service (SAPS). What was once the racist, authoritarian, and violent core of the apartheid state's repressive apparatus, the SAPS is now almost entirely unionised and subject to modern labour relations institutions. As the SAPS struggles to come out from the shadow of its past, it provides a critical case study of the progress in developing public service labour relations today.

Following the democratic elections of 1994, the South African Police (SAP) was given a new name: the South African Police Service (SAPS). In late 1995, all police forces of the previous self-governing 'homelands' were integrated into the SAPS. This chapter explores the history of labour relations between the government and SAP/SAPS, and provides an analysis of the status of those relations. The use of SAP or SAPS will correspond to the year under discussion.

No comprehensive assessment of this labour relations history has been written before. Most analyses have been concerned with the historical role of the service in upholding the apartheid state, or with its transformation and democratisation. The police unions and the challenges they posed to traditional mechanisms of dealing with labour relations in the SAPS are also of very recent origin: the first real union was constituted in 1989 and was recognised only in 1993.

Labour relations in the SAPS should not be examined in isolation. Police personnel are employed by state authorities at the national level, and they render a fundamental service to the public at large. The police are thus part of the public service. Due to the nature of the work they perform, however, they face certain restrictions when it comes to collective action. In South Africa, police work is deemed to be an 'essential service'.

This chapter is divided into three sections:
- the first section surveys the international context of police as public servants
- the second section covers union development and government negotiations with unions in South Africa
- finally, concerns, issues, and the way forward are addressed.

INTERNATIONAL PERSPECTIVES

In western Europe, Asia, and elsewhere, police unions are recognised by the state. The form these unions take and their rights and limits on collective action and organisation differ, however, from one country to another. In the Irish Republic and Singapore, for example, police unions are prohibited, though officers of all ranks belong to associations.

In these countries it is believed that there are adequate mechanisms built into the police service which render the need for unions redundant. Generally police associations have direct access to the commissioner of police and/or the respective minister. Moreover, in most countries police officers are seen as invaluable and their basic needs and concerns are taken very seriously by employers. As a result, in Singapore, for example, government policy states that police officers should receive a salary that is 10% higher than other civil servants. Associations differ from unions in that they are generally organised around profession and skill, and usually have a co-operative rather than an adversarial relationship with management. Associations generally do not engage in militant collective action such as strikes; they are also governed by strict laws internally, and adhere to formal legislation.

Limitations on rights stem from the perception that the status of police officers as law enforcers is incompatible with the use of collective action for the purpose of 'agitation'. It is almost an international norm that police unions are not allowed to strike.

In France, for example, police have the right to protest and demonstrate, but only when off duty. Even in historically liberal countries such as the Netherlands, police unions have the right to demonstrate, but are not allowed to strike, though law does not forbid this. In Britain, where even doctors and prison warders have the right to strike, the police force is the only public or private service denied this right. British police unions are not allowed to affiliate to federations.

All over the world, it is recognised that in the absence of the right to strike, effective and efficient labour relations mechanisms are a must. In Denmark, the leadership of the two key police unions negotiate on a regular basis with top management, as well as with representatives of the responsible ministry. Representatives from the Ministry of Justice, for example, will be present at any negotiations that involve working conditions. In the United States, where police unionisation initially met with great resistance, it has become generally accepted that unionisation gives rise to 'substantial economic benefits ... primarily through the collective bargaining process'. Furthermore, police officers come to appreciate that:

> the value to the community of the job they are performing is recognised in the form of increased benefits. Indeed, police officers and their labour organisations pursue the same economic benefits and working condition improvements as their counterparts in the private sector. (Burpo, 1973: 3)

This realisation, however, has only recently emerged in South Africa.

SOUTH AFRICA

In the past, labour relations in the SAP were under the firm control of police and public service management. This was the result of the autocratic and militaristic nature of the old SAP, and the fact that, prior to 1993, the public service in general had very poor collective bargaining mechanisms. The Police Act No.7 of 1958 stated that 'members of the police force may not unionise without the consent of the Commissioner of Police and, whether on duty or off, may not wear badges or signs which associate them with a trade union' (Christie, 1992). Any grievance, whether collective or personal, was dealt with on an individual basis by a higher ranking official in the police service. This was initially done at station level. If not resolved, it was referred to a district commissioner, and later to the provincial and even the national commissioner of the SAP.

Grievances could relate to anything from personal issues, such as transfers, to potentially collective problems, such as discrimination. Dealing with these problems through an authoritarian ranking system not only individualised issues, but blocked their politicisation.

The situation changed only when South Africa began the transition to a new democratic order. In 1992, the police board looked into recognition of police unions. Recognition was finally granted in late 1993. An informal negotiating forum was set up, but legislation formalising these arrangements was passed only in late 1995.

It was almost inevitable that aggrieved members of the old SAP would come together around a string of common complaints. These included the absence of proper grievance procedures, appalling working conditions and the much-contested political role played by the force. Unity had begun during the period of mass defiance in the late 1980s, when substantial openings emerged for opposition groupings, and continued to build during the democratic transition of the 1990s.

The Police and Prisons Civil Rights Union (POPCRU) was launched on 5 September 1989 and thousands of police and prison wardens took to the streets in support of the new organisation. Lundo Sam, the first president of POPCRU, isolates four main reasons for the formation of the union:

- police and prison workers were the most oppressed workers in the public service
- police and prison wardens were used to uphold apartheid and capitalism
- police workers came to recognise that their needs and interests were in contradiction with police management
- policing in South Africa was seen to deviate from international norms and standards, as typified by the huge distance between the police and the communities they were supposed to be serving (1995: interview).

POPCRU represented the interests of mainly black police officers. It identified itself first as a 'civil rights union', and only in the second instance as a craft-based union. Its 1995 Secretariat Report states that: 'POPCRU was established with the sole purpose of promoting stability, unity, impartiality, and furthermore, to recognise the civil and basic human rights of all South Africans and all people who live in (South Africa)' (POPCRU, 1995: 3).

This conceptualisation, while significant, is limited in terms of a vision for any union, and has had severe consequences for POPCRU's ability to take up shop-floor issues.

Police management did not take POPCRU's formation lying down. In March 1990 about 90 members were dismissed and about 400 were suspended from their jobs. (Those suspended were reinstated in May of that year.) The union was, and still is, widely viewed as ANC aligned.[1] In August 1993, for example, it was reported that 'history was made in Port Elizabeth ... when black policemen were led on a march to a mass rally by a small band of Umkhonto we Sizwe cadres' (*Sowetan*, 9/8/1993). This image was reinforced time and again before the 1994 elections. For example, POPCRU members were reported to have marched in protest on SAP headquarters in Pretoria chanting 'Kill the boer, kill the farmer' – at the time a militant slogan identified with the ANC's Youth League (*Sunday Star*, 22/8/1993). During this action, POPCRU members demanded the removal of white police officers from strife-town townships. It is not difficult to comprehend why the union tended to alienate white police officers.

Though POPCRU was only officially recognised in 1993, it was the only authentic police union in South Africa until then. However, in November 1993, the equally contentious South African Police Union (SAPU) was launched. Many believed that SAPU was set up by management in an attempt to break POPCRU's power and strength. Indeed, there is a popular perception that SAPU's formation is shrouded in secrets, as many of those initially elected to its National Executive Committee (NEC) were high ranking white members of the SAP.

Peter-Don Brandt, SAPU's general secretary, comments that SAPU was formed to allow workers in the police service to have a collective voice in an industrial union that was not politically aligned. Brandt, who has been a member of SAPU since its inception, points out that there were no proper collective bargaining mechanisms for police workers. Gontse

Koitsioe, SAPU communications head, rejects the idea that SAPU was set up by management:

> Nothing has ever been proven to that effect. SAPU was started to take care of the interests of the workers. We are not part of any agenda. People keep asking why, when POPCRU was in existence, SAPU had to be formed. It was fundamentally because of their ideological baggage. It is understandable that POPCRU has a certain ideological bias. But it was urgent that a purely workerist union must be formed and that is why we formed SAPU. SAPU is a union without any adherence to any particular party or political ideology. It looks purely at the interests of workers and the power relationship between workers and government. (Koitsioe, cited in Collins, 1995: 10)

In late 1996, National Police Commissioner George Fivas called for an investigation into the origins of SAPU in response to the union's calls for him to resign (*Natal Mercury* 12/11/1996). According to Bill Dennis, SAPU's general secretary in KwaZulu-Natal, this inquiry failed to establish adequate evidence that SAPU had been set up as a management union with the aim of undermining POPCRU (January 1997: interview).

While POPCRU has remained primarily a civil rights union, SAPU has focused on working conditions. The late 1990s however, have seen changes in the way the unions operate. When POPCRU was formed, much of its collective action was directed at the apartheid state, which it deemed racist, exploitative and oppressive. SAPU was far less combative – hence their label as a reactionary, 'sweetheart' union. After 1994 the political terrain shifted considerably; POPCRU's political ally, the ANC, came to power and SAPU took on the mantle of opposition. Sergeant David Strydom, KwaZulu-Natal correspondent for the official police publication, *Servamus* argued that:

> Morale within the police has sunk to an all-time low, as illustrated by police suicides. Now the South African Police Union has mobilised its estimated 50 000 members to fight the government's lack of concern. This was the role formally filled by the Police and Prisons Civil Rights Union, who

before the April 1994 general elections, had been a troublesome thorn in the side of the Nationalist regime. Once Nelson Mandela's Government of National Unity had been sworn in, SAPU became the more vociferous of the unions ... (1995: 56)

Since the elections, POPCRU has concentrated on internal changes in the SAPS, especially affirmative action. It has formally distanced itself from SAPU's more militant and combative stance. In March/April 1995, SAPU members embarked on a go-slow over salaries and working conditions. POPCRU chastised SAPU, saying that police officers should be less concerned with material gain, and more interested in developing a SAPS centred on human rights for all. In October 1996, when SAPU called for labour action to protest against inadequate overtime pay and the failure of the SAPS to confirm promotions, POPCRU refused to engage in joint action. The union's then-general secretary, Raphepheng Mataka, argued that such action was premature, and would lead to a loss of confidence in the police by the community, which POPCRU argued was not worthwhile over 'such petty issues' (October 1996: interview). Ironically, it is now POPCRU which is branded as a management union.

The picture became even more complex. In March and April of 1998 POPCRU engaged in a number of work-to-rule actions in protest against the appointment of unpopular Indian officers in African townships. The union called for the resignation of KwaZulu-Natal Provincial Police Commissioner, Chris Serfontein.

Organisational structure and capacity

POPCRU and SAPU together represent about 65% of workers in the SAPS. Their membership base differs considerably. By late 1996, SAPU claimed a membership of 56 000 – 60% black and 40% white – figures that serve, albeit in a limited way, to confirm that it is not simply a 'white management' union. In fact, according to Brandt and Koitsioe, the majority of SAPU's membership is ranked at constable or sergeant level or below.

Officers ranked higher than colonel (or senior superintendent) are excluded from membership as they are deemed part of management. All SAPU office bearers are from the police service itself, though there are a number of appointed officials from outside who play a central role in the union, as well as in negotiations. Union leadership, however, remains largely white. Bill Dennis argues that 'black guys tend to take the backseat … This could be because they were always pushed into the background. They haven't learned to assert themselves yet' (January 1997: interview).

POPCRU is essentially a black union. In November 1996, it claimed a membership of 47 000. At the June 1995 national congress, there was only one white delegate, a major from the Eastern Cape.[2] Police officers are in the majority, though there are about 6 000 prison wardens in the union. Most members are from the junior ranks (constable, sergeant and warrant officer). As is the case with SAPU, most of the union's national office bearers and key leadership occupy higher ranks. It was only in late 1997 that POPCRU appointed an education officer and a legal officer, although this was originally agreed upon at its congress in 1995.

According to Brandt, the key issues that members bring to SAPU are promotion, transfers, salaries, overtime pay, and discrimination and victimisation. Sam says that the most pressing issues for POPCRU members are discrimination in all its forms, lack of transport and person-power at station level, improving salaries and narrowing the wage gap. While the membership base of the unions is very different, the issues they take up are compatible. This raises the question as to the appropriateness of two competing unions organising in essentially the same area.

Both unions claim to organise at station level and elect shop stewards at this level. However, neither union was convinced that meetings and report-backs were being held. Both acknowledged a severe lack of union skills and knowledge at the local level. Jacob Tsumane, POPCRU assistant general secretary, stated that 'POPCRU does have shop stewards, but not in all institutions. POPCRU has not identified which stations are not having shop stewards. The priority for the year is to have shop stewards in place' (April 1996: interview).

He said that the union hoped to develop local shop steward councils after its Congress in June 1998. The union's commitment to developing shop steward structures is indicated by their publication of a *Shop Steward Manual* in October 1997. But, by April 1998, there were no full-time shop stewards at police stations.

It would appear that in both unions, the NECs take key decisions. Communication with members is primarily carried out through written media; both unions have negotiated the use of various facilities for communication with police management. Since 1996, SAPU has produced a monthly newspaper, *Union Post*, which gives feedback on union activities and negotiations, insight into problems confronting the SAPS, simplified and summarised police legislation, and information relating to benefits. A similar type of publication was later launched by POPCRU. It is published once every two months, and essentially gives feedback to members on POPCRU's programme of action.

While the two police unions have been able to mobilise effectively a large proportion of police workers, their internal organisational capacities are extremely weak. This is not altogether surprising. Both unions are very young. They have only recently been recognised by management. Labour relations skills are seriously lacking on both sides of the bargaining table. Furthermore, it would appear that police management is not entirely convinced about the role unions could play in improving labour relations. As Sakkie Steyn, head of labour relations in the SAPS puts it:

> Labour relations are still not taken as serious by police management, particularly middle management. It seems they have a difficulty with the change in culture … Unilateral decisions are still taken by management and there seems to be a strong belief in management prerogative. (October 1996: interview)

There has been an ongoing struggle on the part of the unions for the recognition of shop stewards and union officials. Until recently, union officials were only allowed two official working hours per week for union activities. However, in September 1999, the SAPS headoffice sent a circular to the unions and to all national and provincial unit heads that a full-time shop steward should be appointed from each union at both provincial and national level (SAPS, 1999b). (This will be elaborated on in the section concerned with collective bargaining in the SAPS.)

The fact that their services are deemed 'essential' under the Labour Relations Act (LRA) of 1995 limits the capacity of the police unions even further. Police officers are expected to put their service to the public above their union activities. This limits their bargaining power. (The issue of essential services is dealt with in more detail later in this chapter.)

It is also very difficult for police officers to organise at the local level. Attempts at democratisation notwithstanding, police stations still maintain an authoritarian structure and culture, making it very difficult for lower-ranking union officials to challenge higher-ranking officers. According to Sam, 'union members still have problematic relationships with management. Management does not allow them to attend meetings, and tends to respond to union officials as constables rather than union officials.

Officials from both unions speak frankly about weaknesses. Brandt identifies the three main problems facing SAPU as a general lack of knowledge, even amongst union leadership, as to what unionism is about; a lack of understanding as to the role of shop stewards; and a general lack of negotiating skills.

Sam says that POPCRU leaders lack negotiation and mediation skills. There is no effective communication within the union, leading to a lack of transparency around decisions taken in bargaining forums, and contributing to a lack of unity and trust within the union. On the other hand, Mataka points out that: 'police operate on the street and it is hence difficult to have a group coming together to address a particular issue. The police cannot organise as other industries do on the shop-floor. The only time there is convergence is during the changeover of shifts' (October 1996: interview).

The problems experienced by the two unions can be illustrated by a number of incidents. In May 1995, SAPU initiated a work-to-rule action in protest against the lack of overtime pay, particularly for detectives. At the Orlando police station in Soweto, police officers closed the gates of the station and demanded that management re-negotiate overtime pay. Management called in the SAPS's Internal Stability Unit. A gun battle ensued, and a Constable Xaba, who was inside the gates, was killed. POPCRU blamed SAPU for the death of Xaba, who they claimed was one of their members, although it is unclear why Xaba was part of the action if he was a POPCRU member. Neither SAPU nor POPCRU members could say with certainty which union initiated the Soweto action, and what the lines of accountability were (*Sowetan*, 20/5/1995).

In August 1995, the POPCRU general secretary was abducted by members of his own union in the Eastern Cape who insisted on his immediate resignation despite his democratic election into office. In late 1996, members of the old leadership of POPCRU formed a breakaway union, the National Public Police Civil Rights Union (NAPPCRU). According to Mataka, this grouping did not want to organise together with prison wardens. It should also be noted that in KwaZulu-Natal there is another police union, NAPOSU (National Police Service Union), formed in 1994, constituted by ex-members of the KwaZulu police. They are recognised provincially, but not nationally.

The weak organisational capacity of the two unions is also a concern to police management. Imraan Hayden, head of labour relations in the SAPS in KwaZulu-Natal, claims that: 'The police unions suck things out of their thumbs. They are new in the game ... They don't have shop stewards and representatives ... The unions tend to be largely rhetorical, and not equipped to deal with industrial issues' (August 1996: interview).

National police management appears to share these sentiments. According to Sakkie Steyn:

> The different unions have different problems. There is a lack of structure and resources countrywide. The main problem in both unions is that of internal communication. Members do not receive information ... SAPU is a bigger union, and better structured, but they lack sufficient skilled people to participate in joint committees. POPCRU on the other hand lacks infrastructure, and is also plagued with internal revolutions. (October 1996: interview)

While critical of the unions, both national and provincial police management are aware that their own structures also hinder the development of better labour relations. Very little labour relations training has been provided to middle management. It is difficult for the labour relations department within SAPS to monitor local police stations. Mataka says that the department appears to act autonomously from other departments, and from provincial commissioners.

For Brandt of SAPU, police management lacks an understanding of the role of unions, and their potential to improve 'productivity' within the service. It is extremely difficult for the police unions to be effective in an environment that resists equality and joint decision-making. However, the unions have been central to positive changes that have occurred recently in police labour relations.

Relations between unions

By July 1996 some agreement appeared to be emerging between the national leadership of SAPU and POPCRU that a positive working alliance should be developed to present a collective voice in negotiations with police management. However, by 1997 it seemed less likely that the two unions would be able to work together, despite their relatively compatible goals.

While both unions have internally discussed the possibility of a merger, this is not a simple process; both unions have reasons for stalling. In 1995, for example, both Sam and Brandt stated that the two unions did not trust one another. In particular, POPCRU at this time was suspicious of SAPU, believing that its formation was motivated by an attempt to discredit POPCRU. Consequently, POPCRU believed that a merger with SAPU would undermine it's political intergrity. SAPU, on the other hand, believed that POPCRU was seen to be politically motivated, given its alliance with the liberation movement. At this time, SAPU was also concerned that a merger would mean inheriting POPCRU's internal organisational chaos. Such disagreement and tension led to the weakening of representation of the unions during processes of negotiation with police management (Sam and Brandt: interviews).

Over the years, however, both POPCRU and SAPU realised that a positive working alliance was crucial to a strong labour voice during negotiations with police management. If nothing else, they agreed that a tactical alliance during negotiations was needed. By 1998, both unions were prepared to consider a merger process. According to Tsumane, by then POPCRU general secretary, in April 1998 talks about a merger process were initiated. However, both unions were aware that such talks would be controversial given the different political and ideological stances of the two unions (Tsumane, April 1998: interview).

According to Celeste van Niekerk, acting secretary general of SAPU in 1998, the most significant joint initiative between the two unions was the signing of an Agency Shop Agreement with SAPS management in 1998. Presently, there is a general acceptance within the two unions that co-operative working arrangements will be deepened, and that a merger process is probable, although ideological and political tensions between the two unions are likely to persist for some time (Van Niekerk, April 1998: interview).

The existing tensions between the two unions undermine the necessary strength of a collective voice. According to Steyn:

> Non-issues are brought to the negotiating table by the unions.
> The whole question of membership recruitment is taken up

in the Forum. We then have a situation of point scoring ... Positions are hardened, and it is then difficult to reach consensus from all parties. (Steyn, 1996: interview)

While the police service is undergoing major restructuring at all levels, it is in the area of labour relations that change has been slowest. The Safety and Security Act passed by the Cabinet in September 1995 breaks significantly with the past in terms of being more community oriented and sensitive, but it lacks the much-needed creative mechanisms for dealing with labour relations. However, some of the problems are dealt with by the LRA and the South African Police Labour Regulations.

Grievance procedures and collective bargaining negotiating procedures

The first South African Police Labour Regulations were promulgated in November 1993. As a result of this legislation, a South African Police negotiating forum was established on 18 February 1994. Through negotiations in this forum the regulations were changed to exclude a clause stating that all issues dealt with at the forum had to be agreed upon by the SAPS National Commissioner in accordance with the South African Police Service Act (1995). The regulations were also amended to include the former Transkei, Bophuthatswana, Venda, Ciskei (TBVC) states' police organisations (in line with the amalgamation process), and, in September 1995, the new South African Police Service Labour Relations Regulations were promulgated.

The 1993 regulations represent an important break with past mechanisms for dealing with labour-related issues in the SAPS. Firstly, they recognised the right of employees to join organised representative formations. The document states 'employees shall ... have the right to establish and, further only subject to the constitution of the organisation concerned, to join any employee organisation of their own choice' (RSA, 1993a). No member of the police service shall be discriminated against or victimised as a result of joining any such organisation.

According to the 1995 regulations employee organisations shall be recognised if the following conditions are met in the information submitted to the commissioner:

- There must be a proper constitution of the organisations, as well as a

list of the names and details of its office bearers, a physical address and contact number for the organisation concerned.
- A list of members of the organisation must be submitted, accompanied by information regarding the regions members come from, and the units in which they work.
- The employee organisation should be sufficiently representative of the membership concerned.
- The employee organisation should not be affiliated to any political party, nor be financially supported by any such party. (RSA, 1995)

The regulations also contain a new grievance procedure 'aimed at resolving grievances more speedily, and which devolves responsibility for solving problems to the lowest possible level.'[3] The aim is to resolve a grievance in the shortest possible time, up to a maximum of 30 days. If there is still disagreement, the parties concerned go to arbitration. The most common grievances are those pertaining to promotions, salaries (which have to be dealt with at a national level), racism, and irregular selection procedures. A recent SAPS document states that as far as possible, grievances should be resolved via mediation rather than arbitration (SAPS, 1999). The document also allows for an informal grievance procedure whereby an employee is encouraged to raise any grievance verbally with his or her immediate superior, so that a grievance will be resolved before formal grievance procedures are initiated. The grievance procedure should be invoked within 180 days from the date at which the grievant became aware of the grievance. The role of the SAPS Labour Relations Department is to advise workers and management how best to deal with grievances, and in so doing to promote occupational justice and fairness. The department, among its other functions, referees between the two parties, and facilitates and organises arbitration processes.

The most important part of the 1995 regulations was the provision for the establishment of a negotiating forum in the police service at a national level. On 27 September 1995, following consultation between employee organisations and management, the National Negotiating Forum (NNF) was launched and the new labour regulations were inaugurated. This forum was constituted by the employer and recognised employee organisations, and 'any agreement concluded by virtue of proceedings contemplated ... binding on the relevant parties, and the members of the employee organisations involved' (RSA, 1993a). The forum, according to the regulations, should not deal with individual concerns, but with issues of mutual concern to both employer and employee bodies.

Over the years, the NNF has become an arena for dealing with conditions of service as well as with broader transformation questions such as health and safety, affirmative action, equal opportunities, police plans, and the National Crime Prevention Strategy. However, the powers of the NNF were confined to those that could be dealt with by the National Commissioner of the SAPS in accordance with the 1995 Police Act.

While the implementation of the NNF marked a milestone in police labour relations, there were a number of limitations with regards to this structure. Firstly, the NNF was originally established independently of the Public Service Bargaining Council (PSBC) which had authority over remuneration through the Public Service Commission (PSC). This was the result of the exclusion of the police from the Public Service Labour Relations Act of 1993. Secondly, both POPCRU and SAPU were awarded only observer status (with regard to functional members) in the PSBC. Police management had to go back for a mandate from the PSBC on issues pertaining to remuneration.

As a result of these two limitations, both police management and police unions called for the NNF to become a separate bargaining chamber within the PSBC. This was made possible with the promulgation of the Labour Relations Act in 1996. The inclusion of the police in the LRA was very significant. It allowed for the establishment of forums for collective bargaining and negotiations at the local and national level. This meant that the SAPS would be unable to regress into previous modes of unilateral decision-making, dominated by management.

Both police management and police unions welcomed the inclusion of the police into the LRA. They believed that the Act would facilitate less adversarial relations, and that it would encourage good faith bargaining, bilateral agreements, and co-determination. However, both management and unions raised a number of concerns regarding the new Act. Firstly, there were questions as to what issues would be considered as transverse (applying across the public service) and which would be considered sector specific. Both management and the unions wanted to maximise the powers of the NNF, given what they believed were the 'unique and special' service conditions of the police.

For Brandt, the Public Service Co-ordinating Bargaining Council (PSCBC, the PSBC's successor) should deal with as few issues as possible. In terms of the LRA the PSCBC may perform all the functions of a bargaining council, namely it may deal with:

- matters which are regulated by uniform rules, norms and standards that apply across the public service
- matters which apply to terms and conditions of employment applicable to two or more sectors
- matters assigned to the state as employer in respect of the public service, where such matters are not assigned to any particular sector.

But, for the police sector, as no doubt for others in the public service, what is actually defined as transverse or sectoral will be determined only after considerable debate.

A second problem identified with the LRA was the declaration of the entire police service as an essential service. Amongst other things, this denies the police the right to strike. The LRA insists that the police service is essential in its entirety since its key function is maintaining law and order, and the provision of security. The premise, then, is that a strike in the police service would endanger the lives and personal safety of members of the population.

Representatives from both POPCRU and SAPU have called for a distinction between those employees who are merely administrative, and those who deliver a service which, if withdrawn, would be detrimental to the community (Vally, 1993: 71). They stated that many workers in the SAPS do not perform essential services, and should be given the same freedom as other workers. Management, however, according to Steyn, felt that such a distinction would be almost impossible to make. He stated, however, that in the absence of the right to strike, urgent attention should be given to alternative and immediate mechanisms of dispute resolution. The issue of what constitutes essential services in the SAPS is still under discussion.

A third area of concern was around the establishment of workplace forums within the police. There was a lack of clarity on the part of both unions as to how exactly workplace forums would operate in the SAPS. Brandt, for example, posed a question as to who would be delegated authority in the forums, and whether stations would be the correct locations of such forums given their variable size.

Management holds a different view. Imraan Hayden and Mulangi Mphengo of SAPS Labour Relations in KwaZulu-Natal acknowledge the problem of very small numbers at some police stations, but believe that workplace forums could be effective vehicles for consultation and information sharing. A pilot forum has been set up at Durban's main police station, C.R. Swart (though it is called a consultative forum). Issues discussed have included diversity training, the closing of satellite stations, shift work, sector policing, and the setting up of a cultural choir. A formal evaluation has yet to be undertaken, and the police unions will have to develop their own guidelines.

More recently, according to Hayden, participative management forums have been established in the Natal Midlands. These have been constituted by police management and unions, as well as the chairperson of the local Community Policing Forum (CPF) whose role is to provide guidance with regard to service delivery. According to Hayden, the forum has led to a decrease in grievances registered in the SAPS in this area, a decrease in adversarial relationships and an increase in productivity (1999: interview).

To date, the LRA does not provide for workplace forums in the public sector. However, Hayden and Mphengo maintain that, if labour was organised and if there were mature managers and shop stewards, then such forums would be of great benefit to the SAPS. They believe these forums could constitute an excellent internal mechanism for increasing productivity and morale within the police.

Recent changes in collective bargaining and dispute resolution

On 9 September 1999, a circular was sent to all relevant management structures in the SAPS informing them of a number of significant changes with regard to collective bargaining structures.

All workers in the SAPS, whether functional or civilian will now be included in a single collective bargaining forum, the Safety and Security Sectoral Bargaining Council (SSSBC) which was formally constituted on 17 August 1999. This Council will be an equivalent of all other sectoral councils within the PSCBC. These structures are to be replicated at the provincial level. According to the document, the powers and functions of the Council are as follows:

- to negotiate collective agreements on matters of mutual interest
- to implement, monitor and enforce collective agreements
- to implement and monitor those collective agreements that have been concluded in the PSCBC
- to prevent and resolve labour disputes
- to resolve disputes between the employer and trade unions, and between the employer and its employees
- to administer funds to be used for resolving disputes, collective bargaining and general administration of the Council
- to raise, borrow, lend, levy and invest funds
- to develop policy proposals that may affect the sector
- to promote and establish training and education schemes
- to exercise any other power or perform any other function that may be necessary or desirable to achieve the needs of the Council (SAPS, 1999a).

The SSSBC supersedes both the National Negotiating Forum and the Departmental Chamber of the PSCBC. In order for a representative employee organisation to be included in the SSSBC, its membership must be a minimum of 20 000. As a result only POPCRU (with a membership of 39 403) and SAPU (with a membership of 58 998) will be included. The SSSBC is primarily a ratification body. Prior to issues being placed on the agenda of the SSSBC, they are thrashed out in an Executive Committee (EXCO) within the council. The EXCO also decides how unresolved grievances will be mediated or arbitrated. The formation of the SSSBC addresses the previous concerns of the police unions that a sectoral chamber for the police be established within the PSCBC. The SSSBC, it is hoped, will provide for a more informed, streamlined process of collective bargaining. (For more information about the SSSBC, refer to Safety and Security Sectoral Bargaining Council, 1998.)

The appointment of full-time shop stewards (as mentioned above) is also intended to improve collective bargaining and to increase the effective resolution of grievances within the SAPS. According to Hayden, the appointment of full-time shop stewards will speed up these processes since a labour representative from each union will always be available to represent the interests of their respective trade unions in any decision-making process within the SAPS. Shop stewards will also play an important role with regard to dealing with issues that are not formally dealt with in the collective bargaining structures. Such issues could include the drawing up of budgets, developing housing policy, overtime planning, and the utilisation of members in particular police operations. Furthermore, the appointment of shop stewards is aimed at ensuring that consultation with union members takes place, and that as a result, disputes will be minimised (Hayden, 1999: interview; see also SAPS, 1999b).

Finally, the Agency Shop Agreement which was signed in May 1998 by police management and the two registered trade unions is also significant. This agreement formally institutionalises the unions within the SAPS, and provides them with far greater powers as a result. Furthermore, the agreement, it is hoped, will give rise to improved accountability of the unions with regards to their members. The agreement is also advantageous to management who now have clarity as to who their negotiation partners are, and can assume that any agreements concluded are supported by all police members. Should members contest any agreement or decision made, unions will have to account for inadequate consultation.

Issues to address

The political and historical differences between SAPU and POPCRU are most evident in what they regard as the issues to be addressed in light of the concerns of their members, and in how they aim to achieve their goals. SAPU focuses on service conditions such as ensuring that promotions take place in a fair and transparent manner, wage negotiations, overtime payments, and maternity leave. A SAPU representative stated that if basic working conditions do not improve, police officers will continue to be demoralised, and will fail to deliver an optimal service to the community. According to Bill Dennis 'the police cannot fight crime properly because they are under-resourced, and underpaid' (January 1997: interview). SAPU, is, however, also involved in broader issues of transformation such as affirmative action policy, promotion policy, empowerment of women police officers, and better distribution of police resources, especially to historically disadvantaged police stations.

In recent years, SAPU has shown that it is willing to make use of adversarial methods to achieve its goals. Provincial negotiation forums are constituted by recognised employee organisations in that province, a representative of the provincial commissioner's office, area commissioners, and heads of various units (such as visible policing, public order policing, and the detective branch). SAPU has risked antagonising police management, by, for example, being prepared to go to the Supreme Court for 'an urgent interdict when it became clear that management was not willing to promote employees in the police' (*Union Post,* 10/1996). Prior to the 1996 festive season it was reported that:

> Tourists may well be the targets of rampant and unchecked crime over the Christmas period, and the South African Police Union is blaming the situation on National Police Commissioner, George Fivaz. Yesterday Bill Dennis, Provincial Secretary of SAPU, called for George Fivaz to resign immediately. Dennis made the call after revealing that the entire year's police overtime budget for KwaZulu-Natal has recently been spent. (*Saturday Paper,* 9/11/1996)

POPCRU has opposed the militant tactics used by SAPU which antagonise police management. It is this union's belief that militancy should not be employed until labour relations are operating effectively within the SAPS.

POPCRU, as a COSATU affiliate, maintains that the new government should be given a fair chance to implement change. However, POPCRU representatives interviewed were uncertain (as is more broadly the case with COSATU) as to how to deal with conflicts of interest between the union and the ANC-led government (Mataka, 1996: interview). This approach shapes their choice of acceptable tactics. As Mataka argues:

> The police are not like any other civilians in the civil service … If you go on labour actions, it impacts on the service provided. This tends to be a sensitive issue. All demands need to be balanced with the concerns of the community. The police should not be seen to abandon the community, yet at the same time, there should be rights for police workers. (Ibid.)

According to Mataka, the main concern of POPCRU in the future will be that of transforming the police to a representative and effective organisation. He singled out affirmative action and racism as key issues and insisted that while wages and salaries are 'bread and butter issues' of any union, a preoccupation with salaries and wages is shortsighted. POPCRU claims that as an affiliate of COSATU, its demands should be seen in the context of the need for parity between sectors in the public service.

However, POPCRU's actions in KwaZulu-Natal in the early months of 1998 indicated that they are certainly willing to use more hard-hitting tactics than negotiations on these issues. In March and April, POPCRU members at the Durban courts withdrew their services in the hope of changing promotion policy and practice which they deem to favour Indian and white officers. While such action is illegal (owing to the definition of the SAPS as an essential service), police management failed to act in any significant way against these members. Rather ironically, SAPU responded by stating they would launch a protest action in Durban because of the 'unwillingness of the SAPS to enforce discipline' (*Daily News* 30/3/1998).

While SAPU believes that crime cannot effectively be combated while police workers are demotivated as a result of poor working conditions, POPCRU asserts that 'the key issue confronting South Africa is crime. SAPS cannot abandon the primary goal of the government in dealing with crime' (Mataka, 1996: interview).

Both unions' perspectives seem to have validity. In KwaZulu-Natal alone, some 800 police officers have recently requested severance packages. The reasons given are 'dangerous and exhausting work for rotten pay, the stretching of an already stretched service, a sense that odds are continually stacked in favour of criminals ... and, above all, a sense that matters are going to get worse rather than better' (*Daily News*, 13/1/1997).

At the same time, the police service will be able to achieve maximum productivity only with the support and assistance of the communities in which it operates. This is dependent on transforming the SAPS into a service that is representative, accountable, and free of corruption. Service conditions, transformation, and effectiveness are thus inextricably linked.

Police management identify a number of other issues which need to be addressed. Firstly, they make the point that the police service is only one part of the public service. Consequently, they caution that determining salaries and wages falls outside of the power or jurisdiction of both the police unions and police management. It is for this reason, according to Hayden and Mphengo, that it is crucial that the police unions direct their activities away from wage and salary related issues, and focus more on issues of productivity and internal organisational capacity. They argue that:

> The unions should be involved in processes that lead to greater productivity ... they need to develop effective ways of negotiating, and should actively train police on the ground in labour relations ... police officers should also be trained with regards to legislation. Further, the unions should be involved in more policy-related things such as the National Crime Prevention Strategy ... the internal priority for the unions should be to properly organise their structures, and lines of communication. At the moment it is a nightmare dealing with them. (Hayden and Mphengo, August 1996: interview)

Similarly, Sakkie Steyn believes that in the near future negotiations will focus on salaries, promotions, allowances, and the question of sector-specific issues. He adds that decisions made at the PSCBC will bind negotiators.

Both the police unions and police management argued that the provincial forums lack real powers since they are limited to the powers held by the Provincial Commissioners as provided for in the Safety and Security Act (1995). It would appear that at a provincial level, administration is dealt with rather than policy. Issues that have been dealt with in provincial forums in the past include, for example, the allocation of danger allowances, and assessment procedures to be used. When interviewed in October 1996, Mataka of POPCRU argued that provincial forums are a waste of time. He believed that approaching management directly was a far more productive way of resolving grievances and decision-making.

However, unions and management could use the provincial forums to shape the agenda of the SSSBC. These forums could also be used to promote co-determination and participatory management. They have the potential to propel joint training programmes for community policing and to be a key arena for developing provincial police and crime prevention plans. Both the national and provincial negotiating forums (and maybe even workplace forums at the station level) could be used to catapult equity, affirmative action, and fair labour practices in the police service. They could also be useful monitoring tools. Such potential, however, is dependent on the organisational capacity of the unions and the unions' willingness to work collaboratively. It is also dependent on their adeptness in providing guidance and leadership within such forums, which is presently lacking. During an interview in November 1999, Hayden stated that representatives of both unions are unfamiliar with policy and service needs, and have received no training in this regard.

This lack of understanding and familiarity with service needs and policy is also a problem with regards to police management. According to Hayden, most grievances that are lodged in KwaZulu-Natal relate to interpersonal conflict. This, he says, is the result of poor management styles and the unwillingness of police management to undergo a change in 'mindset' with regard to labour relations. He believes that police management at present lack a vision of what labour relations in the SAPS should be. Consequently, training is seen as a key mechanism to remedy such poor labour relations. In KwaZulu-Natal the Labour Relations Department is now providing training for all police managers. This training – which is essentially basic labour relations – deals with the workings of trade unions, the rights of local police managers and the police unions, as well as the process and aims of collective bargaining (Hayden, 1999: interview).

Police management also warn that the Agency Shop Agreement could give rise to unintended consequences. The agreement may lead to a loss of incentive on the part of the unions with regard to mobilising members and providing a proper service to their social bases (Ibid.). In the short term, perhaps the competition which exists between the two unions will act as a catalyst for improved capacity and service delivery, though this is far from certain.

CONCLUSION

The SAPS now has its own sectoral bargaining chamber, the SSSBC, as requested by both police management and the police unions. However, the existence of this forum could lead to complacency. Both parties need to demonstrate that they are able to optimise the potential of this new structure.

For the two police unions to have any real impact in negotiating and decision-making forums, they will need to enhance their internal organisational capacity. They also need to continue with their recent attempts to work collaboratively and to decide whether or not a merger process would be advantageous to their social base. If a merger is agreed upon in principle, other unions in the public service and organisations and individuals who have expertise in labour relations may need to assist them. Thought should be given to inviting unions that have in the past successfully engaged in merger processes to share experiences and provide assistance. This will be a painful process to facilitate, and will require intervention from outsiders who are sensitive to both the political and organisational histories of the two unions. COSATU, as a federation, should be playing a far more active role in developing the police unions, particularly POPCRU. The police unions will never be effective while management remains unconvinced of the need for participatory and democratic labour relations and ill-equipped to take part in them. Police management, in particular the Labour Relations Department, should be actively training managers, particularly at the provincial and station level, in participatory management, collective bargaining, and the proper implementation of relevant legislation. Management needs to be convinced that effective and constructive labour relations will come about only if there is a sharing of both information and resources. Not all managers accept the notion – central to the LRA – that for the police to offer a service which is accountable, transparent, and community-oriented, police workers themselves require a human rights culture within the police department and their own unions.

In order to improve the competence and willingness of police managers in dealing with labour relations, the Labour Relations Departments in all provinces need to prioritise training of all police officers in management positions. Such training should focus on the importance of good labour relations for police productivity, and on informing police managers about the structures and processes pertaining to grievance procedures and collective bargaining. Perhaps the training currently underway in KwaZulu-Natal could provide guidance for other provinces.

Co-determination remains a vision for the future. The unions have repeatedly complained that in all forums and at all levels, police management assume prerogative: this has been particularly so with regards to rationalisation and 'right-sizing'. Management statements have aroused the anger of both unions. In early 1997, National Police Commissioner George Fivaz announced that:

Heads are likely to roll at all levels following a major
evaluation of 'performance service and productivity' by the
police service. The shake-up, he said, was imminent and no
one in the service would be immune, including himself. (*Mail
and Guardian*, 7/2/1997)

The unions' indignant response was primarily the result of the non-
consultative approach to police planning by police management:

The Police and Prison Civil Rights Union accused Fivaz of
bowing to outside pressure. POPCRU Assistant General
Secretary Jacob Tsumane said the union saw the statement
as an 'unnecessary threat that will further demoralise the
police force. Until we see and are allowed to participate in
drawing up such plans, we view his threats as those of a
person playing to the gallery to please the public that he
was fighting crime' (*Mail and Guardian*, 7/2/1997).

Similarly:

SAPU General Secretary, Peter-Don Brandt, said the union
had repeatedly asked police management to present a
comprehensive performance evaluation plan for discussion.
This call was not heeded. 'To suddenly hear through the
media that such ... plans are to be implemented imminently
raises a question as to the seriousness of management to
adhere to the principles of co-determination stipulated in
the new Labour Relations Act'. (*The Star*, 5/2/1997)

The unions seem to have every right to feel resentful. At the very least,
police management should make them aware of upcoming plans.
Management has tended to assume police planning, both for operations
and resource allocation, as its unilateral prerogative. Yet such planning
directly affects union members' working conditions as well as the service
they provide to the community. The unions need to ensure that police
management adheres to the LRA vision of co-determination and
participatory management. They must actively shape the SSSBC agenda,
insisting that any plans or programmes that affect their members must

follow a process of consultation. If this is realised, the unions and their members are likely to respond more positively to proposed strategies, which may in turn result in greater police 'productivity'.

While basic issues such as remuneration will continue to be of concern to police workers, it is precisely in these areas that the two unions are likely to be least effective in achieving demands. This is because they have very little contact with, or control over, the 'real' employer. As a result, the unions should probably focus their attention on the transformation of the police service into one which is representative, upholds equity, and is responsive to public needs and demands. This will mean promoting affirmative action, contesting discrimination in all its forms, and ensuring the transition to community policing. It cannot be denied, however, that as long as grievances around working conditions are not dealt with adequately, real community-oriented policing will be difficult to achieve.

None of this will be easy. It will require multiple strategies such as formal negotiations, collective action, as well as education and training programmes for union officials and management alike.

Labour relations in the SAPS are of grave concern to anyone interested in its transformation into a more effective and transparent organisation. Police workers will be unwilling (and, arguably, unable) to provide a proper service to the communities they are meant to protect as long as they are aggrieved and demoralised. The challenge facing the police unions is that they must simultaneously engage in enhancing the performance of the service, as well as in improving the conditions of service enjoyed by their members.

The unions need to develop constructive relations with each another, as well as with management. They also need to improve their organisational capacity, and prepare their representatives for collective bargaining at both national and provincial levels. Resistance by police management to co-determination may impede meaningful engagement, and will frustrate the unions and their members, which may, in turn, retard the necessary change within the SAPS. Both police unions and management need to acknowledge their immaturity with regard to negotiation and co-determination, and equip themselves to create an institution geared toward effective crime prevention and law enforcement.

NOTES AND REFERENCES

————— ✦ —————

CHAPTER 1

Notes

1 Our choice should not suggest any privileging of the role of the public service within the broad public sector; it is rather a practical choice defined by a series of research imperatives. Given the general shortage of reliable analysis of the public sector as a whole, we felt it wise to cover somewhat less ground, but to do so in greater depth. We hope that the completion of systematic studies of state-owned enterprises and local government will someday allow for a comprehensive assessment of the public sector in its entirety.

2 These included the central administration of the Republic of South Africa and the four provincial administrations of the Transvaal, Orange Free State, Natal, and the Cape Province; the administrations of the 'self-governing territories' of QwaQwa, KwaZulu, Gazankulu, Lebowa, Kwandebele, and KaNgwane; and the administrations of the 'independent states' of Transkei, Bophuthatswana, Venda, and Ciskei, commonly known as the TBVC states.

3 Public Service Labour Relations Act, 1993; the Education Labour Relations Act, 1993; and the South African Police Service Labour Relations Regulations, 1993.

4 The Government of National Unity came into existence following the elections and was comprised of the ANC, the NP and Inkatha Freedom Party (IFP).

5 Though the Presidential Review Commission on the public service acknowledges the existence of 'trade-offs' between transformation priorities, it does not begin to suggest what these should be, nor how they should be determined (PRC, 1998: 2.1.4). Yet this acknowlegement is an important step forward over the earlier White Paper on transformation (DPSA, 1995), which did not even identify the problem.

6 The ANC's concession on 'sunset clauses' granted a measure of job security to public servants from the old order.

7   The PSCBC excludes from its coverage senior management and members of the National Intelligence Agency and Secret Service. A recent Constitutional Court decision granted members of the South African National Defense Force the right to join a trade union, though the court was silent on the extent of rights soldiers would enjoy (Constitutional Court, 1999).

8   For example, De Klerk's above-mentioned unilateral 1993 5% wage implementation included a 20% increase for senior managers.

9   This does not imply that no time was lost due to protest actions and demonstrations as opposed to formal strikes. For example, SADTU used these quite effectively in their winter 1998 resistance to the Department of Education's plans to terminate the contracts of temporary teachers. Such disruptions have been prevalent at the provincial and at enterprise levels – particularly in education – and have a definite, though impossible-to-calculate impact on person days lost. Nontheless, in the first five years of ANC rule there were few – if any – national or sectoral strikes in the public service – a marked improvement over the early years of the transition to democracy.

10   These frustrations intensified after the South African Municipal Workers' Union (SAMWU) concluded a collective agreement which provided impressive increases to nurses working in municipal clinics, who often work in close proximity with those employed by provincial governments. In comparing SAMWU members' improvements with those provided in the PSBC – where nurses' interests were poorly represented – provincial nurses quickly discerned the gains possible through collective action, though not the difficulties involved in developing collective organisation. (See Adler, 1995)

11   For an analysis that misunderstands the dynamics of the nurses' strike see Adam et al., 1997. They claim the nurses struck 'against their own unions', though at the time the vast majority were unorganised. Moreover, they take the event as evidence of 'the inability of emerging corporatist arrangements to cope with a situation bordering on anarchy' rather than as an example of the inevitably messy stages in the evolution of these very same arrangements. (See Adam et al, 1997: 150-151)

References

Adair, B. and Albertyn, S. 1999. 'Collective bargaining in the South African public service: The creation of sector-based bargaining'. NALEDI research memorandum. Johannesburg: National Labour and Economic Development Institute.

Adam, H. Slabbert, F. and Moodley, K. 1997. *Comrades in Business: Post-liberation Politics in South Africa.* Cape Town: Tafelberg.

Adler, G. 1995. 'Govt response to labour unrest is inappropriate'. *Business Day,* 4 October.

Adler, G. and Webster, E. 1995. 'Challenging transition theory: the labour movement, radical reform, and transition to democracy in South Africa'. *Politics and Society*, 23(1).

ANC. 1994. *The Reconstruction and Development Programme: A Policy Framework*. Johannesburg: Umanyano Publications.

Andrew Levy and Associates. 1992-1999. 'Annual report on labour relations in South Africa'. Rivonia: Andrew Levy and Associates.

Baskin, J. 1999. 'The structure of negotiations on salaries in the public service: an assessment'. Research report commissioned by the Department of Public Service and Administration.

Bhorat, H. 1997. 'Public sector raises core labour issues'. *Budget Watch*, 3(3).

Central Statistical Services (CSS). 1997. 'Labour statistics – employment and salaries and wages: public sector (December 1996)'. Statistical release P0251, 24 April. Pretoria: Government Printer.

Constitutional Court of South Africa. 1999. South African National Defence Union versus Minister of Defence and others. Case Cct 27/98. 26 May.

Congress of South African Trade Unions (COSATU). 1997. 'The report of the September Commission on the future of the unions to the Congress of South African Trade Unions'. Johannesburg: Congress of South African Trade Unions.

Department of Public Service and Administration (DPSA). 1995. White Paper on the Transformation of the Public Service. Pretoria: Government Printer.

—————— 1997. 'The provincial review report'. Pretoria: Government Printer.

—————— 1999. 'Report on service and skills audit'. Pretoria: Government Printer.

Fraser-Moleketi, G. 1999. Press statement: Government tables new salary offer to avert strike. Ministry for Public Service and Administration. 27 July.

——————1999a. Press statement: Public service salary negotiations come to an end. Ministry for Public Service and Administration. 7 September.

Friedman, S. 1987. *Building Tomorrow Today: African Workers in Trade Unions, 1970-1984*. Johannesburg: Ravan Press.

Gelb, S. and Bethlehem, L. 1998. 'Macro-economics for the masses?' *Siyaya!* (1), Autumn.

Jacklin, N. and Machin, M. 1998. 'The emperor's new clothes: the government's approach to grading and wage policy in the public service'. Unpublished research report, NALEDI long-term research project on public service labour relations. Johannesburg: National Labour and Economic Development Institute.

Makhura, D and Phadu, T. 1999. 'Lessons from the public service wage dispute'. *African Communist*, 152(3).

NALEDI. 1999. *Unions in Transition: COSATU into the New Millennium*. Johannesburg: National Labour and Economic Development Institute.

Patel, I. 1998. 'Understanding the public service labour market: Prerequisite for its transformation'. Unpublished research report, NALEDI long-term research project on public service labour relations. Johannesburg: National Labour and Economic Development Institute.

Presidential Review Commission (PRC). 1998. 'Developing a culture of good governance: report of the Presidential Review Commission on the reform and transformation of the public service in South Africa'. Pretoria: Government Printer.

Public Servants Association (PSA). 1999. 'In the arbitration between the Public Servants Association of South Africa (and others) and the Government of the Republic of South Africa'. Sandton, 18 October.

Public Service Co-ordinating Bargaining Council (PSCBC). 1999. 'Membership Statistics 1999'. Pretoria: PSCBC.

CHAPTER 2

Notes

1   This chapter treats the apartheid civil service as a case study of the public service broadly. Although there are aspects of the case study which are specific to the civil service it serves to illuminate power relations, as well as a culture of work, within the public service at large.

2   The 1980s ushered in a new phase of collective action within the labour movement generally, with the creation of the Congress of South African Trade Unions (COSATU). The ripple effects of this development within the public service are dealt with in other papers in this collection.

3   Further references to House of Assembly Debates will be abbreviated 'HAD.'

4   Measuring the growth of the public service is complex, however. Different sources produce incompatible statistics, partly because the number of departments that fell under the auspices of the Public Service Commission changed over the years. So the figures cited should be treated as indicators of trends, more than exact measurements.

5   Note that statistics compiled by the PSC after 1967 changed the basis of measurement so that it is not possible to make accurate comparisons before and after 1967.

6   Central Archives Depot, SABK262 99/G/37/9 part 4; file 1/4/71, Committee on Administrative Training for the South African Public Service, 'Konferensie van Hoofde van Departemente,' 1970.

7   This term includes apartheid race classifications 'Indian', 'coloured', and 'African' – although, according to the *Rand Daily Mail* (25/11/1968), by far the majority of black public servants were African. For example, in 1968, out of a total permanent establishment of 326 263, 31 364 were classified as coloured, 7 027 as Indian and 152 507 as African.

8   For more detail see O'Meara, 1996.

9   Central Archives Depot, SABA272, vol. 341, 'Konsultasie tussen owerheid en personeel.'

10   The article quotes Professor B. Roux, of UNISA's Public Administration Department.

References

Adler, G. 1993. 'Skills, control and "careers at work"'. *South African Sociological Review*, 5 (2).

Cloete, J.N.N. 1992. *Public Administration and Management.* Pretoria: Van Schaik.

House of Assembly Debates. 1964. Pretoria: Government Printer.

------1969. Pretoria: Government Printer.

O'Meara, D. 1996. *Forty Lost Years: The Apartheid State and the Politics of the National Party, 1948-1988.* Johannesburg.

Posel, D. 1991. *The Making of Apartheid, 1948-1961.* Oxford: Clarendon.

Republic of South Africa (RSA). 1980. Report of the Commission of Inquiry into Labour Legislation, part 5. (Paragraph 4.65.20).

------ 1962. Public Services Commission: 56th Annual Report, RP 39/168, Annexure A.

Roux, B. 1971. 'The central administration, provincial and local authorities, and the judiciary'. In *South Africa: Government and Politics.* D. Worrall (Ed.) Pretoria.

Seegers. A. 1994. 'The head of government and the executive'. In *Malan to De Klerk: leadership in the apartheid state.* R. Schrire (Ed.) London.

Wilkins, I. and Strydom, H. 1979. *The Super-Afrikaners.* London.

Periodicals

The Public Servant. July 1943. Address of the retiring President.

—April 1944. Address of the retiring President, Mr D. van Wyk.

—March 1961. Editorial.

—September 1962. Editorial.

Rand Daily Mail. 20/11/1958. 'They want right to negotiate'.

—21/7/1959. 'Officials unions avoids politics'.

—7/9/1959. '5 000 needed in public service'.

—21/6/1961. 'Hundreds resign every month'.

—14/4/1964. 'Public service act provision attacked'.

—8/8/1964. 'Public service makes more use of Africans'.

—2/4/1965. 'Staff shortage no better'.

—22/9/1965. 'Officials told to be more tolerant'.

—20/10/1967. 'Many public servants unqualified'.

—1/2/1968. 'Wage freeze under attack'.

—22/2/1968a. 'Calls for public service probe'.

—21/2/1968b. 'Manpower shortage hits Transvaal'.

—22/5/1968. 'Top level checkup on state pay'.

—15/8/1968. 'Shattering staff shortage'.
—30/8/1968a. 'Manpower wasted in public service'.
—24/10/1968. 'All-out bid for state workers'.
—21/1/1969. 'Slipping standards warned'.
—19/3/1969. 'Public service "facing crisis"'.
—21/5/1969. 'Call for change in recruit methods'.
—29/8/1969. 'Questions to public service'.
—17/6/1969. 'Public servants shortage'.
—17/9/1969. 'Public servant shortage'.
—7//1/1975. 'Mulder warns on scramble for staff'.
—7/3/1978. 'Public service employs 1.8 million'.
—8/12/1979. 'No civil servants will lose their jobs'.
—16/7/1980. 'Tortoise remark upsets public servants'.

Rapport. 26/5/1974. 'Ons opname tel koppe'.

The Star. 14/7/1959. 'Domination in public service'.
—1/8/1959. English-speaking customs collector "bowler-hatted"'.
—19/4/1961. 'Staff shortage is "critical"'.
—23/6/1965. 'Public service tries poaching'.
—14/1/1966. 'Essential services'.
—20/9/1967. 'Civil servants not to enter politics'.
—23/3/1970. 'Fear of a stab in the back'.
—2/6/1971. 'Position difficult'.
—11/2/1975. 'Public service gets overhaul'.
—26/2/1976. 'Public service crisis'.
—12/12/1976. 'Few English in top jobs'.
—17/9/1979. 'Revamping the public service- key is speed'.
—25/2/1981. 'The civil service crisis'.

Sunday Express. 14/1/1965. 'No pay rise yet for civil servants'.
—21/2/1965. 'More women in public service'.
—20/12/1970. 'Cabinet staff crisis'.
—14/10/1973. 'Cabinet meddling angers state staff'.
—2/3/1975. 'More black civil servants'.
—21/9/1975. 'Public service takes notice of bonus days'.

Sunday Times. 3/10/1976. 'The little men who are strangling us'.
—30/2/1977. 'Quango', the article quotes Professor B. Roux, of UNISA's
    Public Administration Department.

Interviews

Louwrens, A. Long-serving office-bearer, PSA. 14 May 1996.

CHAPTER 3

Notes

1   The PSPRU publishes widely in these areas. Requests for information
     on its publications should be addressed to:
     The Public Services International
     School of Computing and Mathematical Sciences,
     University of Greenwich
     30 Park Row, London, SEIO9LS
     United Kingdom
     Tel/Fax: +44 208 331-9933
     E-mail: hd39@gre.ac.uk and psiru@psiru.org
2   Harry Kelber's internet news group: WeeklyLaborTalk@igc.org, 18
     September 1996: 'Labor Talk: Privatising Welfare'.

References

Etim, E.U. 1994. 'Structural adjustment programmes and the public sector in
     Africa'. Paper prepared for the Eighth PSI African Regional Conference.
International Confederation of Free Trade Unions (ICFTU). 1996. Trade union
     workplace case studies. Report prepared for the United Nations
     Commission on Sustainable Development by the International
     Confederation of Free Trade Unions.
Martin, B. 1993. *In the Public Interest? Privatisation and Public Sector Reform.*
     London: Zed Books in association with Public Services International.
------ 1996. European integration and modernisation of local public services:
     trade union responses and initiatives. Report for the European Federation
     of Public Service Unions with the support of the European Commission,
     May.
------1996a. Unpublished report to PSI on Commonwealth Local Government
     Forum, Geneva.
ÖTV. 1995. *Modernising the Public Services.* Stuttgart (English translation).
Public Services International (PSI). 1995. 'A public sector alternative strategy'.
     Paper no. 1 in the PSI Policy, Practice, Programme series. Geneva.
------1997. 'Transition Economies. Briefing notes for current public sector
     issues'. Fervey-Voltaire: France.
Public Services Privatisation Research Unit (PSPRU). 1996. *The Privatisation
     Network: The Multinationals Bid for Public Services.* London.
Schick, A. 1996. The spirit of reform: managing the New Zealand state sector in
     a time of change. Report prepared for the New Zealand State Services
     Commission and the Treasury.
Trade Union Advisory Committee (TUAC). 1995. 'Adaptability Versus
     Flexibility'. Paris.

CHAPTER 4

Notes

1 The PSA was exclusively white, the Public Service Union (PSU), which was established under the wing of the PSA, was for Indians, the Institute of Public Servants (IPS) for Africans, and, although the Public Service League (PSL) defined itself as non-racial, it was composed predominantly of coloured members. [Though the term 'coloureds' has the unfortunate effect of perpetuating apartheid concepts, it was the terminology used at the time.]

2 The following draws on Beaumont (1992).

3 This section draws on interviews conducted in 1997 by the authors among organisations party to the PSCBC. Until 1998 the criterion for admittance was a membership threshold of 1 000 members and there were 23 other, smaller organisations that were not covered in the discussion. From that date the threshold increased to 20 000.

References

Blackburn, R.M. 1967. *Union Character and Social Class*. London: Batsford.

Beaumont, P.B. 1992. *Public Sector Industrial Relations*. London and New York: Routledge.

Commission for Administration (CFA). Various years. *Annual Report*. Pretoria: Government Printer.

Community Resource and Information Centre (CRIC). 1990. 'Public sector struggles: an overview'. *South African Labour Bulletin*, 14(8).

De Bruyn, J. 1996. 'Public Service'. In *The Women's Budget*, D. Budlender (Ed.). Cape Town: IDASA.

Department of Public Service and Administration (DPSA). 1995. White Paper on the Transformation of the Public Service. Pretoria: Government Printer.

Friedman, S. 1987. *Building Tomorrow Today: African Workers in Trade Unions, 1970-1984*. Johannesburg: Ravan Press.

Golding, M. 1985. 'Workers in the state sector: the case of the civil administration'. *South African Labour Bulletin*, 10(5).

Mtshelwane, Z. 1995. 'The public sector: the contest for members'. *South African Labour Bulletin*, 19(1).

Public Service Commission. 1977-1995. *Annual Reports*. Pretoria: Government Printer.

Public Service Co-ordinating Council (PSCBC). 1999. 'Membership statistics 1999'. Pretoria: PSCBC.

Standing, G., Sender, J., and Weeks, J., 1996. *Restructuring the Labour Market: the South African Challenge*. Geneva: International Labour Office.

Treu, T. 1987. *Public Service Labour Relations: Recent Trends and Future Prospects*. Geneva: International Labour Office.

Undy, R. et al. 1981. *Change in Trade Unions*. London: Hutchinson.

Wiehahn Commission. 1982. *The Complete Wiehahn Report.* Johannesburg and
Cape Town: Lex Patria.

CHAPTER 5

Notes

1   See also the Green Paper entitled *A New Law for a New Public Service,*
Government Gazette No. 17669, 20 December 1996.

2   The Public Service Act, Proclamation No. 103 of 1994; Employment of
Educators Act, No. 76 of 1998 which amended the Educators Employment
Act, Proclamation No. 138 of 1994; South African Police Services Act,
No. 68 of 1995.

3   The Labour Relations Act, No. 66 of 1995, which came into effect on 11
November 1996.

4   The White Paper on the Transformation of the Public Service was drafted
by the Minister for Public Service and Administration with the COSATU
public service unions, the Parliamentary Portfolio Committee for the
Public Service and members of the government's strategic management
teams.

5   The Constitution of the Republic of South Africa, No. 108 of 1996, Chapter
6, and Schedules 4 and 5.

6   In the case of the *Premier of the Province of the Western Cape vs the President
of the Republic of South Africa and the Minister of Public Service and
Administration,* Case Number CCT 26/88, 29 March 1999, the
Constitutional Court held that the national legislative authority had the
power to determine employment policies and practices (i.e. the Minister
for Public Service and Administration).

7   Schedule 4 and 5 of the Constitution of the Republic of South Africa,
read with Section 3 and Schedule 2 of the Public Service Act.

8   Section 4 of the Employment of Educators Act.

9   Section 24 of the South African Police Services Act.

10   The Public Service Amendment Laws Act, No. 47 of 1997, and Sections 3
and 9 of the Public Service Amendment Laws, 1997.

11   Schedules 4 and 5 of the Constitution of the Republic of South Africa.

12   The Public Service Staff Code and the Public Service Act (before the 1997
and 1998 amendments) contained detailed provisions on discipline of
employees employed in terms of the Public Service Act. This was repealed
by the Public Service Laws Amendment Act, 1998. The Public Service
Co-ordinating Bargaining Council adopted a new Disciplinary Procedure
for the public service as a whole in January 1999, which was implemented
on 1 July 1999. (The PSCBC is the bargaining council that covers the
whole of the public service, Section 36 of the LRA). Chapter 6, Sections
18 to 27 of the Public Service Act, prior to the 1998 amendments, which

repealed these sections, set out an elaborate system for the management of misconduct in the public service.

13   Government Gazette No. 21777.
14   Resolution No. 3 of 1999 of the PSCBC, signed on 4 February 1999, Agreement on Remunerative Allowances and Benefits.
15   Chapter 10, Section 195 of the Constitution of the Republic of South Africa.
16   The Public Service Act as amended, No. 5 of 1999.
17   Section 196 and 197 of Chapter 10 of the Constitution of the Republic of South Africa
18   The Public Service Act, as amended 1997

References

Alford et al. 1993. *The Contract State: Public Service Change in the State of Victoria, Australia.* Center for Applied Social Research: Deakin University.
Ferner, A. and Hyman, R. (Eds.) 1992. *Industrial Relations in the New Europe.* Oxford: Blackwell Business.
Fredman, S. and Morris, G. 1990. 'The state as employer: is it unique?' *Industrial Law Journal* 19.
Hoggett, P. 1996. 'New modes of control in the public service: recent changes in the organisation of the state in the UK'. *Public Administration* (74) Spring.
National Commission of Audit. 1996. *Towards a Best Practice Australian Public Service.* Issued by the Minister for Industrial Relations and Minister assisting the Prime Minister for the Public Service, November.
Schick, A. 1996. The spirit of reform: managing the New Zealand state sector in times of change. Report prepared for the New Zealand State Services Commission and the Treasury.

CHAPTER 6

Notes

1   The four 'states' included Transkei, Bophuthatswana, Venda, and Ciskei; the six territories were QwaQwa, KwaZulu, Gazankulu, Lebowa, Kwandebele, and KaNgwane.
2   The PSC was called the CFA from 1984-1993, and was renamed the PSC under the 1993 Interim Constitution.
3   The countries covered are Australia, Austria, Canada, Denmark, Finland, France, Germany, Greece, Ireland, Italy, Japan, Luxemburg, the Netherlands, New Zealand, Norway, Spain, Sweden, Switzerland, Turkey, the United Kingdom and the United States of America.
4   In general, the definition of a sector is an industry or service. However, the case of the public service, the sectoral bargaining councils for educators and police do not mean a service or industry, but instead are based on

occupation. Thus, cleaners in schools were not part of the ELRC, nor were SAPS administrative staff members of the police bargaining council.

References

Aaron, B., Najita, J.M., and Stern, J.L. (Eds.) 1988. *Public Sector Bargaining*, 2nd ed. Washington D.C.: Industrial Relations Research Association Series, BNA Books.

Adair, B. 1996. 'Collective bargaining in the public service: restructuring the bargaining process in the light of the proposals contained in the White Paper on the Transformation of the Public Service'. Unpublished mimeograph.

Adair, B. and Nyembe, L. 1994. 'Transforming the Public Service Labour Environment'. In *Managing Sustainable Development in South Africa*, Patrick Fitzgerald, Anne McLennan, and Barry Munslow (Eds.). Cape Town: Oxford University Press.

Beaumont, P.B. 1992. *Public Sector Industrial Relations*. London: Routledge.

Coleman, C.J. 1990. *Managing Labour Relations in the Public Sector*. San Francisco: Jossey-Bass Publishers.

Commission for Administration (CFA). Annual Reports, 1984 to 1993. Pretoria: Government Printer.

Davey, H.W., Bognanno, M.F., Estenson, D.L. 1982. *Contemporary Collective Bargaining*, 4th ed. New Jersey, USA: Prentice-Hall.

Department of Public Service and Administration (DPSA). 1996. 'Improved collective bargaining of the central chamber'. Unpublished paper.

International Labour Organisation (ILO). *Collective Bargaining: A Workers Education Manual*. Geneva: ILO.

Many, T.W. and Sloan, C.A. 1990. 'Management and labour perceptions of school collective bargaining', *J Collective Negotiations*, 19(4).

Marks, M. 1997. 'Protecting the police: unions and SAPS'. *South African Labour Bulletin*, 21(1).

Ministry of Labour. 1995. Explanatory memorandum on the draft negotiating document: the new Labour Relations Act. Pretoria: Government Printer.

Organisation for Economic Co-operation and Development (OECD). 1994. 'Public service pay determination and pay systems in OECD countries'. Public Management Occasional Papers, Series 2. Paris.

Olsen, T. (Ed.). 1996. 'Industrial relations systems in the public sector in Europe'. European Public Services Committee. Norway: FAFO Institute for Applied Social Science.

Public Service Bargaining Council (PSBC). 1994. Report on the activities of the Public Service Bargaining Council for the period 28 October 1993 to 31 December 1993. Pretoria: Government Printer.

------ 1995. Report on the activities of the Public Service Bargaining Council for the period 1 January 1994 to 31 December 1994. Pretoria: Government Printer.

------ 1996. Report on the activities of the Public Service Bargaining Council for the period 1 January 1995 to 31 December 1995. Pretoria: Government Printer.

Public Service Commission (PSC) Annual Reports. 1994 to 1996. Pretoria: Government Printer.

------1997. Report on the rationalisation of public administration in the Republic of South Africa, 1994 to 1996. Pretoria: Government Printer.

Rayworth, J.F. 1992. 'Collective bargaining in the Canadian Health Care System'. *Health Manpower Management*, 18(2).

Reddy, P.S. and Sing, D. 1988. 'Employer/employee relations in the South African public service: from joint consultation to collective bargaining'. *South African Journal of Labour Relations*, 10(3 & 4).

Saran, R. and Sheldrake, J. (Eds.) 1988. *Public Sector Bargaining in the 1980s*. England: Avebury-Gower Publishing Group.

Skinner, K. 1997. 'SADTU fights retrenchments', *South African Labour Bulletin*, 21 (1).

Interviews

Biyela, Themi. Chief Negotiator, PSMSA. 12 February 1997.

Brewer, Peter. Legal Adviser, Medical Association of South Africa (MASA). 6 February 1997.

Du Toit, Danie. Former Deputy Director-General – Labour Relations, DPSA. 23 April 1997.

Gwagwa, Thembeka. and Branigan, Eileen. Joint Executive Directors, DENOSA. 6 February 1997.

Hartford, Gavin. National Commissioner, CCMA. 25 March 1997.

Louwrens, Anton. Deputy General Manager, PSA. 29 January 1997.

Maharaj, Norman. General Secretary, HWU. 14 February 1997.

Majola, Fikile. Assistant General Secretary, NEHAWU. 29 January 1997.

McDonald, Netshitenzhe. Member of the Secretariat of the Central Chamber of the PSBC, DPSA. 24 January 1997.

Naiker, Claude. (telephone) Official, PSU. 29 January 1997.

Ngwenze, Solly. DPSA – formerly a NEHAWU Negotiator. 24 January 1997.

Nxele, Mnikelwa. Assistant General Secretary, POPCRU. 23 April 1997.

Pypel, Andrew. Acting Executive Director, NAPTOSA. 24 February 1997.

Sixishe, Nomalizo. Vice-President, NWU. and Balkaran, Alicia Sanjay. General Secretary, NPSWU. 12 February 1997.

Various members, Inter-provincial Labour Relations Forum. 14 February 1997.

Van der Houven, Johan. Secretary, Central Chamber PSBC. 23 April 1997.

CHAPTER 7

Notes

1   Strictly speaking there were three agreements – an initial agreement (known as 1/96) signed on 8 March, the key one (2/96) signed on 29 March, and a follow-up agreement (3/96) signed on 19 April. These agreements were

also supplemented by an agreement reached effective 1 July 1997 (1/97) and another effective 1 July 1998 (1/98), which focused on the actual wage adjustment of those years.

2   In practice it is largely extended by government to SANDF members, with some differences in benefits.

3   Thanks to the many people whose useful comments I have tried to incorporate. The opinions expressed are those of the author.

4   See Agreement 3/96 and especially Annexure A.

5   This was clearly the overall intention even though some clauses of Annexure A suggested that some departments might be justified in having more staff.

6   These are posts on a department's establishment, included within its annual budget, but not filled.

7   This relates to the Voluntary Severance Package (VSP) scheme.

8   Public servants on the payroll but not held against any post on the establishment.

9   Annexure A of agreement 2/96.

10   Clause 2(1) of the agreement implied that 'key personnel' could be turned down, but then implied that this merely justified delaying departure for up to 18 months to ensure adequate succession.

11   See especially Annexures D and E of Agreement 3/96, April 1996.

12   For example Patel has calculated that the minimum salary of police constables immediately increased (in nominal terms) by 56,5% in terms of the agreement, while other ranks in the police saw their minimums increase by anything between 28% and 49% – with the maximums also increasing but by lesser percentages. Lower level nurses, nursing assistants and medical officers also received significant increases in the first year. However, not all occupations received such substantial increases.

13   Strictly speaking the 'special danger' allowance was R300 per month added to the 'danger' allowance of R200 per month.

14   An example of a rank promotion would be the movement from the post of admin clerk to that of chief admin clerk. An example of a leg promotion would be the movement from senior secretary grade 1 to senior secretary grade 2. In each case the employee's job title would change and he or she would effectively move up a grade to a higher salary range.

15   A handful of employees, seven at last count, were on personal notches above the grade 16 maximum.

16   An unpublished overview paper by De Bruyn summarises the target grading system.

17   There are indications that this data is not always reliable or comparable, especially in the earlier years. I will attempt to indicate when figures need to be treated with caution. I have often avoided using the 1995 data.

18   12,5% if the outsourcing of SARS is accommodated.

19   About 81 000 VSPs had been granted, as of May 1999.

20   Over the three year period (1995-98) numbers in the Eastern Cape dropped by 6,3%. But over the 1996-98 period total employment numbers rocketed by 49%. There appears to be something abnormal about the 1996 employment figure.

21   The 1995 data is not relied upon since it appears a bit inaccurate.

22   Given the abandonment of white protected employment in the public service this drop is hardly surprising.

23   Also director level, but the figure excludes items such as the car allowance.

24   In the justice sector similar changes in relative pay have resulted in extensive complaints by prosecutors.

25   See Department of Finance, 1998: 18.

26   The KPMG survey (1997: 78-82) states that public service wages are below market levels but concedes that the data on which this finding is based is inadequate. Surveys repeatedly show the average unskilled wage to be well below the current R21 000 per annum minimum. The latest census, for example, indicates that in October 1996 (when the public service minimum was about R1 500 per month), 62% of all the employed, and presumably a much higher percentage of the unskilled employed, earned less than R1 500 per month.

27   The DPSA's annual Exchequer Report cites personnel figures significantly less than these. This is because DPSA figures only include basic salary and not all costs (such as fringe benefits, pension contributions and so on).

28   See Department of Finance, 1999a: 94.

29   It must be remembered that this is a slightly simplistic calculation since a portion of increased personnel expenditure went towards severance packages and payments towards retirees.

30   See Department of Finance, 1998: 11

31   The source for the above is Department of Finance, 1998. PERSAL is a computerised personnel and salary information system developed in the late 1980s and used in the public service since 1990.

32   Some smaller items (such as medical aid subsidies to retired public servants) may not be included as they are paid directly by the fiscus. The Department of Finance's 1998 Annual Report states that the cost of these medical aid subsidies has risen from R250,7 million in FY 94/95 to an expected R648 million in FY 98/99. See Department of Finance, 1999.

33   There are reportedly instances, especially in certain provinces, where this allowance has been given to more junior officials, although this is probably in breach of the regulations.

34   Figures for non-educators given as answer to National Assembly question by Minister for Public Service and Administration on 10/02/99 listing VSPs granted to 31 July 1998; but including figures for SARS, CEAS and former Deputy President de Klerk's office given in an earlier answer to the National Assembly, and listing VSPs granted up to 30/09/97. Educator information from Department of Education and listed as 'latest available'.

35   It is also not always captured on the PERSAL system.

36   Reflecting early retirement, these amounts are lower than they might otherwise have been. It may be that this is a monthly figure.

37   I make a distinction between the civil service (essentially performing administrative functions), and other components of the public service performing specific sectoral duties such as health or education. In reality there are many grey areas.

38   Although above the projected inflation rate: 5,5% (1999/2000), 4,5% (2000/2001), and 4% (2001/2002). (Department of Finance, 1999a: 16).

39   Not budgeting for these items (or being unable to afford them) has meant that in some cases, such as in the Eastern Cape, these pay promotions have either not been implemented, or they have been at the expense of cuts in service expenditure.

40   Department of Finance, 1998: 18

41   Ibid.: 44

42   Since down-grading is generally nominal and up-grading actual.

References

Crouch, L. 1997. 'Personnel costs in South African education: no easy solutions' (unpublished).

De Bruyn, J. 1995. 'Some of us are not on the gravy train: factors affecting the advancement of lower graded workers in the public service'. NALEDI Research Report. Johannesburg: NALEDI.

------1997. 'An overview of personnel and costs in the South African Public Service' (unpublished).

Department of Finance. 1997. Medium-term expenditure framework: report of the Personnel Management Sectoral Team (unpublished).

------ 1998. Medium-term expenditure review, personnel spending (unpublished).

------ 1998a. Medium-term expenditure review, infrastructure investment (unpublished).

------ 1999. Annual report, 1998. Pretoria: Government Printer.

------ 1999a. Budget review. Pretoria: Government Printer.

Department of Public Service and Administration. Various circulars relating to implementation of PSCBC agreements (such as 'Improvements in conditions of service,' 1 July 1996, Circular No. 1 of 1996).

------ 1995-98. Exchequer reports, annual. Pretoria: Government Printer.

------ 1997. Provincial review report. Pretoria: Government Printer.

------ 1998. 'The observer at collective bargaining' (occasional newsletter).

KPMG. 1997. Public service job evaluation, pay and grading project. Report prepared for Government of South Africa (12 May 1997, unpublished).

Patel, I. 1995a. 'Missing the target: human resource development in the South African public service'. NALEDI research report. Johannesburg: NALEDI.

------ 1995b. 'The labour market of the South African public sector, with particular reference to the public service' (unpublished).

Public Service Bargaining Council. 1996a. 'Agreement reached by Chamber of Public Service Bargaining Council at central level'. Agreement No. 2/96. 29 March.

Siebrits, K. 1994. 'Fiscal aspects of government employment and remuneration in South Africa'. Unit for Fiscal Analysis, Department of Finance (unpublished).

Statistics South Africa. 1998. Census in brief (Report No. 1, 03-01-11: 1996). Pretoria: Government Printer.

CHAPTER 8

Notes

1   Barbara Adair is the former Chief Director: Labour Relations, Department of Public Service and Administration.

2   At the time of writing (1999), proposed legislative amendments that would allow Parliament to make adjustments to the budget were being debated but had not yet been passed.

3   Provincial workshops on the LRA of 1995, facilitated by the author, were held during 1996 as part of the National Hospital Strategy Project.

References

African National Congress. 1994. *The Reconstruction and Development Programme: A Policy Framework*. Johannesburg: Umanyano Publications.

Buhlungu, S. 1998. 'Servicing co-determination'. Report commissioned for the NALEDI long-term research project on co-determination and tripartism in South Africa. Johannesburg: NALEDI.

------ 2000. 'A question of power: co-determination and trade union capacity'. In Glenn Adler (Ed.) *Engaging the State and Business: The Labour Movement and Co-determination in Contemporary South Africa*. Johannesburg: Witwatersrand University Press.

Collins, D. 1994. 'Stuck in the stone age? The public sector in the new South Africa'. *The Shopsteward*, 3(6).

COSATU. 1997. 'Submission to the Presidential Review Commission'. Cape Town: COSATU Parliamentary Office.

Department of Public Service and Administration. 1995. 'White Paper on the Transformation of the Public Service'. *Government Gazette* 16838. Pretoria: Government Printer.

------ 1996. 'Policy framework for transformation units and co-ordinating committees'. Unpublished mimeo.

Dilts, D.A. 1993. 'Labour-management co-operation in the public sector'. *Journal of Collective Negotiations*, 22(4).

Dlamini Zuma, N.C. 1995. 'Speech by the Minister of Health, Dr NC Dlamini Zuma at the opening of the National Consultative Health Forum on 3 November 1995'. Pretoria.

Godfrey, S., Hirschsohn, P. And Maree, J. 1998 'Surrendering prerogatives? Management strategies with regard to worker participation and co-determination'. Report 6 of NALEDI's long-term research project on co-determination and tripartism in South Africa. Johannesburg: NALEDI.

------ 2000. 'Where is management going? Employee strategies with regard to worker participation and workplace forums'. In Glenn Adler (Ed.) *Engaging the State and Business: The Labour Movement and Co-determination in Contemporary South Africa*. Johannesburg: Witwatersrand University Press.

Heinecken, L. 1992. 'Labour rights for the public service: a future challenge'. *Industrial and Social Relations*, 13.

International Labour Office (ILO). 1981. *Workers' participation in decisions within undertakings*. Johannesburg: Skotaville Educational Division.

Kearney, R.C. 1994. 'Labor-management relations and participative decision-making: Toward a new paradigm'. *Public Administration Review*, 54 (1).

Kester, G. and Pinaud, H. (Eds.) 1994. *Trade Unions and Democratic Participation: Policies and Strategies Vol. I*. Paris and The Hague: Institute of Social Studies.

Mazibuko, S. 1996. 'Bringing democracy into the workplace'. *NEHAWU Worker News*, 4(6).

Ministry of Labour. 1995. 'Explanatory memorandum on the draft negotiating document in the form of a Labour Relations Bill'. *Government Gazette* 16259. Pretoria: Government Printer.

NEHAWU. 1996. 'NEHAWU national transformation forum meeting: Main document'. Unpublished mimeo.

Olsen, T. (Ed.) 1996. *Industrial Relations Systems in the Public Sector in Europe*. Norway: European Public Services Committee, FAFO Institute for Applied Social Science.

Patel, I. 1996. 'Changing apartheid's bureaucracy: the transformation of the public service'. In Baskin, J. (Ed.) *Against the Current*. Johannesburg: Ravan Press.

------ 1998. 'Review of public service transformation'. Unpublished commissioned report. Johannesburg: NALEDI.

------ (forthcoming) 'Growing pains: Collective bargaining in the Public Service'. In Adler, G. (Ed.) *Public Service Labour Relations in a Democratic South Africa*. Johannesburg: Witwatersrand University Press.

Satgar, V. 1997. 'The LRA and workplace forums: legislative provisions, origins, and transformative possibilities'. Report 2 of NALEDI's long-term research project co-determination and tripartism in South Africa. Johannesburg: NALEDI.

------ 2000. 'The LRA of 1995 and workplace forums: legislative provisions, origins and transformative possibilities'. In Glenn Adler (Ed.) *Engaging the State and Business: The Labour Movement and Co-determination in Contemporary South Africa*. Johannesburg: Witwatersrand University Press.

Summers, C. 1995. 'Workplace forums from a comparative perspective'. *Industrial Law Journal*, 10(6).

Von Holdt, K. 1995. 'Workplace forums: undermining unions?' *South African Labour Bulletin*, 19(6).

Personal communications

Adair, Barbara. Advisor to the Minister for Public Service and Administration. September 1996.

CHAPTER 9

References

Davies, H. 1997. 'Teacher organisation responses to the resolution of the Education Labour Relations Council'. *Education Africa*, 1(1).

Govender, L. 1996. *When the Chalks are Down*. Pretoria: Human Sciences Research Council.

Nxesi, T. 1997. 'Bargaining round-up 1996: a SADTU perspective'. *Education Africa*, (1).

Patel, I. 1997. 'The labour market of the South African public sector, with particular reference to the public service'. Unpublished NALEDI research paper.

South African Institute of Race Relations (SAIRR) (1985-1996). *South African Race Relations Survey. 1985* (and subsequent years). Johannesburg:

Interviews

Briyrag, R. SACE. January 1997.

Falcon, Roger. Executive Officer, ELRC. 1997.

Govender, Kenny. Deputy Director, Labour Relations, Department of Education. January 1997.

Hofmeyr, Jane. Director, Independent Schools Council. 1997.

Jaff, Rosamund. National Business Initiative, Edupol. 1997.

Maluleka, John. Regional Official, SADTU. 1997.

Martins, Pieter. Chief Executive Officer, SAOU. 1997.

Masigo, Confidence. Teacher, Shamong Primary School, Orlando West. 1997.

Mokgalane, Ella. Researcher, Education Policy Unit. 1997.

Monyokolo, Mareka. Policy Analyst, Centre for Education Policy Development. 1997.

Moon, Sigle. National Coordinator, Education Alliance. 1997.

Nxesi, Thulas. General Secretary, SADTU. January 1997.

SAOU officials. 1997.

Skinner, Kate. Former Media Liaison Officer, SADTU. 1997.

CHAPTER 10

Notes

1   At its general congress in July 1995 POPCRU resolved to affiliate to the Congress of South African Trade Unions (COSATU).
2   Major Thompson was described by Sam as the only real white activist in POPCRU. He was elected in a contested race as the national treasurer of the union at POPCRU's 1995 national congress. According to Sam, most white police officers feel alienated from POPCRU's culture.
3   Taken from the press statement by Minister Sidney Mufamadi concerning labour regulations in the SAPS, 26 September 1995.

References

Burpo, J. 1973. 'Police unions in the civil service setting'. Paper written for the United States Department of Justice.

Christie, S. 1992. 'Collective bargaining in the public service'. Paper written for Centre for African Studies, University of Cape Town.

–––––– 1993. 'Public service employment and the public sector Labour Relations Act'. Paper written for regional workshop, Labour Law and Industrial Relations in a changing Southern Africa, Marine Parade, Durban.

Collins, D. 1995. 'The South African Police Union : transformation from within'. *South African Labour Bulletin*, 19(4).

Cooper, C. 1994. 'Strikes in essential services'. *International Labor Journal*, 13(5).

Fredman, S. and Morris, G. 1989. *The State as Employer: Labour Law in the Public Services*. London: Manse Publishing.

–––––– 1990. 'The state as employer: is it unique?' *Industrial Law Journal*, 19.

International Labour Office. 1975. Article 1, Convention 151 on labour relations in the public service. Geneva: ILO.

International Labour Organisation. 1983. 'ILO freedom of association and collective bargaining document'. ILO Conference, 69th session. Geneva.

–––––– 1988. Record of proceedings. International Labor Conference, 31st Session. San Francisco.

Koitsioe, G. 1995. 'Interview'. *South African Labour Bulletin*, 19(4).

Ozaki, M. 1987. 'Labour relations in the public service: labour disputes and their settlement'. *International Labor Review*, 126(3).

POPCRU. 1995. Secretariat Report. Johannesburg: POPCRU.

Republic of South Africa (RSA). 1993. Public Service Labour Relations Act. Pretoria: Government Printer.

–––––– 1993a. 'South African Police Labour Relations Regulations'. *Government Gazette 5206*. Pretoria: Government Printer.

–––––– 1995. Labour Relations Act. Pretoria: Government Printer.

–––––– 1995a. South African Police Service Labour Relations Regulations. Pretoria: Government Printer.

Safety and Security Sectoral Bargaining Council. 1998. Constitution. Pretoria: SSSBC.

South African Police Service (SAPS). 1999. 'Agreement: South African Police Service Grievance Procedures'. Pretoria.

------ 1999a. 'Memo on the Safety and Security Sectoral Bargaining Council'. Pretoria.

------1999b. 'Labour relations memorandum on the appointment of full-time shop stewards'. Pretoria.

Stewart, A. 1995. 'The characteristics of the state as employer: implications for labour law'. *Industrial Law Journal*, 16(1).

Tiziano, T. et al. 1987. 'Public service labour relations, recent trends and future prospects: A comparative survey of seven industrialised market economy countries'. Paper written for the International Labour Organisation, Geneva.

Vally, B. 1993. 'Employment law in the public and private sectors: a case study for harmonisation'. Unpublished MA dissertation, University of the Witwatersrand.

Periodicals

Daily News, 30/3/1988.
Daily News, 9/11/1997.
Mail & Guardian, 7/2/1997.
Natal Mercury, 12/11/1996.
Saturday Paper, 9/11/1996.
Servamus. 1995. July. [Official police publication]
South African Labour Bulletin 19(4). 1995.
Sowetan, 9/8/1993.
The Star, 5/2/1997.
Sunday Star, 22/8/1993.
Union Post 1 (8), 10/1996.

Interviews

Brandt, Peter-Don. General Secretary, SAPU. January 1997.

Dennis, Bill. General Secretary, KwaZulu-Natal, SAPU. January 1997.

Hayden, Imraan. Head of Labour Relations, KwaZulu-Natal SAPS. August 1996; November 1999.

Mataka, Raphepheng. General Secretary, POPCRU. October 1996.

Mphengo, Mulangi. Labour Relations, KwaZulu-Natal SAPS. August 1996; November 1999.

Sam, Lundo. President, POPCRU. August 1995.

Steyn, Sakkie. Head of Labour Relations, SAPS. October 1996.

Tsumane, Jacob. Assistant General Secretary, POPCRU. April 1996; April 1998.1

Van Niekerk, Celeste. Acting General Secretary, SAPU. April 1998.

CONTRIBUTORS

———— ✦ ————

GLENN ADLER is an Associate Professor in the Department of Sociology and an associate of the Sociology of Work Unit (SWOP) at the University of the Witwatersrand. From 1996 to 1998 he was a part-time senior researcher at NALEDI, where he coordinated its long-term research project on public service labour relations. He recently co-edited *Trade Unions and Democratization in South Africa, 1985-1997* and *From Comrades to Citizens: The South African Civics Movement and the Transition to Democracy* (both from Macmillan). His research interests focus on the impact of social movements on economic and political liberalisation in Africa.

BARBARA ADAIR, an attorney, is a lecturer at the School of Public and Development Management (P&DM) at the University of the Witwatersrand. She also serves as a senior commissioner at the Commission for Conciliation, Mediation and Arbitration, and as national legal adviser to the National Education Health and Allied Workers Union. Before joining P&DM she served briefly as Chief Director in the Department of Public Service and Administration in Pretoria and as legal adviser to the Gauteng provincial government and the Public Service Commission. Prior to entering the public service she worked at the Centre for Applied Legal Studies at the University of the Witwatersrand and practised as an attorney at the Johannesburg law firm, Cheadle Thompson and Haysom, working in the area of public sector employment and acting for trade unions.

SUE ALBERTYN is a Senior Commissioner at the Commission for Conciliation, Mediation and Arbitration (CCMA), based at its national office in Johannesburg. Before joining the CCMA she practised for many years as an attorney, specialising in labour law. At the CCMA she has specialised in public sector labour law, and was appointed to facilitate the establishment of the Public Service Co-ordinating Bargaining Council (PSCBC), the largest bargaining council in South Africa, which was registered in October 1997. Since then she has chaired the Labour Relations Task Team, a sub-committee of the PSCBC which develops policy proposals for consideration by the Council.

JEREMY BASKIN has been involved in South Africa' s democratic union movement since the early 1970s, especially in the paper, printing and wood industries. From 1991 he was national coordinator of the Congress of South African Trade Unions, and in 1993 he was appointed as NALEDI's founding Director. He has written a number of books and articles on labour matters including *Striking Back*, a history of COSATU, and edited *Against the Current*, a collection of essays on labour and economic policy. In 1996 he joined the Department of Labour, where he was in charge of government's labour relations programme. Since 1998 he has been a public policy consultant working on issues related to the public sector labour market.

PHILIPPA GARSON is editor of *The Teacher* newspaper, published by the *Mail and Guardian*. She has worked as a journalist for many years for the *Mail and Guardian*, covering several beats including politics, political violence, and health, specialising since 1993 in education reporting. In 1996 she won the British Council/Sanlam Education Journalist of the Year award, and in 1999 was awarded a certificate of media excellence by the Forum for African Women Educationalists South Africa. She has an Honours degree in political studies, and has published articles in a range of magazines and other publications, both local and international. She wrote the *Sunday Times* Top Schools Survey for 1997, 1998 and 1999 and currently writes the monthly 'Class Struggle' education column in the *Mail and Guardian*.

IAN MACUN is Director of the Skills Development Planning Unit in the Department of Labour in Pretoria. He was previously Deputy Director and a researcher at SWOP, and has published in the areas of labour relations, trade union growth and research methodology. He previously taught Sociology at the University of Cape Town.

MONIQUE MARKS is a Lecturer in the Department of Sociology at the University of Natal, Durban. Her main area of research is on the transformation process within the public order police unit ofthe South African Police Service (SAPS). She has published widely on police transformation in South Africa, including community policing and the role of dissident police groupings in the SAPS. Before joining the University of Natal she was a researcher at the Centre for the Study of Violence and Reconciliation in Johannesburg, where in addition to her work on the police she conducted research on youth politics.

IMRAAN PATEL is Chief Director in the Department of Public Service and Administration in Pretoria, responsible for information and knowledge management. He was previously acting Director and a senior researcher at NALEDI where he worked on public service labour relations and conditions of service. His research interests include co-determination, collective bargaining, wages, employment and public service transformation.

DEBORAH POSEL is an Associate Professor in the Department of Sociology at the University of Witwatersand, and is a research associate of NALEDI. She has written extensively on the apartheid state, including two books, *The Making of Apartheid, 1948-1961* and *Apartheid's Genesis* (co-edited with Phil Bonner and Peter Delius). Her chapter in this collection on labour relations in the apartheid bureaucracy forms part of a larger project which assesses the imprints of the old state in the new one, and their effects on efforts to transform the public service.

CHRISTINE PSOULIS is a Research Officer for the Sociology of Work Unit at the University of the Witwatersrand, where she completed her MA in Sociology in 1995. Her current research interests lie in examining the evolving labour relations system in South Africa, to assess whether these changes are effective in meeting the challenges of efficiency and equity in the workplace. She is also investigating the implications such changes hold for the Southern African region at large.

MIKE WAGHORNE is the Assistant General Secretary of Public Services International (PSI), the international federation for public sector trade unions. He is responsible for much of PSI' s policy development work on public sector reform and modernisation, structural adjustment, privatisation, contracting out and regulatory reform. He also manages the PSI's work on these and related topics at a number of international organisations, where he works with other organisations in the international trade union movement. Prior to joining PSI, he held a number of research and education positions from 1984 to 1989 within the New Zealand Public Service Association, the main public sector trade union in that country.